LIFE SKILLS: A GUIDE FOR PARENTS AND TEACHERS NORMAL & ADHD CHILDREN

Dr. Mina Khatibi, PhD
Educational Psychologist

GULF BOOK SERVICES

Published by Gulf Book Services Ltd
20 - 22 Wenlock Road, London,
NI 7GU, UK
Email: info@gulfbooks.co.uk
GULF BOOK Office No: G23, Sharjah Publishing City Free Zone
SERVICES Sharjah – UAE

First Published by Gulf Book Services Ltd

ISBN: 978-1-917529-16-7
Year: April 2025

Typeset in Garamond by Forging Minds, India
Cover Design by Madhavi. S

CONTENTS

FOREWORD

It gives me a great pleasure to write a foreword to the first edition of this book by Dr. Mina Khatibi, who is an experienced Educational Psychologist.

In the journey of parenthood, few challenges are as complex and nuanced as raising a child with ADHD, especially in the preschool years. This book is a beacon of hope and guidance for parents navigating this landscape, providing insights that are both compassionate and practical.

The early years are foundational, shaping not just our children's development, but also their self-esteem and relationships. For parents of children 2 to 6 years old, with ADHD, these years can be filled with uncertainty and concern. You may find yourself grappling with questions about behavior, learning, and social interactions, often feeling isolated or overwhelmed. This book is here to remind you that you are not alone.

Within these pages, you will discover valuable strategies tailored to the unique needs of children 2 to 6 years old, with ADHD. The author blends research-backed information with real-life experiences, ensuring that her advice is both accessible and relatable. You'll find tools to foster understanding and connection with your child, promoting an environment where they can thrive.

More than just a manual, this book is a source of encouragement. It celebrates the strengths of children with ADHD, offering a fresh perspective that highlights creativity, resilience, and unique problem-solving abilities. As you embark on this journey, may you find solace in knowing that each step you take is a testament to your love and commitment.

Together, let us embrace the challenges and joys of parenting children with ADHD, nurturing their potential and fostering a deeper bond that will last a lifetime.

I would like to congratulate Dr. Mina Khatibi on writing this excellent book which would be of great help to parents, caregivers, and educators as well as children with ADHD.

Best Wishes

Dr. Sohrab N. Tomaraei
Senior Consultant Pediatrician
NMCSH, Dubai, UAE
President of Dubai Pediatric Club

PREFACE TO THE FIRST EDITION

It gives me a great pleasure to write this preface to the first edition of my book. In writing this book, my goal is to provide easy, practical, and scientifically sound educational methods for optimal education and development of basic life skills for normal young children as well as children with special needs, such as children diagnosed with ADHD. It is to provide compassionate guidance for parents who are exploring the complexities and difficulties of raising children diagnosed with ADHD. My intention is not only to share scientific and practical strategies and insights, but also to create a sense of empathy and strengthen mutual support in the community. It is to create greater motivation, encouragement, and empowerment among all parents, educators, and teachers who, perhaps with limited resources, are trying to cope with the difficulties and educational struggles of young children, especially hyperactive children. Since each child is a unique individual, his or her behavioral problems and challenges also manifest themselves in different ways. Recognizing these differences is very important in finding the right approach and support for young children and students who are vulnerable and still dependent on the family.

You will find evidence-based techniques, personal anecdotes and experiences, and scientific and expert advice in these pages. Whether you are looking for tips for managing everyday tasks, cultivating positive behavior, or seeking to understand your child's emotional world, I hope you find this book a practical, useful, and valuable resource.

Remember, you are not alone in this complex and winding path of child rearing, education, and upbringing. Together, we can explore, understand, and solve difficult challenges and problems with exploration, empathy, and companionship. We can navigate the ups and downs of the path to empowering young children with essential life skills with joy, success, and pride, and celebrate victories, nurturing our children's strengths, and helping them thrive.

I would like to thank my family for helping me prepare this book. I am very grateful to my loving children who gave me the gift of parenting experience and strengthened my motivation to write this book.

Wishing all children, their educators, caregivers, and parents all over the world health and happiness.

With empathy and hope,

Dr. Mina Khatibi, PhD
Educational Psychologist

CHAPTER 1: INTRODUCTION

1- THE BASIS OF SUCCESS IN RAISING SOCIAL AND EMOTIONAL EMPOWERMENT OF EARLY CHILDHOOD (2 TO 6 YEARS OLD)

2- AN OVERVIEW OF THE GOALS

1- The Basis of Success in Raising Social and Emotional Empowerment of Early Childhood (2 to 6 Years Old)

In general, the stages of child development include:

1. Infancy (0 to 2 Years): This stage involves rapid physical growth and development, where children begin to explore their environment, develop sensory and motor skills, and form attachment bonds with parents and caregivers.

2. Early Childhood (2 to 6 Years): This stage of development is characterized by rapid growth and learning, where children develop basic skills in language, motor abilities, and social interactions. This is a critical period for cognitive development, emotion regulation, and the formation of social bonds. During these years, children explore their environment, learn through play, and begin to understand their identity and relationships with others.

3. Middle Childhood (6 to 12 Years): During this period, children refine their cognitive skills, develop their emotions, and gradually strengthen their social abilities through interactions with peers and school experiences.

4. Adolescence (12 to 18 Years): This stage of development is characterized by significant physical, emotional, and social changes as children gradually transition into adulthood, establish their identities, and develop independence and deeper relationships.

For various scientific reasons, early childhood (ages 2 to 6) is considered the ideal period for introducing and teaching children to learn social and emotional skills because:

-Rapid Brain Development: Specialized studies in child neuropsychology have shown that during early childhood, children's brains are very flexible and receptive to learning new skills, making it easier for children to absorb and integrate concepts and learn social and emotional skills than at other times in their development. (Neuropsychology is the study of the effects that the structure and function of the brain have on the formation of psychological processes.) The goal of this field of experimental psychology is to understand topics such as how behavior and cognition are processed in the human brain.

-Foundation for Future Learning: Early exposure to learning social and emotional skills helps to lay the groundwork for positive social interactions, emotion regulation, and problem-solving skills, which are essential for a child's later academic and personal success.

-Critical Period of Socialization: This age is a critical time for the development of social skills as children begin to interact more with peers and adults outside their family. Therefore, teaching social and emotional skills during this period helps to establish and strengthen healthy relationships and effective communication.

Based on various research in the field of child development, it has been proven that starting to learn social and emotional skills in early childhood ensures that children develop the emotional and social competencies needed to overcome life's challenges and create a strong foundation for their future growth and well-being.

Although early childhood (ages 2 to 6) is considered a critical and ideal period for teaching children to learn social and emotional skills, we must note that the foundation of this social and emotional upbringing and empowerment of young children is built on the proper understanding of parents, caregivers, and teachers of the importance of early childhood development.

Therefore, efforts to help improve the level of understanding and scientific and practical knowledge of parents, caregivers, and teachers are very important. By further educating and empowering parents, caregivers, and teachers, children's social and emotional skills learning will also be facilitated and strengthened. When children, along with their parents, caregivers, and those around them, feel supported and empowered to express their feelings, build relationships, and gain self-confidence, they are better equipped to overcome personal and social challenges in the home, school, and life environments.

In addition to the scientific and practical educational empowerment of parents, caregivers, and teachers, another key factor in strengthening social and emotional competence in young children is the creation of a supportive and inclusive educational environment suitable for empowering these important and fundamental life skills by parents and teachers. Incorporating activities that promote learning in the area of social and emotional skills, such as role-play, group games, and sensory experiences, can help young children develop essential skills such as empathy, cooperation, and self-awareness.

By prioritizing young children's social and emotional development, we can set the stage for diverse and lifelong success and for each child to reach their full potential. Teaching and reinforcing social-emotional learning is essential and important in early childhood to establish a foundation for social and emotional well-being and development throughout children's lives. By explicitly teaching social-emotional learning skills, teachers can help young children develop a strong sense of self-awareness, recognize and manage their emotions, and build positive relationships with peers and adults. Through appropriate programs and activities, children gradually learn to recognize and identify different emotions in a variety of difficult and easy situations, understand the impact of their words and actions on others, and develop strategies for regulating their emotions and behaviors. By doing so, they become more resilient and better equipped to navigate the challenges of school and life.

Social-emotional learning is often taught to young children through play-based activities (games and discussions designed to promote social-emotional learning). This is important for all children, regardless of cultural, family, or individual differences with other children their age.

The importance of social-emotional learning education is particularly notable for children with ADHD. These children often struggle with self-regulation, impulse control, and emotion regulation, which can lead to problems with social interactions, academic performance, and overall well-being.

Social-emotional learning is not only beneficial for children diagnosed with ADHD, like other children, but is also essential for their academic success. These children often struggle with focus and attention in traditional academic settings, but social-emotional learning activities can help them develop the skills they need to stay focused and engaged. By prioritizing social-emotional learning education for children with ADHD from an early age onwards, parents, caregivers and teachers can specifically prepare them for lifelong success by providing them with the skills they need to navigate social and academic challenges with confidence and resilience, with the guidance of child medical and psychological experts.

2- An Overview of the Goals

1- Purpose: The purpose of this book is to provide guidance and practical solutions for teaching social and emotional learning (SEL) to preschool children, including those with ADHD. It also emphasizes the importance of social and emotional learning in early childhood development and its impact on children's lifelong success and well-being.

A Review of the Objectives of the Book

1. Strengthening the Growth and Development of Basic Life Skills

The central goal of this book is to provide practical, scientific guidance and strategies for teaching social and emotional learning to children aged 2 to 6, including children with ADHD. It also emphasizes the importance of social and emotional learning in early childhood development and its impact on children's lifelong success and well-being.

2. Enhancing the Growth and Development of Essential Life Skills

The connection between social-emotional learning and essential life skills is crucial because it enables children to develop the essential competencies needed to succeed in all aspects of life. By nurturing social and emotional skills, children can build a strong foundation to achieve their goals and overcome the challenges they face. Research has shown that social-emotional learning is closely linked to a wide range of essential life skills, including problem solving, goal setting, time management, and adaptability. By developing these skills in children through social-emotional learning, children can achieve greater success when competing in their personal and professional lives, build stronger relationships, make better decisions, and achieve greater success throughout their lives from early childhood to adulthood. As such, incorporating social-emotional learning into children's education and daily lives is essential to developing the skills they need to thrive in this complex and rapidly changing world.

3. Empowering Parents, Teachers, and Children (Normal and ADHD Children)

Children often learn social skills by observing and imitating the behavior of adults around them. Therefore, parents and teachers can model positive social behaviors such as good communication, empathy, cooperation, and respect, according to the age and level of each child's specific needs.

4. Supporting Positive Communication Channels and Appropriate and Healthy Interactions between Girls and Boys in the Family and Community

In the family and community, by teaching social and emotional skills management, we can support positive communication and appropriate healthy interactions between boys and girls.

5. Providing Useful, Simple, and Practical Strategies

Educational and training guidance along with providing useful, simple, and practical strategies in language that is not too complicated or incomprehensible.

6. Scientific and Practical Guidance for the Social-Emotional Learning of Normal and ADHD Children

Developing educational and training programs specifically for normal and hyperactive young children requires scientific and practical expertise and experience in order to support and guide young children who are at a fragile and vulnerable age, according to the specific needs of each, on the path to empowering their basic life skills, which is one of the central goals of this book.

7. Introducing the Educational Differences in the Social and Emotional Learning of ADHD Children Compared to Normal Children

In this book, an attempt has been made to introduce the educational differences in the social and emotional learning of hyperactive children compared to other children, so that parents and teachers, in addition to applying specific educational principles and methods of social-emotional learning to their hyperactive children and students, can gain a broader perspective to better understand them by comparing the educational differences between hyperactive children and other children, so that they can contribute to the growth and development, learning, academic success, and overall health in the lives of these children with more knowledge and awareness.

8. Creating and Strengthening a Positive, Healthier Overall Atmosphere at Home, at School, and in the Society

One of the general goals of teaching social and emotional skills to young children is to create and strengthen a positive, healthier overall atmosphere in the home, school, and community, which is of great importance in promoting appropriate and pro-social behaviors, overall peace in the family, educational environments, society, and promoting the general health of family members and society.

9. Writing Answers to Common Questions from Parents and Teachers Regarding the Importance of Teaching Social-Emotional Skills to Children Aged 2 to 6 Years

Parents, caregivers, and teachers sometimes face various questions in the process of raising, growing, and developing young children, especially those children who have more specific needs and problems than their peers (such as hyperactive children).

This book attempts to address and answer such questions in a scientific, simple, and understandable language. Also, dear reader, thank you for choosing this book to read. You may have one of the following questions regarding the title of the book:

Why is social-emotional learning mentioned? Why were hyperactive children chosen? Why were young children chosen? Or other questions may arise in this regard, which this book attempts to answer with simple scientific explanations in this section and throughout the various sections.

Why Is Social-Emotional Learning Important?

Positive social and emotional development in the early years provides a vital foundation for lifelong growth and learning. Social development refers to a child's ability to form and maintain meaningful relationships with adults and other children.

Social-emotional learning is vital for students because it teaches them critical life skills, including the ability to understand themselves, develop a positive self-image, take responsibility for their actions, and build relationships with those around them.

Children's social and emotional health affects their overall development and learning from childhood to adulthood. Research shows that children who are mentally healthy are happier, more motivated to learn, have more positive attitudes toward school, and perform better academically than their peers who are less mentally healthy. Social-emotional learning not only improves achievement by an average of eleven percent, but also increases prosocial behaviors (such as kindness, sharing, and empathy), improves students' attitudes toward school, and reduces depression and stress among students (Dorlock et al., 2011). The importance of appropriate and timely interventions in the education and development of social and emotional skills of young girls and boys is an indication of the need to pay attention to their social-emotional learning, which is one of the important goals of this book.

Why Were ADHD Children Selected?

Since, according to the latest statistics and figures from specialized scientific research around the world, approximately 366.3 million adults worldwide (2024) have ADHD (generally also referred to as hyperactivity in this book for short), which includes people who are diagnosed with ADHD regardless of the age of onset, which often begins in childhood. Approximately 129 million children and adolescents worldwide (2024) between the ages of 5 and 19 have hyperactivity disorder. Also, scientific, practical, professional, and specialized research by doctors and psychologists during the growth and development of children with a diagnosis of hyperactivity over the years has shown that early diagnosis and intervention services are essential for recognizing and managing the symptoms of ADHD in children. People with hyperactivity disorder often face numerous important challenges at home with parents, siblings, at school with classmates and other people with whom they interact and communicate. In the absence of appropriate and sufficient knowledge parents, family members, caregivers and teachers, and lack of proper education, these problems often continue from childhood to adolescence and adulthood. Such as difficulty in: concentrating, inattention, listening to parents, elders and teachers, completing daily tasks or controlling emotions, organizing and managing time, which can have a severe impact on their daily functioning at home and school and lead to long-term problems such as academic failure or problems in interpersonal and social relationships.

Studies on children, adolescents, and adults with ADHD have shown that they are more likely than other people to engage in delinquency and addiction, engage in antisocial behavior, drop out of school, and are often less satisfied with their family, social, and professional lives.

In summary, ADHD children were selected because of the significant (and increasing) population of children diagnosed with ADHD, who face numerous challenges, vulnerabilities, and special educational sensitivities.

It is necessary to make efforts and pay attention to the appropriate education and upbringing of these children at home and at school, and the attention and effort in writing this book has also been in this direction.

Why Were Children Aged 2 to 6 Years Chosen?

As explained at the beginning of the book, this developmental period of children is very important for several reasons (such as rapid brain development, the foundation for future learning, the critical period of socialization in enabling the development of children's social and emotional skills). Teaching social and emotional skills at an early age (ages 2 to 6) is essential for overall development, better academic performance, relationship building, and positive long-term outcomes. This is especially true in this age group when children are separated from their parents and family and begin to interact with a wider, unknown community beyond their own family. For example, they may have difficulty paying attention to nonverbal cues from peers and adults or have difficulty identifying and labeling their own and others' emotions (such as sadness, anger, happiness, fear, etc.). There are also other specific social and emotional challenges that they face at this stage of development and development, all of which indicate the need to pay attention to teaching this age group. During infancy, children's brains are very flexible and receptive to learning new skills.

In short, each of us, wherever we are in this vast world, with due regard and respect for national, cultural, social and family differences, can directly or indirectly make a constructive impact on the lives and optimal growth and development of young children in the role of mother, father, guardian, caregiver, sister, brother, teacher, coach, doctor, psychologist, etc. Given the importance of behavioral and emotional sensitivity of children in this age group in imitating and modeling others, each of us can promote and enhance children's social and emotional learning. By strengthening and increasing positive interactions and pro-social behaviors and reducing delinquency and anti-social behaviors in children's lives, we can directly and indirectly strive to shape a safe, peaceful, healthy and happy society through various means until their adolescence and adulthood, and play a very positive, important and constructive role in nurturing and increasing the scientists, geniuses and thinkers of the future.

2- Audience: The audience of the book includes children aged 2 to 6 years with normal and hyperactive behavior and their families and educators, including: parents, caregivers and teachers. This book is designed to be useful and useful for both parents at home and teachers and educators in educational settings in classrooms.

3- Overview: This book covers the basic aspects of social emotional learning such as self-awareness, self-regulation, empathy and other essential social emotional skills appropriate for children aged 2 to 6 years with specialized scientific and practical tips and activities to implement and help parents at home and educators, caregivers, teachers in the school environment.

4- Approach: The approach or framework that the book will follow to teach social emotional learning to children aged 2 to 6 years includes a focus on simplicity, step-by-step guidance and simple scientific and practical activities that are easy to implement in their daily routines.

5- Benefits: The benefits of implementing social emotional learning practices for children aged 2 to 6 years include improved social skills, emotion regulation and overall well-being. Social-emotional learning education can also strengthen parent-child and teacher-student relationships.

6- Empowerment: Parents in the home environment and educators, caregivers, and teachers in the school environment have the power to positively influence children's social and emotional development. This book provides scientific and practical tools and resources to support them on the important path of empowering children 2 to 6 years old with the necessary social and emotional skills and to lay the foundation for success in the education, social and emotional empowerment of normal and hyperactive preschool children.

7- Call for Action: In order to better understand most of the scientific and practical guidance in this book, you can study and review the chapters of this book with sufficient patience, time, and care, and actively engage with its content. Parents at home and educators, caregivers, and teachers at school can actively use the book's content with the help of instructions and examples presented in simple and practical language, and to maximize its benefits, begin to implement strategies and activities related to empowering social and emotional skills for their children and students aged 2 to 6 years.

CHAPTER 2: SOCIAL AND EMOTIONAL EMPOWERMENT OF CHILDREN AGED 2 TO 6 YEARS

1- SOCIAL AND EMOTIONAL SKILLS

2- AN OVERVIEW OF SOCIAL-EMOTIONAL LEARNING

3- UNDERSTANDING ATTENTION-DEFICIT HYPERACTIVITY DISORDER (ADHD)

Social and Emotional Empowerment of Children

The foundation for success in social and emotional empowerment refers to the foundation upon which individuals can thrive and succeed in their personal, academic, and professional lives, including: understanding and managing their emotions, being able to communicate effectively with others, and handling social situations with confidence and kindness. Social empowerment also requires recognizing the importance of diversity, acceptance, and empathy for others, in order to create a supportive and inclusive society. When individuals are socially and emotionally empowered, they are able to make positive choices, set and achieve goals, and overcome obstacles with resilience and determination. The foundation or foundation for success in social and emotional empowerment for children lies in strengthening positive relationships, building resilience, and promoting self-awareness and self-regulation. Ultimately, social and emotional empowerment for children leads to greater self-awareness, self-esteem, satisfaction, and overall well-being in their lives.

The foundation for success in children's social and emotional empowerment is the foundation on which children develop their social and emotional intelligence. Creating this foundation depends on various factors such as children's early life experiences, parenting styles, social environments, cultural and social influences, and the relationships and interactions that shape a child's development from an early age. In short, the foundation for social and emotional empowerment in young children is built on a foundation of various factors, including several key elements:

- Positive Relationships: Children thrive when they have strong, trusting relationships with their caregivers and peers. These relationships provide a sense of security and support, which is crucial for their optimal growth and development.

- Emotional Understanding: Helping children become socially and emotionally empowered is essential for recognizing and labeling their feelings, which includes teaching them the social and emotional skills to understand and manage their feelings in a positive and appropriate way.

- Developing Empathy: Encouraging children to understand and respect the feelings of others helps them develop empathy, which is vital for their social interactions.

- Social Skills: Teaching children how to interact with others, share toys and belongings, understand and respect turn-taking, and understand and gradually resolve conflicts in a positive and friendly manner is important for their social competence.

- Behavior Modeling: Children learn a lot by observing the adults around them. Displaying positive social and emotional behaviors can guide them in developing similar skills.

- Supportive Environment: Creating a supportive and safe environment that encourages exploration, play, and social interaction can foster children's social and emotional development.

Parents, caregivers, and teachers can develop a sense of self-awareness, self-regulation, and self-motivation in children by creating an environment and educational programs for social and emotional skills suitable for each child, at home and school, by creating a strong foundation in children's social and emotional skills. It is critical to their overall well-being, academic success, and future success throughout their lives.

1- Social and Emotional Skills

1. The Concept of Social and Emotional Development

2. Definition of Children's Social and Emotional Skills and their Importance

3. Milestones and Important Social and Emotional Skills of Children Aged 2 to 6 Years and the Role of Play in Strengthening Social Skills

4. Important Theories for Better Understanding Children's Social and Emotional Skills

5. The Most Obvious Difference between Girls and Boys in Social and Emotional Skills

6. The Importance of Boys' and Girls' Social and Emotional Skills at Home and at School

7. Parents' Awareness of the Importance of Children's Social and Emotional Skills

8. Teachers' Awareness of the Importance of Children's Social and Emotional Skills

9. The Role of Parents and Teachers in Strengthening and Developing Children's Social and Emotional Skills

10. The Role of Lifestyle on the Development of Social and Emotional Skills

11. The Role of Parenting Style on Children's Social and Emotional Development

1. The Concept of Social and Emotional Development

Social development refers to the ability to create and maintain meaningful relationships with others. Emotional development is the ability to express, recognize, and manage one's own emotions, as well as respond appropriately to the emotions of others.

The social and emotional development of humans from childhood to adulthood is not linear and direct over the years, but rather has a multi-level process. Children gradually learn various actions, reactions, and behaviors through various means such as observation, imitation, modeling, trial and error, and education and training in the family, school, and community so that they can interact and adapt with others to meet their various needs.

2. Definition of Children's Social and Emotional Skills and their Importance

Social Skills
Definition of Social Skills
The definition of children's social skills is actually related to the definition of children's social development. children's social development refers to the gradual growth and improvement of their ability to interact with others, understand and manage their emotions, and build relationships. Which includes the acquisition of skills and behaviors that enable them to gradually learn how to communicate effectively with others, cooperate with their peers, resolve conflicts, and adapt to social norms and expectations. children's social development is a dynamic process that is influenced by a combination of biological, psychological, and environmental factors and gradually shapes their ability to function effectively in social environments throughout their lives. The key aspects of children's social development include:

1. Social Skills: Learning how to interact appropriately with others, such as taking turns, sharing, listening, and expressing empathy.

2. Emotion Regulation: Developing the ability to understand and manage one's own emotions positively and appropriately, as well as recognizing and responding to positive emotions such as happiness and negative emotions such as anger in others.

3. Relationship Building: Establishing relationships with peers, adults, and caregivers, which requires building trust, loyalty, and understanding.

4. Self-Concept and Identity: Understanding one's strengths, weaknesses, and unique characteristics is self-concept, which influences how one perceives oneself in relation to others, which is identity.

5. Social Cognition: Gaining insight into social situations, including understanding social cues, norms, and in-group roles.

6. Conflict Resolution: Learning strategies for peacefully resolving differences and managing conflicts with others.

7. Peer Interaction: Engaging in play and cooperative activities with other children, which fosters social learning and the development of social skills.

8. Family and Cultural Influences: Recognition and respect for differences in customs, traditions, and social values within the family and broader cultural contexts.

The Importance of Social Skills

The importance of social skills depends on each of its components, the importance of which is gradually determined throughout the life of children in different situations. Therefore, the development of social skills is essential for the overall health of children and their success in life. These skills not only help children to build strong relationships with their peers and adults, but also enable them to adapt better and more easily to different social environments and situations. By teaching children how to communicate effectively and appropriately to partner and cooperate with others, we equip children with the necessary tools to progress in social interactions and create meaningful and positive relationships. In short, children's social skills play an important role in their emotional and social development, and cultivating these skills from an early age is also very necessary and important for creating success in their future personal and professional lives.

Emotional Skills
Definition of Emotional Skills

Children's emotional skills refer to their ability to understand, recognize, and express their own emotions and to appropriately control emotions in different situations and in healthy and appropriate ways. A child's proper recognition and understanding of their own emotions also helps them to correctly recognize the emotions of others, which is an integral part of how they interact with others. These emotional skills are the foundation of self-awareness and mental health. Therefore, children's emotional skills are very important for their overall well-being and personal growth and maturity throughout childhood and adulthood.

The Key Components of Children's Emotional Skills

1. Emotional Awareness: The ability to recognize and identify their own and others' emotions. This skill includes understanding the causes and triggers of emotions (such as understanding facial expressions, body language, tone of voice of others).

2. Emotional Expression: The ability to effectively express their emotions through words, facial expressions, gestures, and body language. children learn to clearly convey their emotions to others (such as happiness by smiling, anger by kicking, hitting or fear by hiding, closing their eyes).

3. Emotion Regulation: Children's ability to manage and control their emotions in different situations. This skill includes coping with stress, frustration, anger, anxiety and sadness (in constructive ways against very emotional reactions) in upsetting situations, calming themselves when upset, adapting to changing expectations and managing frustration without outbursts(for example, when a young child loses his toy, he may become very upset, throw a tantrum, cry for hours, refuse to eat and be stubborn, but as he grows older, he learns to better control and express his sadness and anger, look for the toy or ask adults for help).

4. Empathy: The capacity to understand and share the feelings and perspectives of others. This skill allows children to emotionally connect with others, show compassion, and respond sensitively to their needs (for example, when a child understands his friend's distress when his toy is lost and helps him find it to express empathy).

5. Problem-Solving Skills: Understanding and controlling emotions to resolve conflicts, the ability to manage difficult or unexpected situations, and find solutions to interpersonal challenges. In other words, the ability to

determine the cause of a problem, find different options for a solution, and try a suitable solution until the problem is solved

Young children from the ages of 15 to 18 months use all of their physical, thinking, and language skills to solve a problem through trial and error (for example, when a child has difficulty putting together a puzzle, but eventually learns their place through trial and error to find the right solution).

6. Self-Esteem and Self-Confidence: Self-esteem is loving yourself, creating a good feeling about yourself, and self-confidence is believing in your abilities. This skill helps children manage obstacles and approach new experiences with greater strength and flexibility. If children do not feel loved and valued, they may doubt themselves, their abilities, and their worth, and be afraid and shy away from doing new tasks and tasks.

   Self-Esteem: Includes beliefs about themselves (e.g., "I am loved," "I am worthy," "I am respectable").

   Self-Confidence: It is believing in your abilities (e.g., "I can," "I will succeed," "I can do this new task").

7. Adaptability: The ability to adapt to changes, transitions, and new environments while maintaining emotional stability. This skill describes the ability to identify, understand, and respond to changes in the social environment. Children who are less adaptable experience changes as stressful and often have poorer functioning and tolerance in the face of most changes and challenges (for example, when a child who is non-adaptive is told that playtime or TV time is over, he may react strongly and rebel).

8. Self-Awareness: The ability to understand the child's strengths, weaknesses, values, and beliefs about himself. This skill helps children understand their feelings and behavior more deeply so that they can gradually identify their feelings, thoughts, and values and become aware of the impact of positive and negative emotions on behavior in different contexts, such as home or school. This recognition is actually the first step to regulating their emotions (for example, when a child can answer questions about himself/herself, "Who are you?", "How do you feel right now?", or "Why are you playing this game?" appropriately, according to his/her age).

9. Cognitive Skills: Critical thinking and problem-solving skills that support

emotional understanding and regulation. Emotion regulation is very important in people's cognitive ability to manage and express emotions effectively. Emotions modulate basic cognitive processes. A child's cognitive skills refer to their reasoning, thinking, and understanding. This means how children think, discover, and understand the reasons for things. Emotions and cognition work together to facilitate learning and decision-making. Emotions have a significant impact on human cognitive processes, including perception, attention, learning, memory, reasoning, and problem-solving. Cognitive processing is required to elicit emotional responses.

In defining the relationship between emotional and cognitive skills, the question may arise: which one is activated first, "emotion" or "cognition"?

According to neuroscience research, sensory input always passes through the emotional centers of the brain before reaching the prefrontal cortex (the site of our logical thinking or cognition). Therefore, it is physically impossible for cognition to precede emotion.

In fact, emotional responses modulate and guide cognition to activate adaptive responses to the environment. Emotions determine how a child understands their world, organizes their memory, and makes important decisions. This highlights the necessity of teaching emotional and cognitive skills in children's lives (for example, children aged 3 to 5 years old begin to become more aware of the emotions of their peers, they want to have friends, and if their friend cries, they feel sad and try to solve the problem, for example, by giving him his favorite toy).

In summary, children's emotional skills are influenced by a combination of various cognitive, educational, and genetic factors, environmental, social, and various experiences throughout the child's life. As children grow, they continuously improve these skills through interactions with caregivers, peers, and their environment. Strong emotional skills lay the foundation for resilience, positive relationships, and overall mental health throughout childhood and adulthood.

The Importance of Emotional Skills

The importance of children's emotional skills cannot be overstated as they play a crucial role in various aspects of their development, well-being and overall success in life. To better understand this importance, here are some of the reasons:

1. Healthy Relationships: Emotional skills enable children to form positive relationships with peers, adults and family members. They learn how and

why it is essential to build trust and intimacy to be able to understand the perspectives of others, communicate effectively and resolve conflicts constructively.

2. Social Competence: Children with stronger emotional skills are better equipped to navigate the challenges of social situations, cooperate with others and participate in teamwork. Due to their ability in emotional skills, children's sense of competence increases and grows each time they have a positive experience of overcoming personal and social challenges. As a result, as social competence gradually grows and strengthens, they also better understand, feel, and cultivate empathy, which also strengthens kindness, compassion, and attention to the feelings of others.

3. Academic Success: Emotion regulation and self-management are associated with better academic performance. Children who can better control and manage their emotions have greater focus, motivation, and problem-solving ability when faced with challenges in learning environments.

4. Behavioral Adaptation: The ability to learn a behavior that is appropriate for a given situation is adaptation. In children's emotional skills, adaptation or behavioral adaptation is defined as the process by which children adjust their actions and behavioral responses to adapt to changes in their environment. Emotional skills contribute to more appropriate behavioral outcomes. Children learn to regulate their emotions and impulses (impulsive behavior, sudden emotional responses without pause or thought), reducing the likelihood of destructive behaviors, and increasing their ability to follow rules and norms.

5. Mental Health: Strong emotional skills increase resilience and help children cope with stress, adversity, and emotional setbacks. They are less likely to develop anxiety, depression, or other mental health problems in the future.

6. Conflict Resolution: Children who understand their own and others' emotions can resolve conflicts peacefully. They gradually learn negotiation skills, compromise, and how to find agreed-upon solutions as they grow and develop. Learning conflict resolution skills is essential and important for building and maintaining healthy relationships throughout life from childhood to adulthood.

7. Lifelong Learning and Adaptability: Emotional skills are linked to lifelong learning and adaptability. Children who can manage their emotions and

navigate social complexities are better prepared for future challenges and changes in their environment.

8. Empathy and Global Citizenship: The development of empathy is possible through emotional skills, which, in turn, enhances respect for individual differences, fostering a sense of broader global citizenship. When children understand the differences of others, it promotes tolerance and cooperation with different people in communities. As a result, it reduces the level of disagreements and increases empathy and peaceful coexistence in the wider community.

9. Parenting and Family Dynamics: Emotional skills also affect parent-child relationships and family dynamics. Children who can effectively express their feelings and understand their parents' feelings develop stronger bonds and connections with caregivers, teachers, parents, and others around them. In short, nurturing children's emotional skills from an early age not only enhances their social interactions with peers, but also lays the foundation for lifelong emotional health, resilience, and success into adulthood in a variety of areas of life. These skills are essential for personal growth, interpersonal relationships, and positive contributions to a healthy, peaceful society.

3. Milestones of Important Social and Emotional Skills for Children Aged 2 to 6 Years and the Role of Play in Strengthening Social Skills

Normally, children between the ages of 2 and 6 are constantly learning and developing important social and emotional skills that will lay the foundation for their future success. Here are some key milestones and social and emotional skills for young children at different developmental ages:

Age 2
Social Skills: At this age, children begin to engage in parallel play, where they play alongside others without much interaction. They begin to enjoy simple group activities and show interest in other children, although their direct cooperation is limited.

Emotional Skills: Two-year-old children begin to express their basic emotions more clearly and can recognize emotions such as happiness and sadness. They may show early signs of empathy (such as comforting a friend, and recognizing themselves in mirrors or photos) and begin to develop self-awareness.

Age 3
Social Skills: Engage more in more interactive play, better understand the concept of sharing and taking turns in interactive play with guidance. They enjoy playing with others but may still prefer parallel play.

Emotional Skills: Can identify basic emotions such as happiness, sadness, and anger. They begin to express their feelings using words and actions and show early signs of empathy.

Age 4
Social Skills: Cooperate more in group activities, can follow simple rules in play, and begin to form friendships. They enjoy imaginative play with their peers and often role-play different scenarios.

Emotional Skills: Show better ability to recognize and label their feelings. They can identify some emotions manage stress with strategies such as deep breathing and show greater and more consistent empathy for others.

Age 5
Social Skills: Participate in more complex, collaborative play, understand the concept of rules and fairness, and form stronger friendships. They can resolve minor conflicts with minimal adult intervention.

Emotional Skills: Become more adept at regulating and expressing emotions appropriately. They can discuss their own feelings and understand the feelings of others more deeply.

Age 6
Social Skills: Demonstrate improved teamwork and cooperation skills, can follow more complex social rules, and have a better understanding of social cues. Relationships and friendships become more meaningful and important to them.

Emotional Skills: Demonstrate appropriate and well-developed emotion regulation, can clearly express their feelings, and show a greater ability to empathize with others. They can manage a wider range of emotions and use coping strategies effectively.

The Role of Play in Strengthening Children's Emotional Skills
Play plays an important role in strengthening children's emotional skills.
- Emotional Expression: Play allows children to express and manage their emotions in a safe and controlled environment.

Through play, children learn to gradually express their feelings, whether they are happy, disappointed or afraid, in a safe and controlled environment. This emotional release helps children become more resilient by strengthening emotion regulation.

- Emotion Regulation: Play helps children develop strategies for regulating their emotions, such as deep breathing or talking about feelings. Through play and role-playing, children can have multiple opportunities to experience exploring their different emotions in a safe and understandable environment. Through play, children can learn to express their emotions and regulate their emotions, often through play by modeling emotion regulation on adults and peers.

- Development of Empathy: Play encourages children to consider the feelings of others and fosters empathy and compassion.

Children gradually develop empathy and mutual understanding by playing together. They learn to recognize social cues (including facial expressions, body language, tone of voice, and personal space or boundaries), understand and identify their own and others' feelings, and develop the ability to compromise. These early social interactions and empathy and compassion lay the foundation for positive relationships throughout their lives.

- Self-Awareness: Play helps children develop self-awareness by allowing them to explore their thoughts, feelings, and emotions.

Talking about strengths and challenges while playing can help children become more self-aware. Engaging children in play and doing things they enjoy and are good at can gradually increase their self-awareness and confidence.

- Resilience: Play helps children develop resilience by teaching them how to deal with failure and disappointment.

Play helps children gradually build resilience by developing mutual understanding. It teaches them how to experience more positive emotions when faced with challenges by developing their own solutions to problems. Play allows children to learn why and how they can better cope with difficult issues and various life crises, such as death, grief, and the loss of loved ones.

- Emotional Labeling: Play helps children develop emotional labeling skills by teaching them to identify and name their emotions. "Emotional labeling" is where the brain stores a memory of an event or an action, as well as a feeling associated with that event or action. It is an unconscious process that helps us evaluate a situation and identify an appropriate course of action. Play helps children identify and name different emotions. Like pantomime, it helps children label different emotional faces, happy, sad, angry.

- Emotional Validation or Emotion Validation: Play provides opportunities for emotional validation, where children's emotions are acknowledged and accepted. In fact, validating an emotion is not about agreeing with or rejecting the positive or negative emotions of others, but rather giving value and validity to any emotional expression regardless of how and when it is evaluated. With the help of play, you can teach children that you understand their feelings and perspective, even when you disagree. You build trust, help children feel supported, and help them understand and respect the feelings of others, even when they disagree without agreeing.

By incorporating a variety of appropriate educational games into children's daily routines, caregivers, parents, and teachers can support the development of essential emotional skills so that children can more effectively navigate life's challenges and crises.

Ways to Support Children's Play-Based Social-Emotional Learning
- Encourage Imaginative Play: Provide props such as dolls, blocks, or costumes to encourage a variety of imaginative play.

- Role-Playing: Engage in role-playing games with children to help them practice social skills such as cooperation and conflict resolution.

- Group Games: Play games with children that require coordination and teamwork, problem-solving, or strategy-building.

- Outdoor Play: Encourage outdoor play to promote and reinforce physical activity, exploration, and social interaction.

- Storytelling: Share stories with children through play that promote and strengthen empathy and understanding of different perspectives.

- Emotion Regulation: Teach children simple language techniques for managing emotions, such as deep breathing, counting numbers (for example, from one to five), or talking about how to express feelings, using play.

- Positive Reinforcement: Encourage and praise children in various ways during play for their efforts and progress in social-emotional skills.

In short, by incorporating play into daily routines and providing opportunities for social-emotional learning, caregivers, parents, and teachers can help children develop essential skills that will serve them well throughout their lives.

Considering the individual differences between different children, including girls and boys, educational activities and games can be provided based on their interests, such as:

Girls' Games
- Dressing Up and Role-Playing: Encourages creativity, imagination and social interaction (e.g., princess, superhero).

- Cooking or Pretend Food Play: Develops sharing, turn-taking and cooperation (e.g., making tea for friends).

- Arts and Crafts: Develops fine motor skills, creativity and self-expression (e.g., painting, drawing).

- Doll Play: Encourages nurturing and caregiving skills (e.g., feeding, dressing).

Boys' Games
- Building: Encourages problem-solving, spatial awareness and cooperation (e.g., building blocks, Lego).

- Action or High-Activity Games: Encourages physical activity, coordination with others and social interactions (e.g., chase and run, keep-alive).

- Vehicle and Transportation Play: Develops imaginative play, problem-solving and social skills (e.g., building roads with toy cars).

- Team Sports: Promotes teamwork, cooperation, and good sportsmanship (e.g., soccer, basketball). While these games are not exclusive to girls or boys, they are more popular among both genders. It is important to remember that all children benefit from engaging in a variety of play activities that promote social and emotional development.

To Further Strengthen Social Skills through Play

- Encourage Cooperation: Give children roles or tasks that require cooperation (e.g., solving puzzles together).

- Modeling Appropriate Behavior: Show positive social behaviors yourself (e.g., active listening, cooperation).

- Practice Active Listening: Engage children in conversations and show interest in their thoughts (e.g., use facial expressions that show you are interested and curious as you listen).

- Encourage Empathy: Ask open-ended questions to help children understand others' feelings (e.g., "How do you think your friend is feeling right now?").

- Provide Opportunities for Choice: Allow children to make age-appropriate, reasonable decisions to increase their independence and self-confidence (e.g., ask them, "What do you want for dinner?").

By providing a nurturing environment that supports children's social-emotional development through play, you can help preschoolers build a strong foundation for success throughout childhood and adulthood.

4. Important Theories to Better Understand Children's Social and Emotional Skills

Several theories provide valuable insights into understanding children's social skills and their development. Such as:

Erik Erikson's Theory of Psychosocial Development
Erik Erikson's theory of psychosocial development provides a framework for understanding the social-emotional development of children aged 2 to 6. This period is divided into two key stages:

Stage 1: Autonomy vs. Shame and Doubt Stage (Ages 2 to 3)
Key Task: Gaining a sense of personal control and independence.

Positive Outcome: When caregivers, parents, and teachers provide opportunities for children to make choices and try things for themselves, children develop a sense of autonomy. This sense of autonomy leads to self-confidence and a sense of control over their actions and environment.

Negative Outcome: If caregivers, parents, and teachers overcontrol children or do not allow them to express themselves, that is, express themselves, children may gradually develop feelings of shame and doubt about their abilities and decisions.

Stage 2: Initiative vs. Guilt (Ages 3 to 6)

Key Task: Initiating activities and exercising control through social interactions and play.

Positive Outcome: Whenever children are encouraged and supported in their efforts to take initiative and lead their own activities, they develop a sense of empowerment and initiative. They feel capable of planning and carrying out their own tasks.

Negative Outcome: If children are criticized or controlled too much, they may feel doubtful or guilty about their own desires and initiatives, which can lead to hesitation in pursuing new activities and lack of self-confidence.

The Social-Emotional Development Process in These Stages

Autonomy: Children begin to make decisions and express their preferences and learn to control their own movements and actions.

Initiative: They become more active in social interactions and can participate in role-playing games and express their creativity and ideas in the performance of their roles.

Emotion Regulation: They begin to better manage their emotions and learn to cope with frustration and disappointment.

Social Skills: Children develop basic social skills such as sharing, cooperation, and empathy, which are essential for building relationships with others.

Understanding these stages helps caregivers, parents, and teachers provide appropriate support and opportunities for children to develop a healthy sense of independence and initiative, and to provide a solid foundation for children's future social and emotional development.

John Bowlby's Attachment Theory

John Bowlby's attachment theory emphasizes the importance of early relationships between children and their primary caregivers in shaping social-emotional development. John Bowlby's attachment theory identifies different attachment styles based on the nature of the relationship between children and their primary caregivers. These attachment styles significantly affect children's social-emotional development in different ways, including:

1. Secure Attachment

Characteristics: Securely attached children feel secure and safe in their relationship with their caregiver. They use the caregiver as a safe base from which to explore the environment.

Behavior: They confidently explore and play when the caregiver is present. They may show distress when the caregiver leaves, but quickly calm down upon their return.

Socio-Emotional Impact: These children usually have high self-esteem, better emotion regulation, and strong social skills. They are able to form healthy relationships with their peers.

2. Insecure-Avoidant Attachment

Characteristics: Children with an insecure-avoidant attachment style tend to distance themselves from their caregiver and avoid or ignore their caregiver's presence. They do not seek comfort or much contact with their caregiver.

Behavior: These children are often indifferent to the presence or absence of the caregiver and do not show significant distress when the caregiver leaves or is visibly happy when the caregiver returns.

Social-Emotional Impact: This attachment style may lead to difficulties in forming close relationships, higher levels of aggression, and emotional distancing from others.

3. Insecure-Ambivalent (or Anxious) Attachment

Characteristics: Children with an insecure-ambivalent attachment style are anxious and uncertain about their relationship with their caregiver. They are often clingy and dependent on their caregiver or parents, but do not seem to calm down even when the caregiver returns. In some cases, the child may reject the caregiver or parent and not approach them or may be aggressive towards them. In general, the child's anxiety does not seem to be relieved or calmed down when the caregiver or parent returns.

Behavior: They show significant distress when the caregiver leaves but do not calm down easily when they return. They may be very attached to their caregiver or parent but at the same time sometimes push them away.

Social-Emotional Impact: These children may struggle with anxiety, low self-esteem, and difficulty trusting others, leading to challenges in social interactions and relationships.

4. Insecure-Disruptive Attachment

Characteristics: This style is characterized by a lack of attachment behavior. Children may be confused or fearful of their caregiver, often caused by inappropriate and inconsistent behavior from the caregiver or parent.

Behavior: Children may display a combination of behaviors, including avoidance, resistance, or apparent confusion. They may appear confused or fearful around the caregiver and exhibit conflicting and odd behaviors, such as unexpected silence or crying.

Socio-Emotional Impact: This attachment style is associated with higher risks for behavioral problems, difficulties with emotion regulation, and challenges in forming secure relationships in the future.

Understanding these attachment styles helps caregivers, parents, and teachers provide support and interventions to promote secure attachment and healthy socio-emotional development in children. The relevance of this theory to the social-emotional development of children aged 2-6 years includes:

Key Concepts of Bowlby's Attachment Theory

Attachment Behaviors: Children display behaviors such as clinging, crying, and following their caregivers and parents to get closer to them.

Secure Base: A primary caregiver provides a secure base for the child from which the child can explore the world and return to for safety and comfort.

Internal Working Model: Children create mental representations of themselves, caregivers, and relationships based on their interactions and experiences.

The Internal Working Model is a hypothetical internal map for recognizing and predicting behavior. It is a cognitive framework built on children's past experiences that helps them form their expectations of how people will react and helps them decide how to respond to certain situations.

Separation Anxiety: Children experience fear and distress when separated from their primary caregivers or parents, which indicates a child's attachment to them.

Stages of Attachment Development in Children 2 to 6 Years Old
Ages 2 to 3 Years

Strengthening Attachments: Children develop stronger attachment bonds with their primary caregiver. They show clear preferences and seek comfort and security from their caregiver in unfamiliar or stressful situations.

Exploration and Independence: With a secure attachment, children feel safe to explore their environment because they know they can return to their caregiver for reassurance.

Ages 3 to 4 Years

Understanding Relationships: Children begin to understand the concept of relationships and show interest in peers. They begin to form simple friendships, but they still rely heavily on their primary caregiver for emotional support.

Develops Self-Confidence: Secure attachment builds self-esteem and encourages children to try new activities and interact with others.

Ages 4 to 5 Years

Solid Social Interactions: Children engage in complex social interactions and play. They begin to understand social norms and expectations through the guidance of their caregivers.

Empathy and Emotional Understanding: Children who are securely attached are more likely to empathize and understand the feelings of others because they have experienced consistent and responsive care.

Ages 5 to 6 Years

Increasing Independence: With a secure base, children become more independent and confident in their abilities. They navigate social interactions more effectively and form stronger friendships.

Internal Active Pattern: Children's internal active pattern of relationships influences their behaviors and social expectations in interactions with peers and adults.

The impact of early relationships between children and primary caregivers on children's social-emotional learning includes:

Emotional Security: Secure attachment provides emotional security and helps children manage stress and anxiety.

Self-Regulation: Children with secure attachments are better at regulating their emotions and behaviors because they have learned to trust and rely on their primary caregivers.

Social Competence: Secure attachment leads to greater social competence because children are more confident and empathetic in their interactions.

Resilience: Children with secure attachments are more resilient in the face of challenges because they have a strong foundation of trust and emotional support.

By understanding Bowlby's attachment theory, parents, caregivers, and teachers can foster secure attachment and better support the healthy social-emotional development of young children.

Albert Bandura's Social Learning Theory

Albert Bandura's theory, often referred to as social learning theory, emphasizes the importance of observing, modeling, and imitating the behaviors, attitudes, and emotional responses of others. The relevance of this theory to the socio-emotional development of children aged 2 to 6 years includes:

Key Concepts of Bandura's Social Learning Theory

Observational Learning: Children learn by observing the behaviors and actions of others, especially adults and peers, and then imitating them.

Modeling: Children learn behaviors from role models in their environment, such as the behavior of parents, teachers, and siblings.

Reinforcement: Both positive and negative reinforcers play a role in shaping children's behaviors. Children are more likely to repeat behaviors that are rewarded.

Self-Efficacy: Children develop a sense of self-efficacy, or belief in their abilities, through positive experiences and feedback from others.

The Social-Emotional Development Process of Children

Ages 2 to 3 Years

Imitating Social Behaviors: At this stage, children often imitate the actions and feelings of those around them. They learn social norms and appropriate and inappropriate behaviors by observing and copying the behavior of adults and older children.

The Role of Reinforcement: Positive reinforcement, such as praise and affection, encourages children to repeat desirable behaviors, while negative reinforcement helps them understand behavioral limits and boundaries.

Ages 3 to 4 Years

Developing Social Skills: Children begin to engage in more complex social interactions and learn through observing and imitating their peers. They begin to understand concepts such as sharing, taking turns, and cooperating.

Emotion Regulation: Children learn how to regulate their own emotions and reactions by watching how adults manage their emotions. Modeling calm and constructive responses helps children manage stress and they work to develop these skills.

Ages 4 to 5 Years

Learning through Play: Children at this age engage in pretend play in which they imitate adult roles and scenarios. This type of play helps them understand social roles and strengthens and develops empathy in them.

Building Self-Efficacy: Through successful imitation and positive reinforcement, children gradually gain confidence in their abilities. Encouraging their efforts and providing appropriate, positive, and constructive feedback increases their self-efficacy.

Ages 5 to 6 Years

Solid Social Interactions: Children's social interactions become more complex. They learn to navigate friendships, resolve conflicts, and understand social hierarchies (such as kinship relationships such as aunt, uncle) by observing and participating in group activities.

Internalizing Behaviors: At this age, children begin to internalize the behaviors they observe. They develop a set of social norms and expectations based on the models they see in their environment.

The Impact of Bandura's Theory on Social-Emotional Learning

Role Models: The presence of positive role models is crucial for children's healthy social-emotional development. Children imitate the behaviors of those they look up to.

Consistent Reinforcement: Consistent and appropriate reinforcement helps children understand the positive and negative consequences of their actions and develop appropriate social behaviors.

Appropriate Environment: A supportive and nurturing environment in which positive behaviors are modeled and contributes to children's overall social-emotional development.

By understanding and applying Bandura's social learning theory, parents, caregivers, and teachers can create environments that foster positive social-emotional development in children.

Vygotsky's Sociocultural Theory

Vygotsky's sociocultural theory emphasizes the essential role of social interaction and cultural context in the development of cognition and social-emotional skills in children. The relevance of this theory to the social-emotional development of children aged 2 to 6 years includes:

Key Concepts of Vygotsky's Sociocultural Theory

Zone of Proximal Development: The difference between what a child can do independently on their own and what they can achieve with the guidance and support of others. This range determines the degree of independence or dependence of children in carrying out various activities. Social interactions play an important role in helping children learn and grow within this zone of proximal development and in building their capabilities.

Supportive Scaffolding: The support provided by caregivers, parents, teachers, and peers that helps children achieve higher levels of understanding and skills. As children become more capable, their support is gradually removed.

More Knowledgeable Person: Someone who has a better understanding or higher level of ability than the learner, such as a parent, teacher, or older sibling who can support and guide the child.

Language and Thought: Vygotsky believed that language is the primary tool for intellectual adaptation. Through social interactions, children learn to internalize language, which first takes the form of external thinking or self-talk, and then becomes a tool for internal thinking or inner language and self-regulation.

Application in Social-Emotional Development
Ages 2 to 3 Years

Role of Caregivers, Parents, and Teachers: At this stage, caregivers, parents, and teachers play an important role as the "more knowledgeable person" and provide the scaffolding for children's social and emotional skills to develop.

Language Development: Through interactions with peers, parents, teachers, and peers, children begin to develop the language skills necessary to express feelings and understand social norms.

Ages 3 to 4 Years
Interactive Play: Children become more engaged in interactive and collaborative play and learn social roles and norms through these interactions.

Guided Learning: Adults and older children assist in scaffolding guided activities, guiding children through tasks and helping them understand, control, and navigate social situations.

Ages 4 to 5 Years
Internalization of Social Norms: Through repeated social interactions, children begin to internalize social norms and expectations and learn to control and regulate their behavior accordingly.

Development of Self-Regulation: Language plays an important role in the development of children's self-regulation as children learn to use self-talk (talking to themselves: first out loud then slowly or internally) to guide their actions and manage their emotions.

Ages 5 to 6 Years
Peer Interaction: Peer interaction becomes increasingly important, as children learn from each other and gradually develop their social and emotional skills through play and cooperation with their peers.

The Role of Education: Structured learning environments provide opportunities for children to engage in social learning and develop cognitive and emotional competencies with the support of teachers as "more knowledgeable individuals."

The relationship of social interaction and cultural context to children's social-emotional learning includes:

Participatory Learning: Children learn best in social contexts, where they can collaborate with others and receive guidance from "more knowledgeable individuals."

Cultural Influence: Social and cultural contexts shape the development of social-emotional skills as children learn the norms, values, and behaviors of their society.

Language as a Tool: Language development is closely linked to social-emotional learning, as it enables children to communicate their feelings, understand others, express their feelings and opinions, and better control and regulate their behavior.

Piaget's Theory of Cognitive Development

Jean Piaget's theory of cognitive development focuses on how children acquire knowledge and how their thinking processes change over time. For children aged 2 to 6, Piaget's theory describes the preoperational or "preoperational" stage, which is crucial for understanding their socioemotional development.

Key Features of the Preoperational Stage (Ages 2 to 6)

Symbolic Thinking: Children begin to use symbols, such as words and pictures, to represent objects and experiences. This development is critical for learning language and imaginative play.

Egocentricity: At this stage, children have difficulty seeing things from a perspective other than their own. They believe that everyone else should see the world the way they do.

Animism: Children often attribute human characteristics to inanimate objects, such as imagining that the sun is smiling or that dolls can feel pain.

Focus: Children focus on only one aspect of a situation at a time. For example, they may focus only on the height of a glass of water without considering its width.

The process of social-emotional development in the preoperational stage includes:

Ages 2 to 3 Years

Egocentric Interactions: Children's social interactions are often self-centered. They are trying to understand the opinions of others.

Imaginative Play: Symbolic play, such as pretending to be a cartoon character or using a toy to represent something else, is prominent. This type of play helps children try out and explore feelings and social roles.

Ages 3 to 4 Years

Developing Empathy: Although children are still self-centered, they show early signs of empathy by responding to the feelings of others, even if they do not fully understand them.

Role-Playing: Engaging in role-playing games helps children practice social interactions and experiment with different feelings and behaviors.

Ages 4 to 5 Years
Understanding Rules: Through play and interaction, children begin to understand social rules and norms. They begin to understand the importance of taking turns and sharing.

Forming Friendships: While still functioning largely based on comfort and shared activities, children begin to form simple friendships.

Ages 5 to 6 Years
Understanding others' Perspectives, Perspective-Taking: Children gradually develop the ability to see things from other people's perspectives. Although this skill is still limited, they gradually begin to understand the different perspectives of others.

Complex Social Play: Engaging in more complex social play, such as games with rules and collaborative activities, helps children understand and develop negotiation and conflict resolution skills.

The relationship of cognitive development to children's social-emotional learning includes:
Emotional Expression: Symbolic thinking allows children to express feelings through language and play and facilitates children's understanding and emotion regulation.

Social Skills Development: Interactions during play help children learn essential social skills such as cooperation, sharing, and empathy.

Cognitive Development: As children's cognitive abilities develop, they become increasingly capable of understanding, controlling, and navigating social situations.

By understanding Piaget's theory, parents, caregivers, and teachers can better support young children's social-emotional development through appropriate activities and interactions.

Theory of Mind
Theory of mind refers to the ability to understand mental states such as the beliefs, desires, and intentions of oneself and others. Developed by

psychologists such as David Primack and Alan Leslie, this theory is central to understanding children's development of empathy, perspective-taking, and social understanding.

Theory of mind refers to the ability to understand that others have beliefs, desires, intentions, and perspectives that are different from one's own. It is a crucial aspect of social cognition and plays an important role in the social-emotional development of children aged 2 to 6.

Stages of Theory of Mind Development in Young Children
Ages 2 to 3 Years
Emerging Awareness: Children are beginning to understand that others have different feelings and thoughts, but their understanding is still very rudimentary. They often attribute their thoughts and feelings to others.

Egocentric Perspective: They are largely self-centered, meaning they believe that everyone else sees the world the way they do. For example, they may assume that if they know something, everyone else knows it too.

Ages 3 to 4 Years
Recognizing False Beliefs: Children begin to understand that others can have false beliefs, beliefs that are different from reality. For example, they can recognize that another person may not be aware of a change they have witnessed.

Pretend Play: Engaging in pretend play helps children explore and better understand different perspectives and roles.

Ages 4 to 5 Years
Understanding Different Perspectives: Children become more adept at understanding that others have different perspectives, knowledge, and intentions. They can recognize that different people can see a situation differently than they do.

Advanced Pretend Play: Their pretend play becomes more complex, often involving complex stories and multiple roles, furthering their mental skills.

Ages 5 to 6 Years
Complex Mental Skills: At this age, children can recognize and understand more complex mental states such as intentions, beliefs, and desires and how they influence behavior. They can predict others' reactions in specific situations based on their knowledge and feelings.

Social Interactions: They use their mental skills in social interactions, which leads to better cooperation, empathy, and conflict resolution.

Impact on Social-Emotional Development
Empathy: A well-developed mind allows children to empathize with others, understand their feelings, and share their feelings.

Communication: Children with strong mental skills can communicate more effectively with others because they can consider what others know and adjust their communications accordingly.

Friendship Formation: Mental competence helps children build and guide friendships by understanding the thoughts and feelings of others, making them more adept at resolving conflicts and showing kindness.

Problem-Solving: Children can use their mental abilities to predict the behavior of others and plan their actions accordingly, increasing their problem-solving ability in social contexts.

By supporting children's mental empowerment through activities such as storytelling, pretend play, and discussing feelings and perspectives, parents, caregivers, and teachers can strengthen the ability to understand and interact effectively with others and facilitate and enhance the social-emotional development of children aged 2 to 6.

Emotional Intelligence Theory
Emotional intelligence theory, popularized by Peter Salovey, John Mayer, and Daniel Goleman, focuses on the ability to recognize, understand, and manage one's own emotions as well as those of others. It emphasizes the importance of emotional competence in individual and social success, including the development of social skills such as empathy, communication, and conflict resolution. This theory recognizes the connection between children's social and emotional skills, and that each skill is needed to enhance the development of the other.

Key Components of Emotional Intelligence
Self-Awareness: Recognizing one's own emotions and how they affect behavior.

Self-Regulation: Managing emotions in healthy ways, including controlling impulsive, impulsive emotions and behaviors.

Social Skills: Managing relationships for diverse interactions, communicating clearly, and collaborating effectively in group activities.

Empathy: Understanding and sharing one's own emotions with others.

Motivation: Striving to achieve goals for personal reasons rather than external rewards.

The Relationship between Emotional Intelligence and Social-Emotional Development in Children Aged 2 to 6 Years
Ages 2 to 3 Years
Self-Awareness: Children begin to recognize and label basic emotions such as happiness, sadness, and anger.

Self-Regulation: They begin to learn to manage their emotions with the help of caregivers, parents, and teachers, although behavioral outbursts due to poor emotional control, impulsivity, and impulsivity often occur.

Social Skills: In early interactions, children often prefer to play alongside others. They begin to learn simple social rules such as sharing objects and taking turns.

Ages 3 to 4 Years
Self-Awareness: The enhanced ability to express feelings through words, which indicates a growing emotional vocabulary.

Self-Regulation: Begins to use simple strategies to manage emotions (such as taking deep breaths or asking a caregiver to calm them down).

Empathy: Shows early signs of empathy by responding to the emotions of others (such as comforting a friend who is crying).

Ages 4 to 5 Years
Self-Awareness: Better understanding and a wider range of emotions and their causes.

Self-Regulation: Shows an improved ability to delay gratification and control impulsiveness, impulses with guidance.

Social Skills: Participates in cooperative play, learns how to share things, negotiate, and resolve conflicts with peers.

Empathy: Begins to show genuine empathy by understanding and responding to the emotions of others.

Age 5 to 6 Years

Self-Awareness: Increased awareness of complex emotions and the ability to express emotions more clearly.

Self-Regulation: Can use a variety of strategies to manage their emotions. (such as talking about feelings, problem-solving, and seeking support.)

Social Skills: They build stronger friendships and better understand social dynamics, which indicates improved communication and teamwork.

Empathy: They have a greater understanding of the perspectives and feelings of others, leading to more compassionate and considerate behavior.

Motivation: They begin to set and pursue personal goals, demonstrating intrinsic motivation.

The relationship of emotional intelligence to social-emotional learning includes:

Emotional Literacy: Teaching children to recognize and label emotions helps them build emotional vocabulary and self-awareness.

Coping Strategies: Providing tools and strategies to deal with impulsivity, impulsivity, and behavioral outbursts supports emotional stability and reduces behavioral problems by strengthening self-regulation.

Empathy and Social Understanding: Fostering empathy helps children build stronger, more stable, and more positive relationships with others.

Self-Confidence and Self-Esteem: As children become more skilled at managing emotions and social interactions, their self-confidence and self-esteem grow, contributing to their overall well-being.

By focusing on developing emotional intelligence, parents, caregivers, and teachers can support young children's social-emotional development and set the stage for their future academic and career success, well-being, and happiness.

Social Information Processing Theory

Social information processing theory, developed by Kenneth Dodge and his colleagues, focuses on how children interpret and respond to social cues (social cues are keys or hints that are used from one person to another through hand gestures, facial expressions, and tone of voice to convey a meaning, often indirectly from one person to another) and formulate social goals and strategies. This theory examines and highlights the role of cognitive processes in the formation of children's social skills and interactions.

Developed by Kenneth Dodge, social information processing theory focuses on how children interpret and respond to social cues. This theory describes the mental processes involved in social interactions and how these processes influence behavior. Social information processing theory and the socioemotional development of children aged 2 to 6 include:

Key Components of Social Information Processing Theory
Social Cue Encoding: Paying attention to and interpreting social signals from the environment, such as facial expressions, body language, and tone of voice of others.

Social Cue Interpretation: Understanding social cues and understanding the intentions and feelings of others

Clarifying Goals: Determining one's social goals in a given situation, such as making friends or avoiding conflict.

Behavioral Responses: Generating possible behavioral responses to a social situation based on past experiences and knowledge.

Evaluating Responses: Evaluating responses and choosing the best possible course of action.

Response Execution: Implementing a possible chosen response in different situations in social interactions.

The Relationship between Social Information Processing and Social-Emotional Development in Children Aged 2 to 6 Years

Ages 2 to 3 Years
Early Encoding: Young children begin to notice and respond to early social cues, such as smiles and frowns. However, their ability to interpret and process these cues accurately is still developing.

Imitative Behavior: Most of children's social behaviors at this age are imitative and are learned from observing caregivers and peers.

Ages 3 to 4 Years
Interpretive Skills: Children improve in interpreting and processing social cues, but they may still misunderstand the intentions of others. They begin to understand that others can have different feelings and intentions than they do.

Role-Playing: Engaging in play with peers helps them practice interpreting and processing social cues and responding appropriately.

Ages 4 to 5 Years
Goal Clarification: Children become more aware of their social goals, such as being liked or liked by their peers. They begin to process their information to plan how to achieve their goals.

Complex Social Interactions: They engage in more complex social interactions and can generate a wider range of responses based on processing and interpreting past experiences.

Ages 5 to 6 Years
Response Evaluation: At this age, children become better at processing their information, evaluating potential responses, and choosing the most appropriate course of action. They consider the consequences of their actions more carefully.

Social Problem-Solving: Children develop better problem-solving skills in social situations, which leads to more effective and appropriate social behaviors.

Impact on Social-Emotional Learning
Improved Social Competence: As children become more skilled at processing social information, they are better able to navigate social situations and interact positively with their peers.

Emotion Regulation: Understanding social cues and interpreting them correctly helps children manage their emotions and respond appropriately to others.

Conflict Resolution: Increasing social information processing skills enables children to resolve conflicts more effectively and maintain positive relationships.

Empathy and Understanding: Children learn to empathize with others by accurately processing and interpreting their feelings and intentions, leading to more compassionate and cooperative behavior.

By supporting the development of social information processing skills, parents, caregivers, and teachers can help children strengthen their social-emotional learning and build stronger, more stable, and more positive relationships between the ages of 2 and 6, which will lay a solid foundation for their future academic and career success and success in life.

These theories have evolved over time and are derived from research in developmental psychology, social psychology, and educational psychology. By studying various theories related to children's social and emotional development, parents, caregivers, and teachers can gain a greater understanding of the cognitive and emotional development of children and, with more scientific and practical knowledge and capabilities, teach and support the development and strengthening of basic life skills in children aged 2 to 6.

5. The Most Striking Differences between Girls and Boys in Social and Emotional Skills

The most obvious differences between boys and girls in social skills are:

- Communication Styles: Boys tend to use more physical gestures and action-oriented language, while girls tend to use more verbal and emotional language.

- Aggressive Play: Boys tend to engage in more aggressive play, such as rough and tumble play, while girls tend to engage in more cooperative play, such as collaborative and nurturing activities.

- Group Dynamics: Boys tend to form larger groups and engage in more chaotic play, while girls tend to form smaller groups and engage in more intimate and interactive play.

- Role-Playing: Boys tend to take on more dominant roles in play, such as leaders or heroes, while girls tend to take on more nurturing roles, such as caregivers or lovers.

- Conflict Resolution: Boys tend to resolve conflicts through physical means such as fighting or competition, while girls tend to resolve conflict through verbal communication and compromise.

The most obvious differences between boys and girls in emotional skills are:

- Emotional Expression: Girls tend to express their emotions, both positive and negative, in various ways, while boys tend to suppress their emotions and hide them behind a "mask of indifference." In fact, boys often try to hide their true feelings by showing indifference and masking their emotions, not letting their emotions overcome them.

- Emotion Regulation: Emotion regulation involves awareness, acceptance, and understanding of one's own emotions, as well as the ability to control impulsive behaviors (emotional, thoughtless behaviors). Compared to boys, girls tend to use more emotion regulation strategies. Girls are better at regulating their emotions (for example, when experiencing sadness or anxiety and anger) and use strategies such as talking about feelings or seeking comfort from others, while boys often engage in avoidance emotion regulation strategies to experience fewer negative emotions and tend to struggle with emotion regulation, which leads to impulsive behaviors. As a result, they may resort to maladaptive behaviors, such as harming themselves and others, to cope with overwhelming emotions.

- Emotional Empathy: Emotional empathy is the ability to see things from another person's perspective and understand their feelings. For example, if you are sitting next to a friend and they start crying, you may feel sad too. Girls are more likely to empathize and understand the feelings of others, while boys are more likely to boys are more focused on their feelings and experiences.

- Fear and Anxiety: Girls generally show higher levels of fear and anxiety compared to boys. Girls are more prone to fear and anxiety, especially in relation to social relationships and appearance. Many studies have shown that girls feel more pressure and stress about their body image than boys. According to the cognitive model of social phobia, "appearance anxiety" is a result of people tending to "focus attention" on their "self-image" and experiencing a fear of being negatively evaluated by others, and these behaviors usually increase the severity of social anxiety. "Appearance anxiety" is often higher in girls. In childhood, even jokingly describing them as "ugly girls" can have a negative long-term effect on their "appearance anxiety". While boys feel more pressure and stress about being negatively evaluated by others than about their performance, they are often prone to fears of failure or loss of control and being weak. It seems that boys' deepest fear is often that they are not good enough or that they are incapable. For this reason, it should be noted that "bad boy" is a destructive description for him even in childhood. Because they are often led to negative feelings of self-directed fear and "not being good enough" anxiety. So, they tend to avoid any situation where they feel they will not succeed. So, fear and anxiety in boys and girls are often felt in them for different reasons and in different forms.

Emotional Validation or Confirmation of Feelings

Girls' emotional validation often involves active listening, expressing understanding, and offering supportive words to show understanding of others' feelings. Boys, on the other hand, tend to rely on external sources of validation, such as achievements or competition. Boys may prefer practical advice or solutions to verbal validation when seeking validation of others' feelings. For example, they may find ways to do activities together or offer support in tangible ways rather than verbally.

It is important to note, however, that these differences in emotional skills between girls and boys are less inherent and are not absolute and can vary widely across individuals. Furthermore, these differences are often shaped by social expectations, cultural norms, and individual experiences from early childhood.

6. The Importance of Boys' and Girls' Social-Emotional Skills at Home and at School

Social-emotional skills are very important for boys (2 to 6 years old), such as:
- Building Friendships: Boys need to develop social skills such as sharing, cooperation, and communication to build strong friendships and a sense of belonging.

- Managing Emotions: Boys need to learn to control their emotions such as anger and frustration, avoid violence and chaos, and develop empathy for others.

- Resilience: Boys need to learn to deal with failures and disappointments more flexibly, as experience helps them develop their resilience and growth mindset.

- Building Self-Confidence: Boys need to develop social skills such as assertiveness and self-confidence to participate in group activities with greater confidence and comfort.

- Building Healthy Habits: Boys need to learn healthy habits such as sharing things, taking turns, and cooperating to feel more responsible and socially responsible.

Social-emotional skills are very important for girls (2 to 6 years old), such as:

- Social Interactions: Girls need to develop social skills such as cooperation, communication, and conflict resolution to build strong relationships with peers and adults.

- Emotional Intelligence: Girls need to develop their emotional intelligence by recognizing, understanding, and managing their emotions to prevent them from feeling anxious or overwhelmed.

- Developing Empathy: Preschool girls need to learn empathy by putting themselves in the shoes of others and understanding their feelings. This skill helps them develop self-compassion and kindness.

- Building Self-Esteem: Girls need to develop social skills such as assertiveness and self-confidence to feel confident in their abilities and participate in more group activities.

- Building Independence: Girls need to learn independence skills such as self-care, problem-solving, and decision-making so they can gradually become more autonomous and self-sufficient.

The Importance of Social and Emotional Skills at Home

- Modeling: Parents can model social and emotional skills for their children by demonstrating empathy, kindness, and self-regulation.

- Positive Reinforcement: Parents can reinforce positive behaviors by praising children's social skills, such as sharing or cooperation.

- Redirecting Negative Behaviors: Parents can replace negative behaviors with appropriate, positive behaviors by teaching alternative solutions for dealing with emotions, such as frustration or anger.

The Importance of Social and Emotional Skills at School

- Classroom Dynamics: Teachers can create a positive classroom environment that promotes social-emotional learning through teamwork, role-playing, and class discussions.

- Teacher-Student Relationships: Teachers can build strong relationships with students by demonstrating empathy, understanding, and consistency.

- Curriculum Integration: Teachers can integrate social-emotional learning into the curriculum through games, stories, and activities that foster social skills.

By recognizing the importance of social-emotional skills for children aged 2 to 6 at home and at school, we can create a supportive environment that fosters healthy development and sets the stage for success in later years.

7. Parental Awareness of the Importance of Children's Social-Emotional Skills

Parental awareness of the importance of social-emotional skills for children aged 2 to 6 is crucial for their future development and success.

Why Parental Awareness Matters?
It is important for parents to be aware of the importance of children's social-emotional skills for several reasons:

- Impacts Children's Development: Parents are a child's first teachers, and their awareness of social-emotional skills can have a very positive impact on their child's development from an early age.

- Sets Children's Cognitive Trajectory: Parents' attitudes towards emotions, social interactions, and self-regulation set the stage for their child's understanding of these skills.

- Modeling: Parents' own social-emotional skills serve as a model for their child, teaching them how to control and navigate emotions, relationships, and conflicts.

- Supports the Child's Emotional Intelligence: Parents who are aware of the importance of social-emotional skills can provide a supportive environment that strengthens children's emotional intelligence.

- Increases the Child's Self-Esteem: When parents recognize and validate their child's emotions, it helps to build and strengthen their self-esteem and self-confidence.

- Developing Children's Coping Mechanisms: Parents' awareness of social emotional skills enables them to teach their children healthy coping mechanisms to deal with emotions and stress.

- Building Stronger Parent-Child Relationships: When parents understand the importance of social-emotional skills, they can build stronger and more empathetic relationships with their children.

Ways Parents Can Demonstrate their Emotional Awareness to their Children

- Validate Feelings: Recognize and acknowledge your child's feelings and help them develop emotional awareness and vocabulary for expressing their feelings.

- Teach Social Skills: Model and teach social skills like sharing, turn-taking, and cooperation to help your child build healthy relationships.

- Encourage Emotional Expression: Encourage your child to express their feelings in healthy ways, such as drawing, talking, or writing.

- Practice Mindfulness: Practice mindfulness with your child and teach them to recognize their feelings so they can better control and regulate them.

- Seek Professional Help: If you are concerned about your child's social-emotional development, seek help from a pediatrician, therapist, or counselor.

By understanding the importance of social-emotional skills for preschoolers, parents can provide a nurturing environment that fosters healthy development and sets the stage for their future success.

What's Wrong if Parents Don't Understand the Importance of Children's Social Skills?

If parents do not understand the importance of children's social skills, several problems may arise for their children, such as:

- Difficulty in Forming Relationships: Children with underdeveloped social skills may have difficulty forming and maintaining friendships. They may have difficulty understanding social cues, expressing their feelings effectively, or engaging in frequent interactions with their peers.

- Isolation and Loneliness: Without strong social skills, children may feel isolated and lonely. They may have difficulty fitting in with their peer group, participating in social activities, or connecting with others on an emotional level, leading to feelings of rejection and alienation.

- Poor Communication Skills: Social skills are closely related to communication skills. Children who lack the necessary competence in social skills may have difficulty expressing themselves verbally, actively listening to others, or participating in meaningful conversations, which can hinder their ability to communicate effectively in a variety of social settings, including school, family gatherings, and various social events.

- Difficulty in Dealing with Conflict: Conflict resolution is an essential aspect of social skills development. Children who are unable to resolve conflicts peacefully may resort to aggressive or passive-aggressive behaviors, which can lead to strained relationships with peers and others. They may also often experience high levels of stress and anxiety when faced with interpersonal conflicts.

- Academic Challenges: Social skills are also important for academic success. Children who struggle socially may have difficulty cooperating with classmates, participating in group projects, or getting help from teachers, which can affect their learning experience and academic performance, potentially leading to lower academic success and lower self-esteem.

- Risk of Bullying or Victimization: Children with poor social skills may be more vulnerable to bullying or victimization by their peers or adults. Their inability to assert themselves, communicate effectively, say "no," or set personal boundaries may make them targets of bullying behaviors by their peers or adults, and social problems may exacerbate their emotional distress.

- Emotional and Psychological Impact: Persistent social problems can have significant impacts on children's emotional and mental health. They may experience feelings of inadequacy, frustration, or depression due to poor social interactions and relationships. Over time, these negative experiences can gradually weaken or even destroy their self-confidence and self-esteem, leaving a lasting negative and very damaging impact on their mental health and overall quality of life from childhood through adolescence and adulthood.

In summary, parents' failure to understand the importance of children's social skills can lead to a wide range of problems for their children throughout their lives. These include: challenges in building relationships, feelings of isolation and loneliness, poor communication skills, difficulty dealing with conflict, academic challenges, increased risk of bullying and physical harm, and emotional and psychological crises. Therefore, it is very important that parents understand the importance of developing social skills and actively support their children in acquiring and refining these essential life skills.

8. Teachers' Awareness of the Importance of Children's Social and Emotional Skills

Teachers' awareness of the importance of preschool children's social and emotional skills is crucial for their future development and success.

Why is it important for teachers to be aware of children's social and emotional skills?

- Impacts Classroom Culture: Teachers' awareness of social and emotional skills determines the cultural communication structure of the classroom and creates an environment that promotes more social and emotional learning.

- Supports Children's Development: Teachers can provide targeted support to help children develop their social and emotional skills and better address children when they need more guidance.

- Improves the Learning Environment: When teachers understand the importance of social and emotional skills, they can create a more conducive learning environment to further foster children's emotional security, cooperation, and communication.

- Helps with Classroom Management: Teachers who understand social and emotional skills can use strategies such as positive reinforcement, guidance, and empathy to manage classroom behavior and minimize conflicts.

- Stronger Teacher-Child Relationships: When teachers are aware of social-emotional skills, they can build stronger relationships with their students, understand and identify their individual needs and emotions, and better guide and direct them in resolving conflicts and classroom problems.

- Greater Academic Success: Social-emotional skills are essential for academic success, and teachers who understand their importance can help children succeed and develop these skills in early childhood, building and strengthening the foundation for their future academic success.

Ways Teachers Can Demonstrate Social-Emotional Awareness

- Social-Emotional Learning Activities: Incorporate activities such as role-playing, group games, and storytelling into children's daily classroom routines that promote social-emotional learning.

- Positive Language: Use positive language to praise and encourage children's social-emotional behaviors, such as cooperation and empathy.

- Modeling Social-Emotional Skills: Model social-emotional skills yourself, such as how to manage emotions, resolve conflicts, and show empathy.

- Emotional Support: Provide emotional support to children who may be struggling with feelings of anxiety or frustration.

- Collaboration with Parents: Collaborate with parents to share information about their child's social-emotional development status, updates on their progress, and strategies for continued development of their child's social-emotional skills.

- Professional Development: Seek out professional development opportunities to increase your knowledge of social-emotional skills and learn new strategies to promote children's social-emotional skills.

By recognizing the importance of children's social-emotional skills, teachers can create a supportive environment that fosters healthy development and sets the stage for their future success.

What's Wrong if Teachers Don't Understand the Importance of Children's Social Skills?

If teachers ignore the importance of children's social skills, several important issues may arise for students, such as:

- Difficulty in Collaboration: Strong social skills are crucial for effective collaboration and teamwork. Students who lack these skills may have difficulty collaborating with others, which can lead to challenges in group projects or collaborative learning activities.

- Poor Communication: Social skills are essential for effective communication. Students who often struggle in this area may have difficulty clearly expressing their feelings, opinions, and needs, understanding others, or resolving conflicts peacefully. This can often undermine or even disrupt their academic performance and interpersonal relationships.

- Isolation and Loneliness: Children who lack social skills may have difficulty making friends and forming relationships with peers. This can lead to feelings of isolation and loneliness, which can have negative effects on a child's emotional health and overall development.

- Behavioral Issues: Students with underdeveloped social skills may exhibit behavioral issues such as aggression, defiance, or withdrawal. These behaviors can disrupt the overall learning environment in the classroom and create challenges for the teacher and other students.

- Low Self-Esteem: Difficulty with social interactions can lead to low self-esteem and lack of confidence in one's abilities, negatively impacting various aspects of a student's life, including academic performance, participation in extracurricular activities, and overall well-being. Low self-esteem in preschoolers refers to a negative perception of oneself that can manifest in a variety of ways, even at an early age, including problems such as: feelings of inadequacy, doubt about one's abilities, and a general feeling that others do not see them as good enough or valuable.

In young children, signs of low self-esteem may include:
- Negative Self-Talk or Inner Speech: Children may make critical statements about themselves, such as "I can't do this" or "I'm not good enough."

- Avoidance of Challenges: Children may avoid and refuse to do new activities or tasks that they find difficult or challenging.

- Social Withdrawal: They often have trouble starting or maintaining friendships. For example, they prefer to play alone rather than with others.

- Overly Self-Critical Behavior: They are overly harsh on themselves because of past mistakes or failures.

- Lack of Self-Confidence: Lack of self-confidence in preschoolers can lead to a number of challenges and problems in their school experiences and social environments. Such as:

- Avoiding Challenges: Children with low self-esteem may avoid new activities or tasks because they are afraid of failure or do not believe in their abilities. This problem can make them less willing to participate in class activities, group projects, or even social interactions often and even sometimes disruptive.

- Decreased Academic Performance: A lack of self-esteem can affect children's academic performance. They may be reluctant to answer questions or participate in discussions, which can hinder their learning progress and cause them to fall behind academically compared to their more confident peers.

- Social Withdrawal: Children who lack self-esteem may struggle to start or maintain friendships. They may feel insecure about their social skills, fear rejection, which can lead to social withdrawal or difficulty interacting with peers.

- Increased Anxiety: Low self-esteem can exacerbate anxiety in preschoolers. They may worry excessively about making mistakes, disappointing others, or not meeting their expectations, which can negatively impact their emotional well-being and ability to focus while learning.

- Adult Dependency: Children with low self-esteem may rely too much on adults for reassurance and guidance and become dependent. They may seek constant approval from adults or avoid making independent decisions, which can often hinder their development of independence and problem-solving skills.

- Negative Self-Perception: Over time, persistent low self-esteem can lead to a negative self-image. Children may begin to believe that they are not good enough, valuable enough, capable, or worthy, which can negatively impact their motivation and willingness to participate in activities or challenges.

- Behavioral Issues: Some children may develop various behavioral problems as a result of low self-esteem, such as fighting with classmates and distracting them while doing their homework in the classroom.

In short, if teachers ignore the importance of children's social skills, students may struggle with interacting with their peers, leading to potential isolation or conflict. This can negatively impact their emotional health and academic performance. Ultimately, it hinders the development of essential life skills needed for future success.

What's Wrong if Teachers Don't Understand the Importance of Children's Emotional Skills?

If teachers do not understand the importance of children's emotional skills, several issues may arise:

- Limited Academic Engagement: Children who struggle with managing their emotions may find it difficult to focus and participate effectively in classroom activities. This can lead to lower academic performance and hinder their learning progress.

- Self-Regulation: Students who struggle with self-regulation may have difficulty managing their emotions, leading to outbursts or withdrawal. This can affect their ability to focus and participate in class.

- Empathy: Teachers' lack of attention to students' empathy skills can lead to challenges in forming healthy relationships and understanding the perspectives of the teacher and others, which are crucial for students' social interactions and collaborative learning.

- Behavioral Challenges: Without adequate support from teachers for emotional development, students may exhibit disruptive behavior in the classroom, such as acting out, being aggressive, or withdrawing. This can disrupt the learning environment for all students and hinder the teacher's ability to provide effective instruction.

- Social Isolation: If teachers are not aware of the importance of students' emotional skills, children who lack emotional skills may struggle to build and maintain positive relationships with their peers at school. They may struggle with communication, conflict resolution, and empathy, leading to social isolation and feelings of loneliness.

- Increased Stress and Anxiety: School can be a significant source of stress for children, and those who lack emotional skills may struggle to cope with academic pressure, social dynamics, and other challenges. This can contribute to increased levels of stress and anxiety, affecting their overall well-being and ability to thrive in the school environment.

- Negative Self-Image: Children who do not receive support to develop emotional intelligence may struggle with self-esteem issues and develop a negative self-image. This can affect their level of self-confidence and willingness to participate in classroom activities or interact with their peers.

- Limited Resilience: Emotional skills are essential for building resilience, which is the ability to cope with setbacks and adversity. Without proper support from teachers, students may lack the coping mechanisms and problem-solving skills needed to overcome challenges, leading to feelings of helplessness and reduced motivation.

- Risk of Bullying and Victimization: Children who lack emotional skills may be more vulnerable to bullying or victimization by their peers without proper support from teachers. Their inability to assert themselves, set boundaries, or seek support may make them targets of abuse and exacerbate their emotional problems.

- Long-Term Impact on Mental Health: Teachers' neglect of students' emotional development during childhood can have long-term consequences for their mental health. Students who are not empowered in emotional skills may be at risk for anxiety disorders, depression, and other mental health problems in the future.

In summary, teachers play a critical role in supporting children's emotional development, and a lack of understanding of its importance can have significant consequences for students' academic, social, and long-term mental health success.

9. The Role of Parents and Teachers in Strengthening and Developing Children's Social and Emotional Skills

Both parents and teachers play a crucial role in strengthening and developing children's social and emotional skills in life. Here are some ways they can work together to support children's social and emotional development:

Role of Parents
- Modeling: Parents can model social and emotional skills for their children and teach them through their words and actions in a practical way.

- Emotional Validation: Parents accept and validate their children's feelings and help them develop their emotional awareness and understanding.

- Encouraging Emotional Expression: Parents encourage their children to express their feelings in healthy ways, such as through talking, drawing, or writing.

- Role-Playing: Parents can role-play with their children and teach them how to manage and navigate social situations and emotions.

- Providing Emotional Support: Parents can provide emotional support to their children and help them develop emotional resilience and skills.

Role of Teachers

- Creating a Supportive Environment: Teachers can create a supportive classroom environment to promote social-emotional learning and students' emotional safety.

- Teaching Social Skills: Teachers can teach social skills such as cooperation, communication, and conflict resolution.

- Emotional Intelligence: Teachers can model emotional intelligence and demonstrate how to recognize, understand, and manage emotions.

- Classroom Management: Teachers can use classroom management strategies to positively reinforce and guide students' social-emotional learning.

- Collaborating with Parents: Teachers can collaborate with parents to regularly and daily share information about their child's social-emotional development with them as needed.

Parent-Teacher Collaboration

- Sharing Strategies: Parents and teachers can share age-appropriate strategies and practical ideas to promote their children's social-emotional learning at home and in the classroom, as needed.

- Consistency: Parents and teachers can work together to ensure consistency in the development of children's social-emotional skills in home and school settings, coordinating to support children's optimal social-emotional development.

- Supporting Each other: In your role as a parent or teacher, support each other and understand the importance of each other's contribution to children's social-emotional development.

Working together, parents and teachers can provide a comprehensive approach to supporting children's social-emotional development and equipping, empowering, and preparing them for success in life.

10. The Role of Lifestyle on the Development of Social and Emotional Skills

Lifestyle can affect social and emotional development in various ways, such as:

Home Environment

- Stability and Predictability: A regular, consistent, and predictable home environment makes children feel safe and trusting, which is essential for their social and emotional development.

- Parent-Child Interaction: Children's positive interactions with their parents, such as reading books together, singing songs, and engaging in play, strengthen their sense of attachment and emotional intelligence.

- Family Dynamics: A harmonious family environment with loving and affectionate relationships promotes children's empathy, cooperation, and conflict resolution skills.

Socioeconomic Factors

- Income: Low-income families may face stress, uncertainty, and instability, which can negatively impact children's social and emotional development.

- Education Level: Parents with higher levels of education may be more likely to engage in activities such as reading books and discussing current events, which can further children's social and emotional development.

- Social Resources: Access to resources such as libraries, parks, and community centers can provide opportunities for children to socialize and build skills.

Media Exposure

- Media Screen Time: Excessive screen time (e.g., TV, tablets, mobile phones) can lead to decreased physical activity, increased aggression, and shortened attention spans in children, all of which can negatively impact their social and emotional development.

- Media Content: Exposure to violent or inappropriate media content (e.g., TV, tablets, mobile phones) can promote negative attitudes toward others and reduce or even eliminate children's sensitivity to aggression, causing them to accept aggressive behavior as normal. They may also increase their aggressive tendencies and impair their ability to empathize with others. This exposure to violent or inappropriate media content can lead to long-term behavioral and emotional problems in children into adolescence and adulthood.

Daily Activities

Sleep Patterns: Adequate sleep is essential for cognitive development, memory consolidation, and emotion regulation in children aged 2-6 years.

The Importance of Sleep Patterns for Normal Children

- Emotion Regulation: Adequate sleep helps children better manage their emotions and reduces irritability and mood swings.

- Social Interactions: Well-rested children are more likely to interact positively with their peers, increasing their social and relationship skills.

- Cognitive Function: Adequate sleep supports cognitive development, improving attention, memory, and learning abilities.

The Importance of Sleep Patterns for Children Diagnosed with ADHD

- Symptom Management: Poor sleep can exacerbate ADHD symptoms such as hyperactivity, inattention, and impulsivity.

- Behavioral Problems: Lack of sleep can lead to increased behavioral problems and make it more difficult for children with ADHD to follow routines and instructions.

- Emotional Stability: Consistent sleep patterns can help stabilize mood, reduce anxiety, and improve overall emotional well-being.

Establishing and positively reinforcing a healthy sleep routine is crucial for both normal and ADHD children, as it supports their social, emotional, and cognitive development. Positive sleep patterns can enhance children's social and emotional skills by improving mood, attention, and stress management. Conversely, poor sleep can lead to irritability, difficulty concentrating, and challenges in children's emotion regulation and social interactions.

Positive and Negative Sleep Patterns of Parents of 2 to 6 Years Old Children

Positive Sleep Patterns

- A Consistent Bedtime Routine: Establishing a regular bedtime routine helps children feel secure and have better quality sleep.

- Adequate Sleep for Parents: When parents get enough sleep, they are more patient, attentive, and emotionally better able to care for their children.

- A Healthy Sleep Environment: Creating a calm, comfortable sleep environment for parents and children can improve their overall sleep quality and well-being.

Negative Sleep Patterns

- Irregular Sleep Times: Irregular sleep schedules can lead to sleep disorders and behavioral problems in children.

- Parental Sleep Deprivation: When parents are sleep deprived, they may be less able to respond effectively to their children's needs, which can sometimes lead to increased stress and conflict between them. Negative bedtime habits: Bad habits such as prolonged use of social media, cell phones before bed, can negatively affect the sleep patterns of both parents and children.

Nutritional Pattern (Content and Timing): A suitable nutritional pattern for children aged 2-6 years includes the content of food and the timing of its consumption.

Balanced Nutritional Content

A balanced and appropriate diet plan for the growth and development of children aged 2 to 6 years is very important for several reasons:

General Benefits for All Children

- Growth and Development: Proper nutrition provides essential vitamins and minerals needed for children's physical growth and brain development.

- Energy Levels: A balanced diet ensures that children have the energy they need to participate in daily activities, play and learn.

- Immune System: Foods rich in essential nutrients help strengthen children's immune systems and reduce their risk of various diseases.

- Healthy Habits: Establishing healthy eating habits in early childhood sets the foundation for healthy eating patterns that will last a lifetime.

Specific Benefits for Children Diagnosed with ADHD

- Improved Focus and Attention: Certain nutrients, such as omega-3 fatty acids and proteins, can help improve focus and reduce hyperactivity.

- Stable Blood Sugar Levels: A balanced diet with carbohydrates and proteins helps maintain stable blood sugar levels, which can reduce mood swings and improve behavior.

- Reduce ADHD Symptoms: Avoiding foods with artificial additives, high sugar, and excessive caffeine can help manage ADHD symptoms.

- Overall Health: A balanced diet supports overall physical health, which is especially important for children diagnosed with ADHD who may have additional health concerns.

So, the content of what children eat throughout the day, by incorporating a variety of nutrient-rich foods such as fruits, vegetables, proteins, and whole grains, can make a significant difference in general and specific health outcomes for children aged 2-6 years.

Mealtime Patterns

Nutritional Pattern (Content and Timing): A suitable nutritional pattern for children aged 2-6 years includes the content of food and the timing of its consumption.

General Benefits for All Children

- Growth and Development: Proper nutrition provides essential vitamins and minerals needed for children's physical growth and brain development.

- Energy Levels: A balanced diet ensures that children have the energy they need to participate in daily activities, play and learn.

- Immune System: Foods rich in essential nutrients help strengthen children's immune systems and reduce their risk of various diseases.

- Healthy Habits: Establishing healthy eating habits in early childhood sets the foundation for healthy eating patterns that will last a lifetime.

Specific Benefits for Children Diagnosed with ADHD

- Improved Focus and Attention: Certain nutrients, such as omega-3 fatty acids and proteins, can help improve focus and reduce hyperactivity.

- Stable Blood Sugar Levels: A balanced diet of carbohydrates and proteins helps maintain stable blood sugar levels, which can reduce mood swings and improve behavior.

- Reduce ADHD Symptoms: Avoiding foods with artificial additives, high sugar, and excessive caffeine can help manage ADHD symptoms.

- Overall Health: A balanced diet supports overall physical health, which is especially important for children diagnosed with ADHD who may have additional health concerns.

Therefore, the content of what children eat throughout the day, by incorporating a variety of nutrient-rich foods like fruits, vegetables, proteins, and whole grains, can make a significant difference in overall and specific health outcomes for children aged 2-6 years.

Mealtime Patterns
How family mealtimes are structured can foster social skills like communication, sharing, and taking turns.

Positive Patterns
Positive mealtime patterns, such as regular family dinners, foster better communication and stronger family bonds, and strengthen social and emotional skills.

Negative Patterns
Negative patterns, such as irregular or rushed meals, can lead to stress and reduce opportunities for meaningful interactions. Regular, leisurely meals are key to healthy development.

The Importance of Family Mealtime Patterns

General Benefits for All Children
- Nutritional Intake: Family meals often include more balanced and nutritious options that promote healthy eating habits.

- Social Interaction: Regular mealtimes provide an opportunity for family bonding, increasing communication and social skills.

- Routine and Structure: Establishing regular mealtime schedules helps children feel secure and understand the importance of regular mealtime habits.

Specific Benefits for Children with ADHD
- Predictability and Routine: Regular mealtime routines help children with

ADHD manage their untimely expectations and reduce anxiety due to the predictability, certainty, and consistency of regular meals.

- Positive Role Modeling: Family members can model good eating behaviors and social skills, which children with ADHD can emulate.

- Focused Environment: Mealtimes can be designed to minimize distractions and help children with ADHD better focus on eating and social interaction.

- Nutrition Management: Ensuring a balanced diet can help manage ADHD symptoms, such as improving concentration and reducing hyperactivity.

- Overall, positive, regular family mealtime patterns support children's social, emotional, and physical development and provide a foundation for lifelong healthy habits and positive family and child dynamics.

- Physical Activity: Regular physical activity can improve children's mood, reduce stress, and increase their overall well-being.

General Benefits for All Children
- Physical Health: Improves children's cardiovascular fitness, strengthens muscles and bones, and promotes healthy growth.

- Movement Skills Development: Improves children's coordination, balance, and fine and gross motor skills.

- Social Skills: Encourages teamwork, cooperation, and social interaction.

- Emotional Well-Being: Reduces children's anxiety and stress, boosts and increases their mood and self-esteem.

- Cognitive Development: Boosts children's brain development and improves their focus and attention.

Specific Benefits for Children Diagnosed with ADHD
- Improved Focus: Physical activity helps increase children's attention span and reduces their impulsivity.

- Adaptive Behavior: Reduces hyperactivity and improves overall appropriate behavior.

- Emotion Regulation: Helps children manage their emotions. By controlling and moderating emotions through releasing and discharging energy, it reduces symptoms of anxiety and depression caused by impulsivity or impulsivity by creating greater calmness.

Physical Activities Suitable for Children Aged 2 to 6 Years
At Home
For 2-3 Years: Simple activities such as playing with a ball, running, jumping and dancing to music. Obstacle races and active play with toys are also useful.

For 4-6 Years: More structured activities such as riding a tricycle, catching games, simple exercises and yoga are useful.

At School
For 2-3 Years: Short, guided physical activities such as group ball games, music and movement classes, and supervised playtime with sports instructors are useful.

For 4-6 Years: More organized games such as competitions and simple team sports, activities such as climbing on playground equipment and participating in rhythmic gymnastics or gymnastics classes are also suitable.

For Boys and Girls
General Activities: Appropriate activities such as running, jumping, dancing, playing with balls, and structured games are generally beneficial for boys and girls.

Specific Interests: Encourage activities based on the individual interests of boys (e.g., team competition) and girls (e.g., solo competition), whether they are more physical sports like soccer or creative activities like dance.

Additional Considerations for Children with ADHD
Structured and Routine Activities: Consistent, predictable physical activities help children with ADHD know what to expect and reduce anxiety.

Calming, Focused Activities: Activities such as yoga, martial arts, and swimming can help focus and control thoughts, feelings, and balance excitement.

Short, Frequent Sessions: Short, frequent activities throughout the day can often be more effective than longer sessions at maintaining children's attention and energy levels.

Combining a variety of physical activities that meet the individual preferences and needs of boys and girls can greatly contribute to the physical, social, emotional, and cognitive development of all children, including those with ADHD.

Physical activity strengthens the social and emotional skills of children with and without ADHD by improving mood, reducing anxiety, and increasing self-esteem. It encourages teamwork and social interaction, and helps children develop better communication and cooperation skills. Regular exercise also strengthens children's emotion regulation and resilience.

Tips for Parents
- Establish a consistent and predictable routine at home.

- Engage in positive interactions with your child, such as reading together or playing games.

- Create and foster a harmonious family environment by promoting open communication and conflict resolution.

- Limit media time (such as TV, tablets, mobile phones) and encourage children to be physically active.

- Encourage children to have healthy sleep habits by creating a bedtime routine.

- Prioritize family meals and make them a time for connection and bonding.

- Be an active role model for children by demonstrating your own positive social and emotional skills.

By recognizing the impact of lifestyle factors on social and emotional development, parents can take steps to create a nurturing environment that supports their child's growth and well-being. A positive family lifestyle, with regular routines and strong relationships, strengthens children's social and emotional skills by providing stability and support. A negative family lifestyle, such as incompatibility or conflict, can lead to stress and prevent children from having appropriate emotion regulation and social interactions. A positive, healthy and appropriate nurturing environment is very important for children's social and emotional skills to develop.

11. The Role of Parenting Styles and Educational Methods on How Children Develop Socially and Emotionally

The role of parenting styles and educational methods profoundly affects the social and emotional development of young children. Parenting styles refer to the "how" of parenting, that is, how parents interact, discipline, communicate, and respond to the child's behavior. Parenting style refers to the action parents take to raise their children and meet their needs. Children change as they go through each stage of growth and development. Each child in a family also has a different and unique personality, temperament, interests, and abilities.

Therefore, the role of parents in raising and educating children is multifaceted and complex.

In general, there are four parenting styles:

1. Authoritarian Parenting Style: High control and low affection

2. Permissive Parenting Style: Low control and high affection

3. Abandoning Parenting Style: Low control and low affection

4. Authoritative Parenting Style: High control and high affection

Parenting style plays a significant role in shaping the social and emotional development of young children. Research has shown that parenting style can affect children's growth and development in various ways throughout their lives.

Development of Social Skills

- Authoritarian Parenting: Authoritarian parents often have aggressive, anxious, and withdrawn children.

- Authoritative Parenting: Authoritative parents who balance warmth, affection, and control often have children with adequate ability to cooperate, empathize, and social skills.

- Permissive Parenting: Permissive parents often have children who are aggressive, impulsive, and lack social skills.

- Avoidant Parenting: Permissive parents often have children who are more anxious, insecure, and have poor social skills.

Development of Emotional Skills

- Authoritarian Parenting: Authoritarian parents often have children who show more negative emotions, such as anger and frustration.

- Authoritative Parenting: Authoritative parents often have children who show more positive emotions, such as joy and empathy.

- Permissive Parenting: Permissive parents often have children who exhibit greater emotional instability and mood swings.

- Avoidant Parenting: Permissive parents often have children who exhibit greater emotional distress and anxiety.

Key Features of Effective Parenting Styles for Children 2 to 6 Years Old

- Intimacy: Show affection, empathy, and understanding towards your child.

- Boundary Setting: Establish clear rules and consequences.

- Communication: Communicate openly and honestly with your child.

- Consistency: Consistently enforce rules and consequences for your child's appropriate and inappropriate behavior, and be flexible when necessary.

- Respect: Treat your child with respect and dignity, even when they misbehave.

Tips for Parents

- Practice Positive Reinforcement: Praise and reward your child's positive behavior.

- Set Clear Expectations: Set clear rules and consequences for your child's behavior.

- Be Consistent: Consistently enforce rules and consequences for your child's behavior.

- Be Patient: Practice patience when dealing with your child's tantrums or misbehavior.

- Model Good Behavior: Show your child social and emotional skills yourself.

Challenges for Parents

- Time Management: Set aside time for quality interaction with your child in the midst of a busy schedule.

- Emotion Regulation: Control and manage your emotions when dealing with your child's tantrums or misbehavior.

- Discipline: Set discipline rules that are neither too restrictive nor too restrictive, appropriate for your child's age.

- By understanding the importance of parenting style in social and emotional development, parents can make conscious efforts to adopt effective parenting practices that promote healthy development in their young children.

- Parenting styles significantly influence the social and emotional development of young children. Authoritative parenting, characterized by warmth and firm structure, fosters independence and strong emotional skills in children. Consistent educational approaches that encourage social interaction and emotional expression promote better social competence. Negligent or permissive styles can negatively hinder children's self-regulation and emotional understanding. A balanced and nurturing environment is key to the healthy development and strengthening of preschool children's social and emotional skills.

2- An Overview of Social -Emotional Learning

What is the difference between social-emotional learning skills and children's social and emotional skills?

Social-emotional learning skills and children's social and emotional skills are closely related but not the same. For a better understanding, here is a breakdown of their differences:

Social-Emotional Learning Skills

- Structured Process: A systematic, purposeful approach designed to develop children's social and emotional skills through purposeful instruction and practice.

- Instructional Framework: Typically includes programs implemented in schools and other educational settings to promote children's social and emotional competence.

- Key Components: Includes specific skills such as self-awareness, self-management, social awareness, communication skills, and responsible decision-making.

Children's Social and Emotional Skills

- Natural Development: These skills refer to the abilities that children naturally develop through interaction with their environment and others.

- Daily Interactions: Children's social and emotional skills develop through everyday experiences such as playing with peers, handling conflicts, and expressing emotions.

- Individual Variation: The development of these skills varies widely among children based on their unique experiences and environments.

- Essentially, social-emotional learning provides a structured framework for targeted instruction and reinforcement of children's innate and natural social and emotional skills.

Social-emotional learning helps children develop essential life skills to understand and manage their emotions, set and achieve goals, develop healthy relationships, and make responsible decisions.

Children's Social-Emotional Learning Theory

In general, social-emotional learning refers to the process by which individuals learn and apply a set of social, emotional, and related skills, attitudes, behaviors, and values. It includes the thoughts, feelings, and actions that enable them to succeed in the educational environment, at school, and in life.

Social-emotional learning has its roots in the early 20th century, but it has evolved significantly over the years. Here is a brief history of the development of social-emotional learning:

Early Beginnings (1920-1950)

- Progressive Education: The progressive education movement led by John Dewey and others emphasized the importance of social-emotional learning in educating children.

- Character Education: The character education movement, launched in the 1920s, focused on teaching children moral values and social skills.

Middle Years (1960-1983)

- Social Learning Theory: Albert Bandura's (1961) social learning theory stated that children learn behaviors through observation, imitation, and reinforcement.

- Emotional Intelligence: Howard Gardner's (1983) concept of emotional intelligence introduced the idea that children need to understand and manage their emotions in order to succeed.

Modern Era (1990-2010)

- CASEL (Partnership for Academic and Social-Emotional Learning): CASEL is a leading organization in the field of social-emotional learning (CASEL, 1994) that provides research-based guidance and resources.

- Frameworks: CASEL developed the social-emotional learning framework, which includes five competencies: self-awareness, self-management, social awareness, communication skills, and responsible decision-making.

- Whole Child Approach: The whole child approach, popularized by the Association for Curriculum Oversight and Development (ASCD, 2007), emphasized the importance of children's social-emotional learning in education.

Recent Developments (2010s to Present)

- Increasing Focus on Social-Emotional Learning: Growing recognition of the importance of social-emotional learning in education has led to increased investment in research, curriculum development, and teacher training.

- Integration with Academic Learning: Social-emotional learning is now recognized as a critical component of academic success, with research showing that social-emotional learning skills can improve academic achievement and reduce achievement gaps.

- Digital Tools and Resources: The development of digital tools and resources has made it easier to teach and assess social-emotional learning skills.

- Social-emotional learning has evolved throughout its history through the contributions of many researchers, educators, and organizations. Today, it is widely recognized as a vital component of education that is essential for promoting children's overall well-being, academic success, and lifelong learning.

Social-emotional learning focuses on teaching children the following skills:

- Self-Awareness: Recognizing and understanding one's own emotions, strengths, and weaknesses.

- Self-Regulation: Managing and regulating emotions, thoughts, and behaviors in different situations.

- Social Awareness: Showing empathy and understanding for others, recognizing social cues, and understanding cultural and social differences.

- Communication Skills: Building and maintaining healthy and meaningful relationships, including effective communication, teamwork, and conflict resolution.

- Responsible Decision-Making: Weighing the pros and cons of different personal and social choices and considering their ethical implications.

- These components collectively help children navigate their social world, build positive relationships, and effectively manage and resolve challenges with greater independence.

- Social-emotional learning is a powerful approach to education that focuses on helping students develop the skills necessary for success in school and life. By integrating social-emotional skills into the curriculum, schools can create a more supportive and inclusive learning environment that fosters the growth, development, and overall development of the whole child.

- Social-emotional learning is not just about teaching children kindness and respect, it is about equipping them with the tools they need to navigate the complexities of life in this modern world.

Benefits of Social-Emotional Learning for Young Children

Social-emotional learning is essential for young children because it lays the foundation for their future academic, social, and emotional success. Here are some of the benefits specifically for young boys and girls at home and at school, considering the personality and structural differences of children:

Benefits of social-emotional learning for boys aged 2-6 years include:

- Improved Emotion Regulation: Helps boys develop emotional awareness, understanding, and control, and reduces anger and aggression.

- Enhanced Problem-Solving Skills: Teaches boys to better identify problems, think critically, and develop appropriate solutions.

- Better Social Skills: Helps boys build friendships, collaborate with peers, and communicate effectively.

- Increased Empathy: Strengthens boys' compassion, understanding, and kindness toward others.

- Reduced Aggression: Reduces boys' aggressive behavior by teaching them to manage emotions and resolve conflict peacefully.

Benefits of social-emotional learning for girls aged 2-6 years include:
- Increased Self-Confidence: Helps girls develop self-awareness, self-acceptance, and self-confidence.

- Improved Communication Skills: Enhances verbal and nonverbal communication skills, leading to better relationships.

- Increased Creativity: Encourages girls to express their feelings creatively and fosters imagination and innovation.

- Better Conflict Resolution: Teaches girls to resolve conflicts in a peaceful and respectful manner.

- Increased Empathy: Helps girls develop a deeper understanding of the feelings and perspectives of others.

Benefits of Social-Emotional Learning at Home
- Stronger Parent-Child Bonding: Strengthens the bond between parents and children and fosters a sense of security and trust between them.

- Emotional Intelligence: Parents can model and teach social-emotional learning skills such as empathy, self-awareness, and self-regulation to children.

- Reduced Anger: By teaching children to recognize and manage their emotions, parents can reduce their tantrums and outbursts.

- Improved Relationships: Promotes positive relationships between children and parents in the family by encouraging active listening, cooperation, and respect.

Benefits of Social-Emotional Learning at School (e.g., Kindergarten, Preschool)
- Classroom Atmosphere: Creates a positive classroom atmosphere and promotes a sense of belonging and learning for children.

- Teacher-Student Relationships: Fosters strong teacher-student relationships based on trust, respect, and understanding.

- Academic Performance: Linked to improved academic performance, as emotionally intelligent students tend to perform better academically.

- Development of Social Skills: Schools can provide opportunities for socialization, collaboration, and teamwork through social-emotional learning activities.

- Bullying Reduction: Social-emotional learning programs can help reduce bullying in children by teaching empathy, self-awareness, and conflict resolution skills.

By incorporating social-emotional learning into the home and school environment, parents and educators can help boys and girls aged 2-6 develop essential social-emotional skills that will serve them well throughout their lives.

3- Understanding Attention-Deficit Hyperactivity Disorder (ADHD)

1. What Is Meant by ADHD?

2. What Are the Main Symptoms of ADHD?

3. What Are Some Common Symptoms of ADHD in Boys and Girls Aged 2-6 Years?

4. Why Is It Important to Understand ADHD?

5. How Common Is ADHD in Children Aged 2-6 Years?

6. What Percentage of High Achievers Have ADHD?

7. How Can Parents and Teachers Support Children with ADHD?

8. What Are Some Common Misconceptions about ADHD?

9. What Are the Specific Behavioral Symptoms of ADHD in Boys Compared to Girls Aged 2-6 Years?

10. What Are the Differences between the Behavior of Children Aged 2-6 Years with ADHD at School and at Home?

11. Is there a Significant Difference in the Development of Social and Emotional Skills in Children with ADHD Compared to Normal Children?

12. How Does Social and Emotional Learning in Children with ADHD Compare to Normal Children?

13. How Does the Brain Function in Social and Emotional Development in Children with ADHD?

14. What Are the Potential Challenges in Children with ADHD?

15. What Are the Distinct Strengths of Children with ADHD Compared to other Children at the Same Age?

16. What Are the Apparent Weaknesses of Children with ADHD Compared to other Children at the Same Age?

17. How Is ADHD Diagnosed in Children?

18. What Are the General Strategies for Managing ADHD in Children?

1. What Is Meant by ADHD?

ADHD stands for attention-deficit hyperactivity disorder. In children aged 2-6, it is usually characterized by a pattern of inattention and distractibility (inability to maintain focus), hyperactivity (excessive movement that is inappropriate for the environment), and impulsivity (rapid, hasty actions that occur in the moment without thinking). It is often abbreviated as ADHD (also in this book).

These symptoms are often caused by problems and disorders in the cognitive activities of the brain (such as: thinking, problem solving, attention, reasoning, memory) and other behavioral and emotional functions of the brain (such as: controlling behavior and emotions). Attention deficits and problems in emotion regulation are often considered the main symptoms of hyperactivity, which have very important and significant effects on the way relationships, interpersonal interactions, family, social, health and in general the growth and development of children.

Although over the past years, experts and researchers have often proposed proven reasons based on the involvement of various genetic, hereditary and environmental factors for the development of hyperactivity disorder and have discussed them in detailed research, in most cases the exact cause of hyperactivity remains unknown.

For example, a specific event, such as traumatic brain injury, exposure of the fetus to biological hazards during the mother's pregnancy, a genetic defect or mutation, severe nutritional deprivation of the mother during pregnancy or early in the child's life may play a role in the development of hyperactivity.

2. What Are the Different Types and Main Symptoms of ADHD?

There are three types of ADHD:

1- Combined: Hyperactivity-Impulsivity-Inattentive: This is the most common type. Children with this type are hyperactive and impulsive. They also have trouble paying attention and concentrating and are easily distracted.

2- Hyperactivity-Impulsivity: This is the least common type. Children with this type are hyperactive and impulsive. But they do not have trouble paying attention and concentrating.

3- Inattentive: Children with this type are often inattentive and easily distracted and lose focus. They may not be lively or even calm and are not hyperactive. Many people with ADHD also have problems with hyperactivity or impulsivity, but this is not always the case. For example, about 2 to 3 out of 10 people with ADHD have difficulty concentrating, but with hyperactivity or impulsivity they do not have problems.

The main symptoms of ADHD include:

The main symptoms of ADHD and the main focus of most behaviors of hyperactive children often include:

- Inattention: They have difficulty maintaining attention and concentration, are easily distracted by external stimuli or different thoughts, often make careless mistakes.

They usually have difficulty concentrating on tasks or activities, such as playing with toys or listening to stories. They often have difficulty following instructions or completing tasks.

- Hyperactivity: Restlessness, hyperactivity, difficulty sitting in inappropriate positions.

  Often restless or fidgety, especially when expected to sit still (such as when eating, playing quietly).

- Impulsivity: Often acts quickly without thinking about the consequences, interrupts conversations or activities of others, has difficulty waiting for turns in activities or games.

- Affective Disorganization: Often has frequent mood swings. Is impatient and impatient in managing frustration or anger, and often has difficulty controlling their emotions, leading to anger or outbursts.

- Forgetfulness and Disorganization: Often misplaces or loses toys, books, or other items. Has difficulty following routines or completing daily activities that require organization. For example, misplacing a book, losing a pencil, forgetting to brush your teeth, or having trouble tidying up your school bag or messy room.

3. What Are the Common Symptoms of ADHD in Boys and Girls Aged 2-6 Years?

ADHD symptoms may appear differently in boys and girls (ages 2-6) for a variety of reasons (e.g., personality and cultural differences), with girls often exhibiting more internalizing behaviors, which can sometimes make it more difficult to diagnose ADHD at an early age. Some of these differences in ADHD symptoms in boys and girls aged 2-6 include:

Boys (2-6 Years Old)
- Hyperactivity: Boys are more likely to exhibit more lively hyperactive behaviors than girls their age (such as running, fidgeting, and difficulty sitting still).

- Impulsivity: They may act more thoughtlessly than girls their age, interrupt others, and have trouble waiting their turn.

- Disruptive Behavior: Boys often exhibit more externalizing symptoms and engage in negative or inappropriate behavior in settings such as preschool or daycare to a significantly greater extent than girls their age.

Girls (2-6 Years Old)

- Inattention: Girls are more likely than boys to show signs of inattention, such as difficulty concentrating, being easily distracted, and not following instructions.

- Internalizing Symptoms: They may appear more withdrawn than boys their age, have lower self-esteem, and struggle with internalizing their frustration.

- Verbal Aggression: Girls may show more verbal aggression and emotional outbursts than boys their age, compared to the physical aggression of boys their age.

- These differences can sometimes lead to misdiagnosis of ADHD in girls, because their ADHD symptoms are less obvious. These are general patterns of ADHD, but it is important to remember that every child is unique and ADHD symptoms can vary greatly.

4. Why Is Understanding ADHD so Important?

Understanding ADHD is important for several reasons. These include:
For Parents
Early Intervention
Reason: Early identification of ADHD allows parents to seek appropriate interventions and supports for their child. Appropriate early intervention can significantly improve a child's development and quality of life.

Impact: Timely support can help manage symptoms, improve children's behaviors, and enhance their learning and social interactions.

Better Parenting Strategies
Reason: Understanding ADHD allows parents to better adopt effective parenting strategies tailored to their child's needs.

Impact: Positive parenting techniques can reduce stress for both the child and the parents and create a more positive and harmonious family environment.

Emotional Support
Reason: Children with ADHD often struggle with self-esteem and emotion

regulation. Understanding their condition helps parents better provide them with the emotional support they need.

Impact: A supportive home environment fosters resilience, self-confidence, and emotional well-being.

Advocacy

Rationale: Awareness of ADHD enables parents to advocate for their child's needs in a variety of settings, including healthcare and education.

Impact: Advocacy ensures that children receive the facilities and supports they need to thrive.

Stress Reduction

Rationale: Understanding the nature of ADHD can reduce parental frustration and stress by setting realistic expectations and adopting effective management strategies.

Impact: A firm, calm management approach, coupled with appropriate parental awareness of each child's needs, helps the entire family dynamic.

For Teachers
Individualized Teaching Strategies

Rationale: Understanding ADHD helps teachers develop and implement individualized teaching strategies that meet the specific needs of children with ADHD.

Impact: Tailored instruction improves academic performance and appropriate classroom behavior.

Classroom Management

Rationale: Awareness of ADHD enables teachers to adopt effective classroom management techniques that minimize children's behavioral disturbances and support all students.

Impact: A well-managed classroom benefits both the child with ADHD and their normal peers.

Promoting Inclusion

Reason: Educators who understand ADHD can create an inclusive learning environment where all students feel valued and supported.

Impact: Inclusion fosters a positive school culture and reduces conflict and conflict among students.

Early Identification and Referral

Reason: Teachers are often the first to notice signs of ADHD. Understanding this condition allows them to identify potential cases earlier and refer students to specialists for further evaluation.

Impact: Early identification of ADHD leads to timely support and intervention.

Partnering with Parents

Reason: Teachers who understand ADHD can effectively communicate with parents and work with them to support the child's development.

Impact: Strong partnerships between home and school enhance the educational experience and the child's health and academic achievement.

Understanding ADHD in young children is crucial to providing appropriate support and creating an environment in which they can thrive. By becoming aware, both parents and teachers can make a significant positive impact on the lives of children with ADHD.

By recognizing the signs and challenges of hyperactivity, you can help children develop the social-emotional skills they need in life and work together to create a positive learning environment.

Without understanding, identification and appropriate and appropriate solutions, hyperactivity can have serious negative and lasting consequences including school failure, family stress and disruption, depression, relationship problems, substance abuse, delinquency, accidental injuries and career failure from childhood, adolescence and adulthood.

5. How Common Is ADHD in Children 2 to 6 Years Old?

ADHD is relatively common in children aged 2 to 6, with an estimated prevalence of 2% to 7.9%. Boys are more likely to be diagnosed with ADHD than girls, and older children (ages 4, 5, and 6) are more likely to meet ADHD criteria than younger children (ages 2 and 3).

However, diagnosing hyperactivity in children aged 2 to 6 can be challenging because the symptoms of the disorder can be confused with the normal behaviors of normal 2- to 6-year-olds. In addition, children aged 2 to 6 may have difficulty expressing their symptoms, making it difficult for healthcare providers to accurately diagnose the disorder.

Early identification and intervention in the management of hyperactivity in children aged 2 to 6 is critical. Without early intervention, children with hyperactivity may struggle academically and socially, leading to long-term problems in their academic and personal lives.

Important considerations challenging the diagnosis of ADHD in children aged 2 to 6:

- Age-Related Development: Preschool children are still developing their attention skills, and their ability to sustain attention and complete tasks may not be as mature as older children.

- Diagnostic Challenges: Diagnosing ADHD in children aged 2 to 6 can be challenging due to their limited ability to communicate and follow instructions.

- Co-Occurring Problems: Many hyperactive children aged 2 to 6 may also have comorbid conditions such as autism spectrum disorder, anxiety, or sensory processing disorder, which can interfere with their development and behavior and cause additional behavioral and learning problems for children.

It is important to remember that each child develops at their own pace, and some children aged 2 to 6 may exhibit behaviors that resemble hyperactivity symptoms that are transient due to age-related developmental factors. Therefore, an accurate diagnosis and evaluation of ADHD in children requires a comprehensive evaluation by a qualified physician and psychologist.

6. What Percentage of Gifted Children Have ADHD?

ADHD is often seen as a barrier to academic success and achievement. However, some studies have shown that there may be a unique relationship between hyperactive children and excellence and genius, as many children with ADHD appear to be creative, innovative, and able to think outside the box than other normal children their age. These traits can lead to extraordinary success in areas such as art, music, technology, and entrepreneurship. Children with ADHD may also have high levels of curiosity, energy, and enthusiasm, which can lead them to pursue their interests and excel in their chosen fields.

In this regard, we should pay attention to this very important educational and nurturing point that instead of focusing solely on the challenges and deficiencies of hyperactive children, we should pay more attention and focus on recognizing and cultivating their talents and strengths, because by providing these children with appropriate support, facilities and opportunities to direct their energy and creativity, they can achieve very important and great achievements throughout their academic and social lives and make a significant contribution to the progress of society. With the right guidance and encouragement from parents, supervisors and teachers, hyperactive children can use their unique abilities to achieve their full potential and progress in a world that values diversity and innovation. In this way, the relationship between hyperactive children and excellence and genius can be seen as a significant, powerful and transformative relationship. For example, a study in 2003 in South Korea showed that 9.4% of the outstanding children they studied had hyperactivity. Also, at the Center for the Development of Excellence in Denver, about 10% of the 3,000 gifted children studied were diagnosed with ADHD.

Overall, various international studies 2023 show that about 8.8% of gifted children have ADHD. However, some research suggests that up to 50% of gifted children may show symptoms similar to ADHD, which does not necessarily mean that all of them have a formal diagnosis of ADHD.

In short, children diagnosed with ADHD often show strong energy and motivation, which, if positively directed, can turn into excellence and genius. Their ability to think quickly and act quickly can lead to problem-solving and innovative creativity. However, providing structured environments and supports to help them effectively use their potential is crucial.

7. How Can Parents and Teachers Support Children Aged 2 to 6 Years Diagnosed with ADHD?

Parental and teacher support is crucial for the academic and personal development of children diagnosed with ADHD. Parents play a critical role in providing a nurturing and understanding environment for the hyperactive child. They can work closely with teachers to create an appropriate plan to support their child's needs, such as providing extra help with homework, implementing behavioral strategies, and ensuring they have access to necessary resources. By working hand in hand with teachers, parents can help create a consistent and structured approach to learning that benefits the hyperactive child.

Teachers also play a vital role in supporting hyperactive children in the classroom. They can create a supportive and inclusive classroom environment, use differentiated instructional strategies, and provide resources to help these children succeed academically. Teachers can also work with parents to share information about their child's progress and behavior, allowing for a unified approach to supporting the child at home and at school. By fostering a strong partnership between parents and teachers, children with ADHD can receive the support they need to reach their full potential and succeed in their academic and personal lives.

Supporting children diagnosed with ADHD requires a collaborative effort between parents, teachers, and healthcare professionals. Here are some ways parents and teachers can support preschoolers with ADHD:

Parents
- Create a Daily Routine: Establish a consistent daily schedule, including set times for meals, naps, and activities.

- Provide Structure and Boundaries: Establish clear rules and consequences and enforce them consistently.

- Encourage Physical Activity: Regular physical activity, such as outdoor play or dance classes, can help reduce symptoms of ADHD.

- Use Visual Aids: Visual aids such as charts, pictures, and schedules can help hyperactive preschoolers understand and follow daily routines.

- Provide Positive Reinforcement: Praise and reward good behavior, such as using a sticker or star on a chart.

- Communicate with Teachers: Communicate with teachers regularly to stay informed about your child's behavior and progress in the preschool setting.

- Seek Professional Help: If your child has significant attention or behavior problems, seek professional help from a pediatrician or psychologist.

Teachers
- Create a Nurturing Environment: Create a warm, welcoming, and predictable classroom environment that promotes social-emotional learning.

- Use Positive Behavioral Supports: Use positive behavioral supports, such as reinforcement systems and redirection techniques, to promote good behavior.

- Provide Individualized Support: Provide individualized support and accommodations to help hyperactive preschoolers succeed in the classroom.

- Encourage Active Participation: Encourage active participation in group activities and games to help hyperactive preschoolers stay engaged and focused.

- Give Regular Breaks: Help hyperactive preschoolers regulate their behavior.

- Collaborate with Parents: Work with parents to develop strategies to support their child's behavior and learning in the classroom.

- Be Patient and Understanding: Be patient and understanding when working with hyperactive preschoolers, as they may need more time and support to complete tasks.

Common Strategies

- Use Movement-Based Activities: Use movement-based activities, such as music or dance, to help hyperactive preschoolers stay focused and engaged.

- Suggested Choices: Offer choices throughout the day, such as "Do you want to play with blocks or puzzles?" to help hyperactive preschoolers feel more in control.

- Use Visual Reminders: Use visual reminders, such as pictures or charts, to help hyperactive preschoolers remember routines and tasks.

- Provide Frequent Feedback: To help hyperactive preschoolers stay motivated and engaged, provide frequent feedback and encouragement.

- Encourage Social Skills: Encourage social skills like sharing and turn-taking through play-based activities.

- Parents and teachers working together can provide the support and accommodations needed to help hyperactive preschoolers succeed in the classroom and develop important social-emotional skills.

Parents and teachers can ensure that their support strategies promote independence rather than dependency by focusing on fostering self-regulation and problem-solving skills in children with ADHD.

- Gradual Independence: Gradually reduce the level of support as children become more able to complete tasks independently. This helps build their confidence and self-sufficiency.

- Empowerment: Encourage children to make their own choices and take responsibility for their actions when making decisions to choose or do something with the supervision of their parents or teachers. This promotes their decision-making skills and responsibility.

- Skill Building: Focus on teaching coping strategies, i.e., ways to cope, confront and overcome stress and life problems (e.g., finding a quiet place to do homework to deal with distractions) and organizational skills, i.e., ways to create structure and order and prioritize tasks and assignments (e.g., prioritizing tasks based on importance or interest) that the child can use on their own (rather than having tasks done for them).

- Positive Reinforcement: Use praise and rewards to reinforce independent behavior and effort, and emphasize the importance of spontaneity.

- Adaptation: Maintain regular expectations and routines, which help children cope with difficult and challenging situations with greater adaptability and independence and internalize adaptability.

By gradually reinforcing these skills and promoting independence, parents and teachers can help children with ADHD strengthen and develop the ability to manage their behavior and responsibilities independently.

8. What Are Some Common Misconceptions about ADHD?

Many parents and teachers still have misconceptions about ADHD. Studies show that about 50% of them believe that ADHD is just an "excuse for bad behavior" or "poor parenting," and 30% think that children with a diagnosis of ADHD simply have to work harder to focus. These misconceptions can hinder effective support and intervention for children with a diagnosis of ADHD.

There are several common misconceptions about children with ADHD that can reinforce the misunderstanding and stigma surrounding ADHD. Often parents and teachers assume that all hyperactive children display the same symptoms and behaviors. This is not true. In fact, hyperactivity is a spectrum disorder and symptoms can vary greatly from child to child. Some children may struggle with hyperactivity and impulsivity, while others may have difficulty paying attention and concentrating. It is important to recognize and acknowledge individual differences in how children display hyperactivity in order to provide appropriate support and understanding.

Here are some common misconceptions that parents and teachers may have about children with ADHD:

Parental Misconceptions
- ADHD Is Just a Phase: Many parents may think that hyperactivity is a phase that children will outgrow, but symptoms of hyperactivity can persist throughout childhood, adolescence, and even adulthood.

- ADHD Is Caused by Poor Parenting: Parents may feel guilty or blame themselves for their child's hyperactivity, such as "I am a bad parent because my child is hyperactive." But in reality, hyperactivity is not caused by poor parenting. It is considered a neurodevelopmental disorder that affects children's brain function and behavior.

- ADHD Is a Lack of Discipline: Some parents may think that hyperactive children just need stricter discipline, but in reality, they often need specific strategies to help them focus better and have more control over their emotions and behaviors.

- ADHD Children Are Just "Lazy": Hyperactive children often have trouble getting started and staying on task, but they are not lazy. They need help breaking tasks down into smaller steps and finding ways to stay engaged in tasks and activities.

- ADHD Children Are Unable to Learn: This is a common misconception. Hyperactive children can learn and achieve a lot with the right support and accommodations.

- My Child Is Hyperactive Just Because He or She Is Overactive: While in reality some children with ADHD may be hyperactive, others may not be. In addition to hyperactivity, inattention, disorganization, or difficulty maintaining attention are also common symptoms, so some may be calm but struggle with inattention, disorganization, or difficulty maintaining attention.

- Medication Is the Only Solution for ADHD: While medication can be helpful in managing some symptoms, behavioral therapy, lifestyle changes, and alternative treatments such as diet and exercise can also be effective in addition to medication.

- My Child's ADHD Is Not Severe Enough to Require Treatment: Every ADHD child is unique, and the severity of symptoms can vary greatly. Even mild symptoms of ADHD can significantly impact a child's daily life, requiring their own specific behavioral training and treatments.

- ADHD Can Be "Cured" with Willpower or Discipline: While behavioral therapy and self-regulation techniques can help manage symptoms, there is no definitive cure for hyperactivity. Medications and other treatments can help manage symptoms, but they are not a definitive cure.

Teachers' Misconceptions

- ADHD Children Are Just "Noisy": Teachers may view hyperactive behaviors more as intentional misbehavior than as unintentional and symptomatic of ADHD.

- ADHD Children Can Never Sit Still or Pay Attention: While it is true that ADHD children often have trouble sitting still or concentrating, many can learn strategies to help them sit still or pay attention.

- ADHD Children Are "Unmotivated": Teachers may think that ADHD children lack motivation to do homework, but they often need help to feel interested in starting activities and finding ways to stay engaged in homework.

- ADHD Children Are Only Distracted by Media Technology: While media technology can be a challenge for ADHD children, it is not their only source of distraction. They may be distracted by their own thoughts or external sensory stimuli in their environment.

- ADHD Is Just a Behavioral Problem: Teachers may see ADHD as simply a behavioral problem, but it is a neurodevelopmental disorder that affects executive function, attention, and the control of impulsive behavior.

- ADHD Children Can Never Fully Learn or Achieve Significant Academic Success: With the right support, accommodations, and strategies, they can make academic progress and develop important life skills just like everyone else.

What Can We Do to Combat These Misconceptions?

To combat these misconceptions, we can:

- By eliminating these common misconceptions and gaining a better understanding of ADHD, we can help create a more inclusive and supportive environment for children with the disorder.

- Educate ourselves about ADHD with the help of doctors, psychologists, and expert counselors.

- Work together as parents, teachers, and healthcare providers to provide appropriate support and accommodations for children with ADHD.

- Focus on the strengths and abilities, rather than the deficiencies, of children with ADHD.

- Provide individualized support and strategies that are appropriate for each child to help children with ADHD succeed.

- Support educational programs that understand and accept children with ADHD through collaborative home-school communication.

9. What Are the Specific Behavioral Symptoms of ADHD in Boys Compared to Girls between the Ages of 2 to 6 Years?

In children between the ages of 2 and 6, both boys and girls can show symptoms of ADHD. However, the symptoms of ADHD may differ somewhat in boys and girls. Here are some specific behavioral signs of ADHD in boys aged 2 to 6 compared to girls aged 2 to 6 years:

Boys Aged 2 to 6 Years

- Increased Hyperactivity: Boys with ADHD are more likely to show excessive physical activity, such as running, jumping, or climbing, which can be distracting and disrupt classroom activities.

- Irritability: They may fidget with their hands, feet, or other objects and often have difficulty sitting still for long periods of time.

- Difficulty Following Directions: They may have trouble following multi-step instructions or may forget to complete tasks altogether.

- Impulsivity: They may interrupt others to get their answers out or have difficulty self-regulating and controlling their emotions.

- Aggressive Behavior: They may exhibit more aggressive behavior toward girls (such as hitting, pushing, or throwing toys), which can be distressing and intolerable to parents and teachers.

Girls Aged 2 to 6 Years

- Daydreaming and Inattention: They may exhibit more internalizing behaviors (such as daydreaming, staring into space, or getting lost in their thoughts) than boys.

- Social Problems: They may struggle with social skills such as sharing, taking turns, or cooperating with peers.

- Emotional Dysregulation: They may experience more emotional disturbances than boys (such as irritability, mood swings, or extreme reactions to minor disappointments).

- Perfectionism: They may exhibit perfectionistic tendencies. When tasks are not performed to their high standards, this often leads to increased anxiety and stress.

- Avoidance Behaviors: They may avoid activities that they find challenging or overwhelming, which can lead to missing out on learning and socializing opportunities.

It is important to note that these symptoms are not specific to boys or girls and can vary in severity and symptoms from child to child. Furthermore, while Some symptoms may be more common in boys aged 2 to 6, but can also occur transiently in girls aged 2 to 6.

10. What Are the Differences between the Behavior of Children with ADHD at School and at Home?

Children aged 2 to 6 with ADHD often exhibit different behaviors at school and at home, which can be attributed to a variety of factors. Here are some differences you may notice:

At School

- Structured Environment: Schools provide a structured environment with established schedules, routines, and rules, which can help these children be more organized and focused.

- Teacher Support: Teachers may be more aware of a child's ADHD symptoms and provide resources such as extra attention, visual aids, or motor breaks to help them stay engaged.

- Social Interactions: School provides opportunities for social interaction with peers, which can help these children develop social skills and learn how to manage and direct their relationships with others.

- Emotion Regulation: Teachers may be more experienced in managing children's emotions and behaviors, which can help reduce tantrums and behavioral and emotional meltdowns.

At Home
- Unstructured Environment: Homes often have a more relaxed atmosphere, with fewer rules and structures, which can make it challenging for preschoolers with ADHD to regulate their behavior.

- Parental Stress: Parents may experience more stress and anxiety at home, which can lead to increased frustration and conflict with their child with ADHD.

- Emotion Regulation: Parents may be more emotionally sensitive to their child's behavior and may feel and express more emotional distress when their child exhibits challenging behaviors.

- Frequent Mood Swings: Preschoolers with ADHD are often more prone to tantrums and behavioral and emotional meltdowns at home due to increased emotional intensity and lack of structure at home.

Differences between School and Home Behavior
- Excitement: They may show more excitement at home where there is less structure.

- Inattention: They may show more inattention at home, where they may have more freedom to engage in preferred activities or avoid their primary responsibilities.

- Impulsivity: Impulsive behaviors (such as interrupting others) may be more likely to occur at home, where there is less structure and fewer consequences.

- Emotion Regulation: They may struggle more with emotion regulation and controlling emotions at home, where they may be more emotionally demanding from their caregivers.

It is important to recognize that these differences are not unique to ADHD, but are also a natural result of different environments and expectations. By understanding these differences, parents, caregivers, and teachers can work together to develop strategies that support the child's unique needs and help them thrive in both the school and home environments, and to increase home-school communication.

11. Is There a Significant Difference in the Development of Social and Emotional Skills in 2 to 6 Years Old Children with ADHD Compared to Normal Children?

Research shows that children aged 2 to 6 with a diagnosis of ADHD may have delays or differences in the development of social and emotional skills compared to their peers who do not have ADHD. Examples include:

Social Skills
- Delayed Development of Social Skills: They may have delays in developing social skills, such as starting or maintaining friendships, understanding social cues, and cooperating with peers.

- Difficulty in Emotion Regulation: They may have trouble recognizing, understanding, and managing their emotions, which can lead to impulsive reactions and problems with social interactions.

- Difficulty in Empathy: They may have trouble understanding and responding to the emotions of others, which can affect their ability to form and maintain relationships.

Emotional Skills
- Increased Anxiety and Stress: They may experience higher levels of anxiety and stress due to problems with executive function, attention, and self-regulation.

- Disturbance in Emotion Regulation: They may have trouble controlling and managing their emotions, which can lead to mood swings, irritability, and outbursts.

- Difficulty in Self-Awareness: They may have trouble recognizing and understanding their emotions, which can make it challenging for them to develop emotional intelligence and self-awareness.

Why Is This so?
- Neurodevelopmental Factors: ADHD is a neurodevelopmental disorder that affects executive function, attention, and impulse control systems. The brain is affected. These systems also play a role in social and emotional development.

- Executive Functioning Deficits: Children diagnosed with ADHD often struggle with executive functioning deficits such as planning, organization, time management, and self-regulation, which can affect their ability to develop social and emotional skills.

- Environmental Factors: Environmental factors such as disorganization and maladjustment or exposure to trauma (physical and psychological injuries) can also lead to delays or problems in social and emotional development in children with ADHD.

What Can We Do?
- Early Intervention: Early identification and intervention can help address social and emotional skill deficits in preschool children with ADHD.

- Individual Support: Provide individual support and facilitation to help children with ADHD develop social and emotional skills.

- Parent-Teacher Collaboration: Appropriate and regular collaboration between parents and teachers in the home-school relationship is necessary to provide ongoing support and strategies to address the development of social and emotional skills.

- Treatment: To help children with ADHD develop their social and emotional skills, consider treatments such as play therapy or cognitive-behavioral therapy, as needed, with the advice of a specialist doctor and psychologist.

- By acknowledging these differences and providing targeted support, we can help preschool children with ADHD to develop the social and emotional skills they need to thrive.

12. How Is Social-Emotional Learning in 2 to 6 Years Old Children with ADHD Compared to Normal Children?

Social-emotional learning is essential for all children, including those diagnosed with ADHD. While both normal children and children with ADHD can benefit from social-emotional learning, the approach and strategies required for children with ADHD may be slightly different. Here is a comparison of the benefits of social-emotional learning for normal children and children with ADHD aged 2 to 6:

Characteristics and challenges of normal children and children with ADHD in social-emotional learning:

Characteristics of Normal Children Aged 2 to 6 Years
- Curiosity: Normal children aged 2 to 6 are often naturally curious and eager to learn.

- Collaboration: They often tend to cooperate with peers and teachers and show an understanding of social norms.

- Emotion Regulation: Normal children aged 2 to 6 can regulate and control their emotions with some occasional behavioral and emotional outbursts and outbursts.

- Empathy: They can often recognize and respond appropriately to the emotions of others.

- Communication Skills: They often have basic communication skills such as verbal and nonverbal cues.

Common Challenges of Normal 2 to 6 Years Old Children
- Temperament: They may occasionally have tantrums due to frustration or overstimulation.

- Frustration with Rules: They may sometimes struggle with following rules or transitions, leading to frustration and resistance.

- Sharing and Turn-Taking: They may need guidance in sharing and taking turns with peers.

- Separation Anxiety: They may experience separation anxiety when leaving their parents or caregivers.

Characteristics of 2 to 6 Years Old Children with ADHD

- High Energy Levels: They have high energy levels that make it challenging for them to concentrate.

- Impulsivity: They often act impulsively, interrupting others.

- Difficulty Transitioning: They may struggle with change, resisting changes in routines or activities.

- Affective Dysregulation: They often experience more frequent and intense emotional outbursts due to difficulty regulating their emotions.

- Social Problems: Young children with ADHD may struggle with social interactions, such as starting or maintaining conversations.

Common Challenges for Children Aged 2 to 6 Years with ADHD

- Following Directions: They may have difficulty following multi-step instructions or remembering instructions.

- Staying Focused: They often struggle to maintain focus during activities, which often leads to restlessness or indifference.

- Self-Regulation: They often need more support with self-regulation strategies, such as deep breathing or visualization techniques.

- Lack of Social Skills: They may need explicit instruction in social skills such as cooperation, empathy, and conflict resolution more often.

- Sensory Sensitivities: Some may be sensitive to certain sounds, lights, or textures, which can affect their ability to focus or participate in activities.

Understanding these characteristics and challenges is essential for parents, caregivers, and teachers to provide individualized support and accommodations for children aged 2 to 6 who are normally developing and who are diagnosed with ADHD in social-emotional domains.

Comparison of social-emotional learning skills and strategies for normal and ADHD-diagnosed children aged 2 to 6 years:

- Emotion Regulation: Normal children have some emotion regulation but need better emotion regulation skills such as recognizing and managing their emotions better, while children with ADHD may struggle with emotional disorders.

- Self-Awareness: Normal children have some self-awareness but tend to have a better understanding of their strengths, weaknesses, and emotions, while children with ADHD may struggle with self-awareness.

- Empathy: Normal children have some empathy but tend to have a greater desire to develop empathy to better understand other people's perspectives, while children with ADHD may have difficulty understanding empathy and responding to other people's emotions.

- Social Skills: Normal children have some social skills but tend to strengthen their social skills further so that they can more easily succeed in social relationships (such as starting and maintaining friendships, cooperating with peers) and following social norms, while children with ADHD may often struggle with these skills.

Comparison of social-emotional learning teaching strategies for normal children and children with ADHD:

Mindfulness: Normal children tend to use mindfulness strategies naturally (such as taking deep breaths or counting to 10 before reacting to an emotion). Children with ADHD may need explicit instruction in mindfulness strategies.

Labeling Emotions: Normal children tend to identify and label their emotions accurately, while children with ADHD may have difficulty labeling emotions.

Problem-Solving: Normal children tend to use problem-solving strategies more effectively (such as breaking problems down into smaller steps or asking for help from others). Children with ADHD may have difficulty solving problems due to problems with executive function.

Self-Regulation: Normal children have better self-regulation skills (such as taking breaks when needed or using coping mechanisms such as deep breathing). Children with ADHD may need more specific instruction and support to develop self-regulation skills. In short, teaching social learning strategies to children with ADHD often need special training and additional support. For example, strategies such as:

- Use Visual Aids: Use visual aids such as pictures or diagrams to help them understand and identify emotions.

- Break Down Tasks: Break down complex tasks into smaller steps so they can better develop problem-solving skills.

- Provide Frequent Feedback: Provide frequent feedback and encouragement to help them develop self-awareness and self-esteem.

- Use Movement-Based Activities: Use movement-based activities to help them release their excess energy more easily and improve their concentration.

- Modeling: Model social-emotional learning skills yourself (such as taking breaks when needed) to help them learn the skills better by example. By acknowledging these differences and using targeted teaching strategies, we can support the social-emotional learning of normal and hyperactive preschoolers and help them strengthen and further develop the social-emotional skills necessary for success throughout life.

13. How Does the Brain Function in Social and Emotional Development in Children with ADHD?

Brain Development in Normal Children 2 to 6 Years Old
Toddlerhood (ages 2 to 3) is a critical period for brain development. During this time, the brain undergoes significant changes that lay the foundation for future cognitive, social, and emotional skills. Changes include:

Rapid Growth: The brain continues to grow rapidly, forming billions of new connections between neurons.

Synaptic Pruning: Unused connections in the nervous system are removed, making the brain more efficient.

Prefrontal Cortex Development: This area, which is responsible for decision-making, self-control, and social behavior, continues to grow.

Language and Social Skills: Children develop language and social interaction skills that are crucial for communication and relationships.

Emotion Regulation: The ability to manage emotions improves, helping children respond more appropriately to situations.

Brain Development in Children with ADHD at Ages 2 to 6 Years
Brain maturation in children aged 2 to 6 with ADHD is often delayed compared to their normal peers. This delay is most pronounced in the frontal cortex, which is responsible for executive functions such as attention, planning, and impulse control. Their brain development pattern:

Delayed Maturation: The brains of children with ADHD often mature several years later, especially in the frontal regions.

Similar Development Pattern: Despite the delayed brain development, their overall brain development pattern follows a similar trajectory to that of normal children without ADHD.

Impact on Symptoms: This delay can exacerbate ADHD symptoms such as inattention, hyperactivity, and impulsivity.

Potential for Improvement: As children with ADHD grow older, their brain development can progress. This growth can indicate the potential for improved brain function.

Understanding these differences in brain development can help create targeted interventions and support for children with ADHD so that they can receive timely care and appropriate resources for growth and development.

Research has shown that brain function in social-emotional development in ADHD children is characterized by the following:

Neurobiological Abnormalities
   - Prefrontal Cortex Dysfunction: The prefrontal cortex, which is responsible for executive functions, impulse control, and emotion regulation, is often underactive in children with ADHD. The prefrontal cortex and its connections may be associated with hyperactive symptoms (symptoms such as distractibility, forgetfulness, impulsivity, poor planning, and hyperactivity).

   - Amygdala Hypersensitivity: The amygdala, which is responsible for processing emotions, is often more active than normal in children with ADHD, leading to increased emotional reactivity and impulsivity in children with ADHD.

   - Dopamine Imbalance: An imbalance in the secretion of the neurotransmitter dopamine is common in children with ADHD. They often have low levels of dopamine in the brain. Imbalanced function in dopamine signaling leads to symptoms such as impulsivity, inattention, and difficulty in decision-making in children with ADHD.

   - Neurotransmitters: Are chemicals that are secreted from one neuron of the nervous system and affect the activity of another neuron.

- Dopamine: A neurotransmitter that plays a role in motivation, reward processing, and attention.

Functional Brain Imaging Studies
- fMRI Studies: fMRI studies have shown that children with ADHD show less activity in the frontal cingulate cortex and basal ganglia during social and emotional tasks.

- Functional Connectivity Analysis: Functional Connectivity Analysis has shown altered connections between brain regions in children with ADHD, along with greater activity between several subcortical regions and the frontal cortex than in the brains of normal children.

Neural Mechanisms
- Emotional Processing: Children with ADHD may have difficulty processing emotions due to altered neural activity in the amygdala and prefrontal cortex.

- Impulse Control: Impulse control deficits in children with ADHD may be related to neural mechanisms such as reduced activity in the anterior cingulate cortex.

- Social Cognition: Children with ADHD may have difficulty with social cognition due to altered neural activity in the prefrontal cortex and temporal regions of the brain.

Social and Emotional Development Implications
- Challenges in Emotion Regulation: Children with ADHD may experience difficulties in emotion regulation due to altered neural activity in the amygdala and prefrontal cortex.

- Impaired Social Skills: Impaired social skills in children with ADHD may be related to reduced activity in the prefrontal cortex and anterior cingulate cortex of the brain.

- Increased Risk of Mental Health Problems: A combination of neurobiological abnormalities and functional brain imaging findings suggest that children with ADHD may be predisposed to mental health problems.

Some Specialized Interventions to Help Children Diagnosed with ADHD
- Behavioral Therapy: Behavioral therapy can help ADHD children improve emotion regulation, impulse control, and social skills.

- Cognitive Training: Cognitive training programs can help improve attention, working memory, and executive functions in ADHD children.

- Neurofeedback Training: Neurofeedback training (training the brain to create healthier brain activity patterns) can help people with ADHD self-regulate their brain activity.

To conduct neurofeedback to monitor brain waves, sensors are placed on the child's scalp to monitor brain wave patterns associated with different mental states (such as calm, focused, or restless).

For example, during neurofeedback sessions, the child might watch a fun animation that responds to their brain waves and rewards them for creating calm and focused brain activity through a process of monitoring and feedback at specific times. Over time, this training can help the child maintain focus and control impulses more effectively.

Or, if a child is playing a video game in which a character only moves forward when the child is calm and focused, they learn to maintain this state until the character in the game moves. This practice helps the child gain better control over their attention and behavior in everyday situations. Over time, with repeated practice, the child learns to produce these brainwave patterns consistently.

Therefore, neurofeedback can help hyperactive children by teaching them to regulate their brain activity to improve their attention and concentration difficulties, reduce hyperactivity, and increase their control over impulsivity.

By understanding the neural mechanisms underlying social and emotional development in hyperactive children, we can provide targeted interventions to support their social and emotional development.

14. What Are the Potential Challenges of ADHD in Children Aged 2 to 6 Years?

Children aged 2 to 6 with ADHD can face a number of challenges that affect their daily lives and development. Such as:

- Inattention: Difficulty paying attention and focusing on tasks, following instructions, and staying on task.

- Hyperactivity: Excessively active, have trouble staying still, and are constantly "on the go."

- Impulsivity: Often react quickly, act without thinking, and interrupt others. Have trouble waiting their turn.

- Emotion Regulation: Struggle to manage emotions, which can lead to frequent tantrums and emotional outbursts.

- Social Skills: Difficulty making and maintaining friendships, understanding social cues, and cooperating with peers.

- Behavioral Issues: Often cause problems in educational settings such as daycare or preschool due to inappropriate and sometimes disruptive behaviors.

- Learning Difficulties: Often have difficulty learning new concepts and keeping up with academic tasks.

- Injuries: They often suffer various injuries due to hasty or impulsive actions and lack of awareness of danger.

Early diagnosis and intervention are essential to help children aged 2 to 6 with ADHD learn the skills needed to manage these challenges in a timely manner.

15. What Are the Distinctive Strengths of Children with ADHD Compared to Normal Children of the Same Age (Ages 2 to 6 Years)?

While children with ADHD may face challenges in certain areas, they often have unique strengths that can be used to support their development and success. Here are some of the distinctive strengths of children with ADHD compared to normal children of the same age:

Cognitive Strengths
- Creative Problem-Solving: They often think outside the box, tend to be creative problem solvers, and come up with interesting, innovative solutions.

- Improved Memory: They may have an increased ability to recall verbal information, especially when the information is presented in a novel or unexpected way. For example, when a teacher uses an engaging story instead of just listing scientific facts about a subject. The novel and unexpected elements of the story capture the attention of the child with ADHD, and he or she remembers the information with greater accuracy and detail than with traditional teaching methods.

- Increased Attention: While they may struggle with inattention and persistent focus, they can focus intensely on subjects that interest them and show remarkable attention to detail.

- Improved Spatial Skills: They may be somewhat superior to normal children in tasks and skills related to spatial perception, such as puzzles, mazes, or building games.

(Spatial Perception: The ability to locate, move around, orient, make multiple decisions, analyze situations, and represent the surrounding environment and the body's relationship to it.)

Socio-Emotional Strengths
- Eager to Take an Action: They are often eager to take an action, which can lead to a sense of adventure and exploration in them.

- Fearlessness: They may be more willing to take risks and try new things, which can help them develop greater resilience and self-confidence.

- Empathy and Understanding: Despite struggling with emotion regulation, they often strive to show empathy and understanding towards others, which can lead to strong social connections in them.

- Natural Curiosity: They are naturally curious and interested in learning, which can lead them to ask questions and seek out new experiences.

Behavioral Strengths
- Resourceful: They often find ways to adapt to situations and use their creativity and resourcefulness to overcome obstacles.

- Quick-Thinking: They tend to They are quick to think and react quickly to changing situations or unexpected events.

- Motivation: Despite challenges with organization and planning, they can be highly motivated to do a task or activity when they are interested in it.

- Positive Attitude: Many have a positive outlook on life that can help them maintain a sense of humor and optimism despite challenges.

Teaching strategies include:
- Play to their Strengths: Identify their strengths, such as creative problem solving or spatial skills, and build teaching strategies around them.

- Provide Choices: Provide reasonable choices, allowing them to make their own decisions and demonstrate independence.

- Use Movement-Based Activities: Incorporate physical activity into lessons or activities to help them release excess energy and stay more focused.

- Encourage Independence: Encourage independence by providing opportunities for self-directed play or projects that allow them to showcase their creativity.

By recognizing and valuing these strengths, you can create a supportive environment that fosters growth, confidence, and success for preschoolers diagnosed with ADHD.

16. What Are the Obvious Weaknesses of Children with ADHD Compared to Normal Children of the Same Age (Ages 2 to 6 Years)?

While children with ADHD often have unique strengths, they also face specific challenges that can affect their development and behavior. Here are some of the more obvious weaknesses of children with ADHD compared to normal children aged 2 to 6:

Cognitive weaknesses include:
- Trouble with Sustained Attention: They often struggle to focus on a single task for long periods of time, which leads to difficulty with sustained attention. For example, they may start a task but quickly become distracted and lose track of what they were doing. This can make it challenging for them to complete assignments, follow instructions, and stay engaged in activities that require long-term focus. Their attention tends to wander and they seek out new stimuli to keep their minds engaged.

- Impulsivity: Impulsive behaviors, such as interrupting others, making unexpected responses, or making hasty decisions, can be challenging for them.

- Working Memory Challenges: They often face working memory challenges that affect their ability to retain and manipulate information for short periods of time.

For example, an ADHD child may have difficulty remembering a series of teacher instructions, such as "First put your books away, then get your art supplies ready, and finally sit down at your desk." They may quickly forget the steps in the instructions, which leads to incomplete or incorrect completion of the task. This difficulty can negatively affect their performance in academic and daily tasks where retaining and using information is critical.

- Organization and Planning: Difficulty organizing and planning can lead to disorganization, losing their personal belongings, and missing deadlines.

Social emotional weaknesses include:
- Emotion Regulation: They often struggle with emotion regulation, leading to mood swings, irritability, or intense emotions.

- Self-Doubt and Low Self-Esteem: Frustration from executive functioning challenges can lead to self-doubt and low self-esteem.

- Difficulty in Cooperation: Problems following rules can make it challenging for them to cooperate with others.

- Social Skills: Difficulty with social skills, such as starting or maintaining friendships, can be a challenge for them.

Behavioral weaknesses include:
- Impulsivity: They may act without thinking (such as interrupting others or making hasty decisions).

- Restlessness: Constant restlessness, moving around, and difficulty sitting still are common behaviors.

- Emotional Outbursts: They may have trouble controlling their emotions, leading to frequent tantrums or mood swings.

- Trouble Following Rules: Hyperactive children may have trouble sticking to rules and instructions, often because they forget or get distracted.

- Social Challenges: Their impulsive and lively behavior can make it challenging for them to make and maintain friendships.

Teaching strategies include:

- Break Tasks into Smaller Steps: Break complex tasks into smaller, manageable steps to help them stay focused and avoid feeling overwhelmed.

- Provide Visual Reminders: Use visual reminders, such as charts or graphs, to help them remember Use important information or tasks.

- Encourage Self-Monitoring: Teach them to monitor and control their behavior by setting goals and tracking their progress.

- Provide Regular Feedback and Encouragement: Provide regular feedback and encouragement to help build their self-confidence and self-esteem. By acknowledging these weaknesses and using targeted strategies, you can help support the overall development and well-being of preschoolers with ADHD.

17. How Is ADHD Diagnosed in Children Aged 2 to 6 Years?

Diagnosing ADHD in children aged 2 to 6 can be challenging due to the natural variability in their behavior and developmental stages. However, a comprehensive diagnostic evaluation can help identify potential signs and symptoms. Here is an overview of the diagnostic process:

The evaluation process includes:

- Parent-Guardian Questionnaires: Parent-guardian questionnaires, such as the Vanderbilt Assessment Scale or the Connors Rating Scale, are used to gather information about the child's behavior and symptoms.

- Clinical Interview: A full clinical interview is conducted with the parent-guardian or child to gather more detailed information about the child's behavior, sleep patterns, and developmental milestones.

- Observations: Observations of the child's behavior in various settings such as home, school (kindergarten, preschool) are made to assess attention, control of impulsivity or hyperactivity.

- Developmental Screening: Developmental screenings are done to rule out other developmental disorders or conditions that may help diagnose symptoms.

Diagnostic Criteria

The American Academy of Pediatrics recommends that the diagnosis of ADHD in children aged 2 to 6 years should be based on the following criteria:

- Persistent Symptoms: Symptoms must be present for at least 6 months before diagnosis.

- Six or More Symptoms: The diagnosis includes six or more symptoms from the following categories:

- Inattention: The child often does not pay attention to details, has difficulty maintaining concentration, or is easily distracted.

- Hyperactivity: The child is restless, taps his hands or feet, has difficulty sitting still, or has difficulty doing quiet activities.

- Impulsivity: The child often interrupts others, has trouble waiting for their turn, or has difficulty responding.

- Severity: The symptoms must cause significant impairment in the child's social, academic, or daily functioning.

Best methods for assessment include:

- Multi-Source: Gather and compile information from multiple sources, including parents/guardians, teachers/caregiver, preschool, and trained observers.

- Standardized Assessments: Use standardized assessments such as the Vanderbilt Assessment Scale or Connors Rating Scale to assess the child's symptoms and behaviors.

- Consider Comorbid Conditions: Consider the child's other developmental disorders or conditions that may contribute to or accompany the symptoms.

- Monitor Progress Over Time: Monitor progress over time to determine if symptoms remain persistent and affect the child's daily functioning.

- Work with a Multidisciplinary Team: To ensure a comprehensive assessment and treatment of the child, a multidisciplinary team of professionals, including a pediatrician, psychologist, and educator, often collaborates and collaborates.

18. What Are the General Strategies for Managing ADHD in Children Aged 2 to 6 Years?

Here are some immediate strategies to help manage ADHD in children aged 2 to 6 in emotional and critical situations, such as:

Immediate emotion regulation strategies include:
- Deep Breathing: Encourage your child to take slow, deep breaths, inhaling through their nose and exhaling through their mouth.

- Counting: Ask your child to count slowly to 10 or 20 to help them calm down.

- Visualizing a Calm Place: Ask your child to imagine a calm place, such as a beach or a forest, and visualize themselves in that environment.

- Physical Touch: Gently hug your child, hold their hand, or pat them on the back and caress them to help them feel calm.

Immediate strategies for behavioral challenges include:
- Redirect Your Child's Attention: Direct your child's attention to a different activity or toy to help them refocus.

- Offering Choices: Give your child options, such as "Do you want to play with blocks or dolls?" to give them a sense of control.

- Use Positive Language: Instead of saying "don't cry," use positive, calming language, such as "I know you're upset, but it's okay, my dear, calm down!"

- Provide Sensory Relief: Provide a soft toy or stuffed animal to help your child control their emotions and behavior and provide sensory relief. A soft stuffed animal or a familiar blanket can be comforting for a child in stressful moments and help your child feel safe and calm in those situations. This feeling of comfort can reduce the child's anxiety and is considered a sign of a calm and safe environment for the child, and in most cases, it can bring emotional peace to an angry or anxious child.

Immediate strategies for disruptive behavior include:
- Set Clear Boundaries: Set clear boundaries and consequences for your child's disruptive behavior, while also showing empathy and understanding.

- Use Diversion: Direct the child's energy and attention to a more appropriate and interesting activity or toy. In that critical situation, distracting the child from explanation and discussion works faster.

- Provide an Alternative Outlet: Provide an alternative outlet for a more appropriate release of the child's energy (such as running around in a designated area or playing with play dough).

Additional Tips

- Keep Your Intervention Brief: Keep unnecessary interventions brief as much as possible and focus on the immediate issue and problem at hand. Long and unnecessary discussions often cause the child to become stubborn, intensify destructive behavior, and prolong the crisis. To better control the crisis situation and manage the child's behavior, it is better to react firmly but calmly.
(Aim for 1 to 3 minutes of intervention and then reassess the situation before continuing to manage your child's behavior.)

- Be Calm and Patient: When dealing with challenging behaviors, it is very practical, important, and essential to remain calm and patient. While addressing a child's behavior problem, be calm and patient, avoid yelling or punishing. Expressing your uncontrolled anger and rage, even if understandable and justified due to the child's inappropriate behavior, often reinforces children's destructive behaviors. So, considering this important parenting point, manage your and your child's behavior control calmly and calmly as much as possible to calm down the difficult situation.

- Follow Up on Behavioral Consequences: After the child's problem is resolved immediately, follow up on the consequences of inappropriate behavior, such as taking away privileges (such as limiting a child's favorite activity) or creating clear expectations for the child's future behavior with certainty and without interruption.

Since each child is unique and what works for one child may not work for another child, be flexible and adapting these strategies to meet the individual needs of each child aged 2 to 6 is essential. Always remember in very difficult and challenging times that parenting is a very sensitive and important skill to the extent that sometimes even a small uncontrolled reaction of parents has a very destructive and dangerous impact on the whole personality and life of the children. Therefore, your tolerance and resilience to get through critical and unbearable and difficult moments in managing the destructive behavior of children aged 2 to 6, especially children with ADHD, is very necessary, vital and commendable.

CHAPTER 3: THE RELATIONSHIP BETWEEN SELF-AWARENESS AND EMOTIONAL UNDERSTANDING

1- EMOTIONAL UNDERSTANDING OF CHILDREN 2 TO 6 YEARS OLD

2- ACTIVITIES TO HELP CHILDREN TO IDENTIFY AND LABEL THEIR EMOTIONS

3- SELF- REFLECTION, RECOGNITION OF ONE'S OWN STRENGTHS AND WEAKNESSES IN CHILDREN 2 TO 6 YEARS OLD

4- ACTIVITIES TO HELP CHILDREN ENCOURAGE BEHAVIORAL REFLECTION AND SELF-ASSESSMENT

5- POSITIVE REINFORCEMENT AND PRAISE FOR CHILDREN'S PROGRESS AND ACHIEVEMENTS

6- WHAT IS THE RELATIONSHIP BETWEEN SELF-AWARENESS, EMOTIONAL UNDERSTANDING, AND MINDFULNESS PRACTICES?

7- SIMPLE MINDFULNESS PRACTICES SUCH AS ABDOMINAL BREATHING AND MINDFUL LISTENING FOR SELF-AWARENESS

Self-Awareness

Definition

Self-awareness in social-emotional learning for children aged 2 to 6 involves recognizing and understanding their feelings, strengths, and preferences. For example, a child might say, "I feel happy when I play with my friends," indicating that they can identify their feelings and why. This awareness helps them navigate social interactions and manage their emotions effectively.

Components of Self-Awareness

While it is ideal to introduce all components of self-awareness to children aged 2 to 6, it is essential to consider their developmental stage and abilities. Children typically are 2 to 6 years old, and are still developing their cognitive, emotional, and social skills. They can learn some, but not all, of the components of self-awareness.

In social-emotional learning for children aged 2 to 6, self-awareness includes several essential components:

- Emotional Cognition: The ability to identify and label their own emotions, such as knowing when they are feeling happy, sad, angry, or scared.

- Sensitivity: Recognizing what triggers their emotions, such as realizing that they feel angry when someone takes a toy without their permission.

- Body Awareness: Being aware of how their emotions affect their bodies, such as noticing that their heart rate increases when they are excited. Developing an awareness of their own body, how they move, and how they feel physically, is crucial for self-control and managing reactions.

- Sense of Identity: Understanding personal characteristics, such as name, likes, dislikes, and preferences, that help a child feel.

- Expressing Emotions: Learn to express their feelings in appropriate ways, such as using words to express their discomfort instead of hitting.

- Reflecting on Behavior and Self-Evaluation: Begin to reflect on their actions, thoughts, and feelings to assess their impact on others.

Encouraging children to think and reflect on their actions and the consequences of those actions helps them learn from experiences and develop a deeper understanding of themselves. Identify what they are good at and what they are weak at and need to strengthen and improve. This builds a sense of self-confidence and realistic self-evaluation.

These components help children aged 2 to 6 years to advance their interactions with the world and strengthen the early stages of self-awareness, which will continue to develop with age-appropriate instruction. So, to teach self-awareness to children aged 2 to 6, focus on these components.

The level of self-awareness in children aged 2 to 6 includes the following characteristics:

In 2-Year-Old Children
Early Self-Awareness: Begins to recognize themselves in mirrors and photographs. They may begin to use pronouns such as "I" and "mine."

Simple Preferences: Show simple preferences for specific toys or activities they enjoy and begin to express their independence.

Emotional Triggers: Have a limited understanding of what makes them feel. They react strongly to immediate needs such as hunger or tiredness.

Body Awareness: Begins to recognize the different major body parts and senses, but their ability to understand and express these feelings is still developing.

Limited Reflective Behavior and Self-Evaluation: At this age, children have the least ability to evaluate their actions or feelings. They primarily react to immediate experiences and feelings.

In 3-Year-Old Children

Identifying Emotions: Can identify and label their basic emotions, such as happiness, sadness, or anger.

Understanding Personal Characteristics: Begin to understand simple personal characteristics, such as being big or small, and may describe themselves using terms such as "I am big."

Emotional Triggers: Begin to recognize simple triggers for their feelings, such as knowing that not getting a toy makes them sad. They still need guidance to understand and manage these triggers.

Body Awareness: With better awareness of their body, they can identify more body parts, and may begin to understand basic physical needs, such as knowing when they are hungry or tired.

Emerging Reflective Behavior and Self-Evaluation: Begin to demonstrate early reflective behavior and self-evaluation. They may recognize when they have done something wrong (such as spilling juice), but their understanding is still very simple and immediate.

In 4-Year-Old Children

Sophisticated Self-Concept: They demonstrate a more complex self-concept and understand aspects such as their abilities and characteristics.

Empathy and Roles: They demonstrate empathy and can imagine themselves in different roles during play, such as pretending to be a doctor or a parent.

Emotional Triggers: They show greater awareness of what makes them feel (such as understanding that sharing can lead to both positive and negative feelings). They begin to verbalize these triggers.

Body Awareness: They show a better understanding of their body's feelings and needs. They can more clearly express feelings such as pain, hunger, or fatigue.

Developing Reflective Behavior and Self-Evaluation: They begin to show greater awareness of their actions and the consequences of their behavior. They can recognize how their behavior affects others and may feel pride or regret for their actions. They can begin to talk about the causes of their behavior, such as what they did and why they did it.

In 5-Year-Old Children

Detailed Self-Description: They can describe themselves in more detail, including likes, dislikes, and personal characteristics

Understanding Differences: They recognize differences between themselves and others, such as their own abilities or personal preferences.

Emotional Triggers: Complex emotional triggers They begin to identify and express their feelings, including social interactions and personal successes or failures. They begin to use coping strategies to manage and control their emotions.

Body Awareness: They have a good understanding of their physical needs and can express their own feelings. They understand the importance of activities such as exercise and rest.

Improved Reflective Behavior and Self-Evaluation: Demonstrate an increased ability to self-evaluate and reflect on their own behavior and feelings. They can discuss past experiences and express how they felt and why they felt that way. They begin to understand the concept of improved reflective behavior and can talk about what they can do differently next time.

In 6-Year-Old Children

Advanced Self-Concept: They have a full understanding of their identity, including their strengths and weaknesses.

Social Comparison: They begin to compare themselves to peers, understand people's social interactions, and their place in social groups.

Emotional Triggers: They demonstrate a high level of understanding of emotional triggers, including subtle social cues and internal factors such as self-esteem. They can discuss these triggers and use more complex strategies to manage their emotions.

Body Awareness: They demonstrate a keen awareness of their body and their physical needs. They can participate in activities that promote their physical health and understand the impact of physical activity on their health.

Advanced Reflective Behavior and Self-Evaluation: They demonstrate a more developed sense of reflective behavior and self-evaluation. They can evaluate their actions in a variety of contexts and understand the consequences. They can set simple goals for themselves and discuss how to achieve them. They are also beginning to understand their strengths and areas for improvement in their weaknesses. These levels of self-awareness reflect the gradual and significant growth that occurs in early childhood, ages 2 to 6, helping children develop a strong sense of identity and a sense of their place in life.

The importance of self-awareness includes:

- Improved Relationships: Self-awareness helps people understand themselves better, which can lead to more authentic and meaningful relationships with others.

- Better Decision-Making: Self-awareness can help people make more informed decisions by recognizing their own perceptual errors and motivations.

- Emotional Intelligence: Self-awareness is a key component of emotional intelligence, which is essential for effective communication and conflict resolution.

- Personal Growth: Self-awareness is a key factor in personal growth and development, as it allows people to recognize their strengths and weaknesses and work towards self-improvement.

- Mental Health: Self-awareness can help people better understand their mental health needs and seek appropriate support.

In the context of children aged 2 to 6, self-awareness is an essential skill that can be developed through play-based activities, social-emotional learning curricula, and guidance from parents and teachers. By fostering self-awareness in children aged 2 to 6, we can help them become emotionally intelligent, confident, and empathetic individuals.

What Is the Relationship between Self-Awareness and Emotional Understanding in Children Aged 2 to 6 Years?

In children aged 2 to 6, self-awareness and emotional understanding are closely intertwined and mutually reinforce each other. This mutual reinforcement includes:

- Self-Awareness: When children recognize their own emotions, they become more self-aware. This recognition is the first step to emotional understanding and their own reactions.

- Emotional Understanding: With greater self-awareness, children can better understand and express their emotions. This helps them manage their emotions and respond appropriately to different situations, which increases their emotional understanding.

For example, a child who can recognize when they are feeling frustrated (self-awareness) can learn to express this frustration with words rather than acting out (emotional understanding). This mutual reinforcement helps them navigate social interactions more effectively.

1- Emotional Understanding of Children Aged 2 to 6 Years

Emotional awareness and understanding refer to the ability to identify and understand their own and others' emotions. This is the ability to recognize emotional cues, express emotions in a healthy way, and develop empathy for others.

Emotional awareness and understanding are very important for children aged 2 to 6 because they help them:

Develop Social Skills: Improve relationships with peers and adults.

Manage Emotions: Regulate their own emotions and develop healthy coping strategies.

Develop Empathy: Understand and respond to the emotions of others.

Improve Academic Performance: Increase focus, attention, and problem-solving skills.

Children's emotional understanding and recognition of emotions gradually develop as they grow and mature. Here are some examples of emotional understanding levels for children aged 2 to 6:

For 2-Year-Old Children

At this age, children are in the early stages of recognizing and expressing emotions. Characteristics you can typically expect include:

Early Recognition of Emotions: Children begin to recognize basic emotions such as happiness, sadness, and anger in themselves and others. For example, they may be able to point to a happy or sad face in books or real-life situations.

Simple Emotional Expression: They are often able to express their feelings through basic words, gestures, and facial expressions. For example, they may say "happy" or "angry" and show the corresponding facial expressions.

Developing Empathy: Early signs of empathy begin to emerge. For example, a 2-year-old may comfort a crying friend by hugging or giving them a toy.

Emotion Regulation: While they can express their feelings to some extent, managing and regulating these feelings is still challenging for them. For example, tantrums are common when arguing with others because they are still struggling with self-control.

For 3-Year-Old Children

By the age of 3, children experience significant growth in their understanding and expression of their emotions. Characteristics you can typically expect include:

Identifying Emotions: They can identify a wider range of emotions in themselves and others, including happiness, sadness, anger, and fear.

Verbal Expression: Children begin to use words to express their feelings more clearly, making statements like "I am sad" or "I am angry."

Empathy: Empathy continues to develop. They may comfort a friend who is upset, share their toys, or express concern for others.

Emotional Responses: They begin to understand the causes and effects of different emotions. For example, they may recognize that a friend is crying because they have fallen.

Emotion Regulation: They begin to use simple strategies, such as asking for help or getting help from a caregiver, to manage their emotions.

These advances in emotional understanding and expression often represent important milestones in a 3-year-old's ability to navigate their emotional world and lay the foundation for more complex emotional and social skills.

For 4-Year-Old Children

By age 4, children's emotional understanding deepens significantly. Characteristics you can typically expect include:

Complex Emotions: They begin to recognize and understand more complex emotions, such as jealousy, pride, and guilt.

Verbal Expression: They can express their feelings more clearly and explain why they feel a certain way.

Empathy: They show more consistent empathy and can comfort upset friends and family members to some extent.

Emotional Causation: They understand a wider range of reasons for feelings, such as recognizing that someone may be upset because they miss a loved one.

Emotion Regulation: Gradually uses strategies to manage their emotions, such as taking deep breaths or seeking comfort from an adult or favorite toy.

These milestones reflect an important step forward in their ability to navigate and express their feelings, preparing them for more complex social interactions and relationships in the future.

For 5-Year-Old Children

By age 5, children's emotional understanding becomes more complex. Characteristics you can typically expect include:

Recognizing Complex Emotions: They can recognize and name a wider range of emotions, including pride, shame, and guilt.

Verbal Expression: Children can clearly express their feelings and explain why they feel a certain way.

Empathy: Show greater empathy and compassion, and can offer comfort and support to their upset peers, and demonstrate a deeper understanding of the feelings of others.

Social Awareness: Understand the impact of their actions on the feelings of others and can modify their behavior accordingly.

Emotion Regulation: Use more effective strategies to manage their emotions, such as talking about their feelings, asking for help, or using self-soothing techniques like deep, slow breathing.

These developments reflect significant progress in 5-year-olds' emotional literacy and social competence, allowing them to act with greater skill and sensitivity in their emotional and social worlds.

For 6-Year-Old Children

By age 6, children have developed a more nuanced understanding of emotions. Here are some of the characteristics you can typically expect from their emotional development at this age:

Identifying Emotions: Six-year-olds can recognize and name a wide range of emotions, such as happiness, sadness, anger, fear, and surprise. They can also understand more complex emotions, such as jealousy and pride.

Understanding Causes: They begin to understand the causes of emotions and realize that certain events or situations can trigger certain emotions. For example, they know that losing a toy can make them sad or that winning a game can make them feel happy.

Empathy: Children at this age begin to show empathy and understand that others have feelings and that their actions can affect those feelings. They can often comfort a friend who is upset or share in someone else's happiness.

Emotion Regulation: Six-year-olds are developing the ability to better manage their own emotions. While they may still struggle with controlling their impulsivity, they are learning coping strategies (such as deep breathing or seeking help from an adult) to cope with strong emotions.

Social Awareness: They are becoming more aware of social norms and expectations regarding emotional expression of their emotions and feelings. They are beginning to understand the appropriate situations (the right time and place) to express their specific emotions in order to establish and maintain their connections with others.

It is important to remember that these are general milestones in children's emotional development and that each child is unique. Some children may develop their emotional understanding earlier or later than their peers, depending on a variety of factors such as family parenting styles, temperament and individual differences, and the environment and circumstances of each child's development.

2- Activities to Help Children Aged 2 to 6 Years to Identify and Label their Emotions

Remember, every child develops at their own pace, so be sure to tailor activities to your child's unique needs and abilities. For example, for children diagnosed with ADHD:

- Keep activities short and engaging.

- Incorporate movement and physical activity into your play and practice.

- Use visual aids and assistive devices to increase their focus.

- Offer choices and allow them to make choices and decisions.

- Provide positive reinforcement and encouragement.

Teach Emotional Understanding Strategies to Children Aged 2 to 6 Years

- Identify Emotions: Teach them to recognize and label their emotions.

- Express Emotions: Encourage healthy expression of emotions through art, music, or talking.

- Emotion Pantomime: Play a game where they act out different emotions without speaking.

- Emotion Chart: Create an emotion chart with pictures or words to help them identify emotions.

- Storytelling: Share stories that highlight different emotions and how characters deal with them.

- Role-Playing: Participate in role-playing activities that involve emotional scenarios.

- Emotional Cue Recognition: Teach them to recognize emotional cues in themselves and others.

- Empathy: Teach them to understand and respond to the emotions of others.

- Breathing Exercises: Practice deep breathing exercises to calm down when you feel overwhelmed.

Teaching Appropriate Emotional Understanding Strategies for Children Aged 2 to 6 Years with ADHD

Visual Aids: Use visual aids such as pictures or charts to help recognize emotional cues.

Movement-Based Activities: Incorporate movement-based activities that help release excess energy while also promoting emotion regulation.

One-on-One Support: Provide one-on-one support and guidance during emotional awareness activities.

Positive Reinforcement: Provide positive reinforcement and praise for efforts made to develop emotional awareness skills.

Fidget Toys: Let fidget toys or other sensory tools help them regulate their emotions.

Parents and teachers can play an important role in helping children develop a deeper understanding of their emotions. Here are some examples of strategies for teaching children to improve emotional understanding at home and at school:

At Home
- Labeling and Validating Emotions: When your child expresses an emotion, acknowledge it and label it so they learn the name of each feeling. For example, are you "angry" right now? or I can see that you are really "happy."

- Modeling Emotional Awareness: Children learn by observation, so make sure you model healthy emotional expression for them yourself. Share your feelings with your child using "I" statements, such as "I" feel "sad" when I am tired.

- Talk about Feelings: Engage in conversations about feelings, using stories, books, or scenarios to explore different feelings. Open-ended questions like "How do you think he or she might be feeling?" or "What do you think would make you feel better?"

- Teach Emotional Vocabulary: Expand your child's emotional vocabulary by teaching them new words and phrases like "frustrated," "excited," or "scared."

- Encourage Empathy: Role-play different scenarios where children can practice putting themselves in someone else's shoes. For example, "How would you feel if your friend lost their favorite toy?"

- Create a Feeling Chart: Create a chart or poster with different feelings and ask your child to identify which one they are feeling.

At School (Kindergarten, Preschool)
- Emotional Education: Incorporate emotional education into the curriculum using lessons and activities that help children understand and manage their emotions.

- Emotional Stories: Use stories to teach children about different emotions and the feelings of characters.

- Role-Play: Engage children in role-playing activities that help them practice empathy and understand different emotions.

- Feelings Notebook: Create a feelings notebook for children to express their feelings through writing, drawing, or art.

- Class Discussions: Encourage class discussions about emotions using open-ended questions to foster empathy and understanding.

- Emotion Regulation Strategies: Teach children specific strategies for managing and controlling their emotions, such as deep breathing, counting, or relaxing.

- Emotion Recognition Games: Play games that help children recognize and identify different emotions, such as "Emotions Pantomime" or "Emotions Card Game".

Additional tips for parents and teachers include:
- Be Patient and Consistent: Developing emotional intelligence takes time and practice. Be patient and consistent in your approach.

- Use Positive Language: Focus on positive language and reinforcement when teaching emotional intelligence.

- Encourage Self-Reflection: Encourage children to think about their feelings and thoughts to build self-awareness.

- Involve the Whole Family: Involve the whole family in teaching emotional understanding to create a supportive and emotionally understanding family.

By implementing these strategies, parents and teachers can help children develop a deeper understanding of emotions, which leads to improved relationships, better emotion regulation, and increased emotional understanding.

3- Self- Reflection, Recognition of One's Own Strengths, and Weaknesses in Children 2 to 6 Years Old

Self-reflection is the process of deliberately examining one's own thoughts, feelings, and behaviors to gain a deeper understanding of oneself. Through self-reflection, individuals reflect on and analyze their experiences, actions, and feelings to gain deeper understanding and insight. In children, self-reflection involves considering their behavior, emotions, and the consequences of their actions, even though their cognitive abilities to do so are still developing.

Self-reflection can be a challenging but rewarding process that helps individuals do a variety of things, such as:

- Develop Self-Awareness: Gain a better understanding of their own thoughts, feelings, and motivations.

- Identify Patterns and Habits: Recognize repetitive behaviors, thought patterns, or emotional reactions to better understand themselves.

- Set Goals and Make Changes: Use their own thinking to set goals, develop strategies for improvement, and make positive changes in their lives.

- Improve Relationships: Build more empathetic and understanding relationships by understanding how your actions and behavior affect others.

- Develop Emotional Intelligence: Develop emotional intelligence by recognizing and managing your own emotions as well as understanding the emotions of others.

(Emotional intelligence is the ability to manage your own emotions and understand the emotions of those around you. It has five key elements: self-awareness, self-regulation, motivation, empathy, and social skills.)

Self-reflection is an ongoing process that can be applied to various aspects of life, including personal growth, relationships, career development, and problem-solving. By incorporating self-reflection into everyday life, young children can gain a deeper understanding of themselves and improve their overall well-being.

Self-Reflection in Children 2 to 6 Years Old
In young children, children's level of self-evaluation or self-reflection is still developing. At this stage, they may not have the cognitive ability to engage in complex self-reflection like older children and adults. However, they can still demonstrate a level of self-awareness and reflection and self-evaluation through play and interaction with others.

Levels of Self-Reflection in Children 2 to 6 Years Old

In 2-Year-Olds

Basic Awareness: At this stage, children begin to develop basic self-awareness. They recognize themselves in mirrors and photographs and can recognize simple emotions.

Behavior: Self-reflection in 2 years old is very limited and is mainly expressed by immediate experiences. They may express basic feelings, such as "I feel happy" or "I don't like that," but deeper analysis of feelings is beyond their ability.

In 3-Year-Olds

Emerging Self-Awareness: Children begin to express more emotions and can sometimes explain simple reasons for their feelings, such as "I feel sad because I lost my toy."

Behavior: They may begin to understand the immediate consequences of their actions, such as knowing that hitting a friend will make them feel sad and cry, but their ability to reflect on these actions in a deeper context is limited.

In 4-Year-Olds

Developing Empathy: Four-year-old children are better at recognizing the feelings of others and can begin to empathize. They begin to think about how their actions affect those around them.

Behavior: Their self-reflection includes simple thoughts about their behavior and its impact, such as "I made my friend sad because I didn't give my toy."

In 5-Year-Olds

Complex Feelings: Children at this age have a broader emotional vocabulary and can reflect on more complex feelings and social interactions.

Behavior: They may think about past experiences and consider how they would have acted differently in similar situations. For example, "Next time, I will ask my friend if she wants to play with my toy."

In 6-Year-Olds

Advanced Self-Reflection: Six-year-old children can engage in more complex self-reflection, considering long-term consequences and more abstract concepts such as fairness and justice.

Behavior: They are able to analyze their actions more deeply and may express thoughts such as "I was wrong to take the toy because it wasn't mine," which indicates a better understanding of social norms and ethics.

Self-reflection in children is a gradually developing skill that becomes more complex with age. By nurturing this ability, parents, caregivers, and teachers can help children become more self-aware, empathetic, and able to make better thoughtful decisions.

Here are some ways to encourage self-reflection in young children:
Encouraging self-reflection in young children involves using age-appropriate strategies that help them better think about their actions, feelings, and experiences. Here are some ways to foster self-reflection in children aged 2 to 6:

For 2-Year-Olds
Labeling Feelings: Help them identify and label their feelings by saying things like, "You look happy because you're laughing" or "I see you're upset about breaking your toy."

Simple Choices: Offer simple choices and discuss the outcomes. For example, "Do you like the red cup you chose?"

Mirror Play: Encourage play with mirrors to help them talk and see and recognize their own reactions.

For 3-Year-Olds
Emotional Faces: Use picture cards with different facial expressions and ask your child to identify and talk about different emotions.

Role-Play: Engage in pretend play where your child can act out different scenarios and think about how the characters are feeling.

Imitation: Children at this age are beginning to understand that others have their own thoughts and feelings. They may imitate the feelings and behaviors of those around them, which can be a form of personal reflection.

Play-Based Exploration: Encourage children to engage in pretend play, which can help them develop a sense of identity and explore different roles and feelings.

Simple Questions: Ask simple questions like "What are you doing?" or "How are you?" to encourage them to learn to think about their actions and feelings.

Storytime Reflection: After reading a story, ask simple questions about the characters' feelings and actions, such as "Why do you think the bear was sad?"

For 4-Year-Olds

Daily Summary: At the end of the day, ask them to share one thing they liked and one thing they didn't like about their day.

Feelings Chart: Use a chart with different feelings and encourage your child to point out how they felt throughout the day and explain why.

Puppet Play: Use dolls to role-play different situations and talk about how the dolls might be feeling and why.

Verbalization: Children at this age may begin to use simple words to express their thoughts and feelings, such as "I am happy" or "I am angry."

Emotional Labeling: Encourage children to identify and label their emotions, such as "You feel sad because your friend is leaving."

Role-Play: Continue to engage children in role-play activities that promote empathy and understanding of different emotions.

For 5-Year-Olds

Reflective Questions: Ask open-ended questions about their experiences, such as "What made you happy today?" or "How did you feel when you helped your friend?"

Drawing Feelings: Encourage them to draw pictures that represent their feelings and discuss the drawings together.

Journal: Create a simple journal where your child can draw or write about his or her daily experiences and feelings.

More Complex Thinking: Children at this age may begin to demonstrate more complex thinking and problem-solving skills, which can lead to a greater sense of self-awareness, a higher level of self-evaluation, or personal reflection.

Self-Description: Encourage children to describe themselves using simple statements, such as "I am a kind person" or "I like playing with blocks."

Conversation about Feelings: Engage children in conversations about their feelings using open-ended questions such as "How did you feel when…" or "What do you think would happen if…"

For 6-Year-Olds

Cause and Effect: Discuss the cause and effect of their behavior, feelings, and actions. For example, "What happened when you shared your toy with your friend?" and "How did you feel? How did your friend feel?"

Self-Assessment: After completing a task or activity, ask your child what they think they did well and what they might do differently next time.

Group Discussions: In group settings, such as classrooms, facilitate discussions where children talk about their experiences and think about them together.

Journaling: Provide a journal where children can draw or write about their day's activities. Encourage them to express their feelings during the different activities and what they learned.

Discussion Circles: Have regular family or class discussion circles where children can talk about experiences, feelings, and things they enjoy or find challenging.

"Feelings" Chart: Use a chart with different feelings and ask children to choose or point to how they are feeling at certain times of the day. This exercise helps them identify their feelings and learn about them and the consequences and reflections of each behavior.

Storytime Reflection: After reading a story, ask questions like, "How do you think the character in the story felt?" and "What would you have done if you were in that situation?" This exercise helps children connect with the story and learn about their feelings and the consequences and reflections of each behavior.

Role-Play: Participate in role-play games where children can act out different scenarios and then talk about what they did and how they felt. This encourages empathy and self-reflection in them.

Goal Setting and Review: Help children set small, achievable goals and review them regularly together. Discuss what they did well and what they could improve on to foster a growth mindset (focusing on effort, not just results).

Art Activities: Use art as a vehicle for children to reflect. Ask them to draw or paint something that represents their day or their feelings, and then discuss their artwork.

"Two Stars and a Wish": Encourage children to identify two things they did well ("stars") and one thing they would like to improve ("wish"). This exercise helps build self-awareness and motivation with a positive approach.

By incorporating these activities into your daily routine, you can help children develop the habit of self-reflection, which leads to greater self-awareness and emotional intelligence. Remember that each child develops at their own pace, and some may demonstrate more advanced levels of self-reflection than others. By providing a supportive and nurturing environment, you can help build a strong foundation for emotional understanding, emotional intelligence, and self-awareness in young children.

4- Activities to Help Children Encourage Self-Reflection

Here are some home and school activities to encourage self-reflection in children aged 2 to 6:

Home Activities
- Mirror Talk: Use a mirror to talk to your child about their appearance, actions, and feelings. For example, "You have big brown eyes" or "You're really good at playing with blocks."

- Different Feelings: Display different emotions (e.g., happy, sad, angry) and ask your child to guess how you're feeling.

- Emotion Cards: Create a set of cards with different emotions (e.g., happy, sad, excited) and ask your child to categorize them or explain why they might be feeling that way.

- Personalized Storybooks: Create a storybook with your child as the main character. Ask them to describe their actions, thoughts, and feelings in the story.

- Role-Playing: Engage in role-playing activities with your child (such as feeding a doll or pretending to be a doctor). This can help them develop empathy and understanding of different perspectives.

School Activities (Kindergarten, Preschool)

- Self-Portrait Drawing: Provide materials for children to draw a self-portrait and ask them to describe their drawing.

- Emotion Craft: Gather a variety of materials (such as construction paper, glue, scissors) and ask children to make a craft that represents their current feelings.

- Emotion Sorting: Prepare a set of emotion cards or pictures and ask children to sort them into categories (e.g., happy, sad, angry).

- Self-Assessment Time (Personal Reflection): Set aside time each day for children to think about their day and write down what they did, what they liked, and what they didn't like. Share and evaluate.

- Role-Play: Set up a role-play space (such as an office or store) in the classroom that encourages social skills and empathy.

- Personal Bookmaking: Have children create their own books about their daily tasks or favorite activities.

- Discussion Circles: Hold regular discussion circles so children can share and evaluate their thoughts, feelings, and experiences with their peers.

Self-Awareness Games: Play games that promote self-awareness, (such as "Red Light: Stop and Green Light: Go"), that ask children to think about the appropriateness or inappropriateness of their actions and feelings.

Tips for teachers include:

- Encourage children to use "I" statements when expressing their thoughts and feelings to become more self-aware by encouraging self-evaluation (self-reflection).

- Use "Open-Ended Questions" that encourage self-reflection, such as "What do you think would happen if…" or "How did you feel when…"

- Provide opportunities for children to express themselves through art, music, or writing.

- Create a safe and supportive environment where children feel comfortable sharing their thoughts and feelings.

- Remember to tailor these activities to your child or student's developmental level and individual abilities. The goal is to develop self-reflection and emotional intelligence and self-evaluation. Encourage self-reflection in a fun and engaging way.

5- Positive Reinforcement and Praise for Children's Progress and Achievements

Providing positive reinforcement and praise for progress and achievements is crucial in encouraging a growth mindset, building self-confidence, and fostering a love of learning and emotional intelligence in children. There are several ways that parents at home and teachers at school can provide positive reinforcement and praise, such as:

Parents at Home
- Specific Praise: Instead of general praise like "Good job!", use specific praise that highlights what your child did well, such as "You did a great job using your counting skills to solve that puzzle!"

- Verbal Affirmations: Use verbal affirmations to boost your child's self-confidence, such as "I'm proud of you for trying your best" or "You're getting better at reading every day!"

- Nonverbal Cues: Use nonverbal cues such as "hugs" or "handshakes" to show appreciation and encouragement.

- Written Messages: Leave sweet notes or drawings for your child to find and show how proud you are of their accomplishments.

- Special Treats: Offer special treats or privileges as rewards for good behavior or accomplishments, choosing a dinner menu, or having a special outing.

Teachers at School (Kindergarten, Preschool)
- Individual Praise: Offer individual praise that recognizes each child's unique strengths and achievements.

- Verbal Affirmation: Verbal affirmation can be powerful, so make sure you acknowledge children's efforts and achievements during lessons, class discussions, or during individual interactions.

- Visual Reminders: Use visual reminders like stickers, stamps, or stars on charts to track each child's progress and reinforce positive behavior.

- Classroom Board: Create a classroom board that displays children's artwork, art projects, or achievements, giving them a sense of pride and accomplishment.

- Celebrations: Celebrate milestones and achievements with small parties, special activities, or treats to make children's learning fun and rewarding.

Tips for Effective Praise
- Specific Praise: Offer specific praise for each specific task to highlight exactly what the child did well.

- Authentic Praise: Make sure your praise is genuine and sincere. To maintain the credibility of your praise with the child.

- Avoid Over-Praise: Avoid giving too much praise or too much attention to a child, as this can cause imbalance and lead to jealousy or resentment in others.

- Focus on Effort: Instead of simply emphasizing natural talent or ability to encourage children, emphasize effort to create a growth mindset (the belief that their most basic abilities can be developed through dedication and hard work).

- Progress Praise: Instead of just encouraging the end result of progress, encourage them to constantly strive for continuous improvement and improvement.

Remember, positive reinforcement, praise, and praise must be given consistently and genuinely to have a lasting impact on children's self-esteem, confidence, and motivation.

6- What Is the Relationship between Self-Awareness, Emotional Understanding, and Mindfulness Practices?

Self-awareness, emotional understanding, and mindfulness practices are closely related and reinforce each other in several ways:

-Self-Awareness: Mindfulness practices, such as meditation, help people to become more aware of their thoughts, emotions, and bodily sensations by focusing on them. This practice increases self-awareness by encouraging a deeper understanding of themselves.

-Emotional Understanding: Through mindfulness practices, people learn to notice their emotions and observe them without immediate reaction or judgment. This increased emotional understanding helps them to recognize and name their feelings, which leads to better emotion regulation and better control of their emotions.

-Mindfulness Practices: Regular mindfulness practice promotes a state of moment-to-moment awareness of what is being felt in the moment, helping people to focus on their current experiences without interpreting or judging themselves. This focus helps develop self-awareness and emotional understanding, allowing people to perceive their internal states more clearly.

For example, a mindfulness practice such as focused breathing can help a child become aware of their anxious feelings and understand how they are affecting their body, thereby promoting self-awareness and emotional understanding. They may become aware of tension in their muscles, a racing heart, or shallow breaths, all physical signs of anxiety. They learn that by controlling their breath, they can calm their body and mind.

Here is a definition and benefits of mindfulness exercises for children aged 2 to 6 to better understand their social-emotional learning:

Mindfulness

Definition
Mindfulness is a type of meditation in which a person focuses on being aware of what they are feeling in the moment, without interpretation or judgment.

Benefits of Mindfulness for Children Aged 2 to 6 Years
The benefit of mindfulness for children is that it helps them feel more relaxed. Then they can learn to notice their feelings, even uncomfortable ones, with a little focus and pause before reacting to any stimulus.

Mindfulness is a powerful tool that can be helpful for both typically developing children aged 2 to 6 and children diagnosed with ADHD. Some of the benefits for both groups include:

Benefits of Mindfulness for Normal Children Aged 2 to 6 Years
- Improved Emotion Regulation: Mindfulness helps children aged 2 to 6 develop their emotional awareness, allowing them to recognize, understand, and manage their emotions more effectively.

- Enhanced Focus: Regular mindfulness practice can improve attention and focus in children aged 2 to 6, leading to better performance in school and their daily activities.

- Reduced Stress and Anxiety: Mindfulness can help children aged 2 to 6 to cope with stress and anxiety by teaching them to focus on the present moment, the now, and let go of worries about the past or the future.

- Better Social Skills: Mindfulness can improve social skills by increasing empathy, self-awareness, and understanding others' perspectives.

- Increased Self-Awareness: Mindfulness helps children aged 2 to 6 gain a better understanding of themselves, including their strengths, weaknesses, and feelings.

- Improved Behavior: Regular mindfulness practice can lead to improved behavior, including reduced impulsivity, aggression, and anger.

Benefits of Mindfulness for Children Aged 2 to 6 Years with ADHD
- Improved Attention and Focus: Mindfulness is especially beneficial for children with ADHD, as it helps them develop attention control and reduce distractions.

- Reduce Impulsivity: Mindfulness can help children with ADHD regulate their impulsivity and make more thoughtful and appropriate decisions.

- Improved Emotion Regulation: Children with ADHD often struggle with emotion regulation. Mindfulness can help them develop more appropriate strategies to manage their emotions more effectively.

- Increase Self-Awareness: Mindfulness can increase self-awareness in children with ADHD and help them recognize their strengths, weaknesses, and areas for improvement.

- Better Relaxation and Sleep: Regular mindfulness practice can improve the quality of sleep in restless and lively children by creating and practicing greater relaxation, which is essential for children's overall health throughout life.

How to Introduce Mindfulness to Children Aged 2 to 6 Years?
- Start Small: Start with short mindfulness exercises and gradually increase

the duration as children become more comfortable with the practice (maximum 5-10 minutes initially).

- Use Simple Language to Explain: Use simple language and examples that children aged 2-6 can understand and grasp easily.

- Make the Exercises Fun: Incorporate games, songs, and activities that make mindfulness fun and engaging for children aged 2-6.

- Model: Demonstrate mindfulness yourself by modeling, as children often learn by observing adults.

- Be Patient: Be patient and consistent when introducing mindfulness to children aged 2-6, as mindfulness can take time to learn, so you need to be patient and persistent in teaching this new skill and developing it in young children.

Tips for Practicing Mindfulness with Children Aged 2 to 6 Years

- Breathing Exercises: Do deep breathing exercises together (such as taking a deep breath through your nose and exhaling slowly through your mouth).

- Body Scan: Paying attention to different parts of the body and bodily sensations in order and gradually from head to toe. Ask children to lie down or sit comfortably while you guide them to scan their bodies from head to toe, noticing without judgment any internal feelings (such as happiness, discomfort) or bodily sensations (such as heat, cold).

- Sensory Exploration: Engage children's senses by exploring their surroundings (e.g., the real sound of a car, a bird, or children playing in the street) during mindfulness practice.

- Guided Imagery: Use guided imaginative imagery exercises during mindfulness practice that include visualization techniques to help children relax and focus their minds (e.g., imagining and visualizing a forest with colorful trees, different bird sounds, a river).

By incorporating mindfulness practice into your daily routine with young children, you can help them develop essential social-emotional learning skills, self-awareness, and emotional understanding that will serve them well throughout their lives.

Appropriate Mindfulness Practice for Children Aged 2 to 6 Years

For children aged 2 to 6, it is essential to use simple, engaging, and fun mindfulness techniques that can capture their attention and imagination. Here are some examples of mindfulness exercises suitable for children aged 2 to 6:

For 2-Year-Olds

Deep Breathing with a Stuffed Animal: Have your child lie on their stomach with a stuffed animal. Encourage them to watch the toy rise and fall as they take deep breaths.

Simple Sensory Play: Engage in sensory activities with your child, such as playing with water, sand, or play dough. Focus on the textures of the toys and the different senses.

For 3-Year-Olds

Deep Breathing: Encourage them to take deep breaths. and breathe slowly and count their breaths.

Balloon Blowing: Encourage them to blow up balloons with their own breath and ask them to focus on the sensation of blowing up the balloon and the sound it makes.

Sensory Play: Engage in sensory play with play dough, sand, water or rice and encourage them to explore and focus on comparing the different textures.

Nature Walk: Take a short walk outside with your children and encourage them to pay attention to the sights, sounds and smells around them.

Soothing Music: Listen to soft music together and encourage them to move their bodies to the rhythm of the music.

For 4-Year-Olds

Body Awareness: Practice simple yoga poses together (such as "tree pose").

Mindful Walking: Walk together and focus on the feel of each step and the sounds around you.

Finger Play: Play with rice or dough with your fingers and encourage them to focus on their fingers and their feelings.

Guided Imagery: Use guided imagery exercises to help them visualize peaceful scenes, such as the beach or forest.

Emotional Movement: Act out different emotions (such as happiness, sadness, anger) without talking through nonverbal body movements (pantomime) and encourage them to identify and express different emotions.

For 5-Year-Olds
Mindful Coloring: Engage in coloring activities with children, focusing on the colors, shapes, and textures of the paper.

Nature Explorer: Create a nature exploration game and encourage children to explore the sights and sounds of nature. Focus on your surroundings.

Mindful Listening: Listen to soothing music or nature sounds together and focus on the different sounds you hear.

Yoga Games: In simple yoga games for preschoolers, for example, one person stands in front of the group as the yogi and tells the others what yoga pose to repeat and do. Play simple yoga games like "Yogi Says" or "Yoga Freeze Dance."

In "Yogi Says," the yogi stands in front of the group and tells the others what yoga pose to do. Players just have to obey the instructions that start with "Yogi Says," or they're out of the game.

In "Yogi Freeze Dance," play some fun music and have the kids dance freely. Suddenly "stop" the music and say, "Stop, freeze!" Encourage children to hold a specific yoga pose (such as tree pose or warrior pose) while frozen in place. Count to 10 and then say "Move!" and let them go back to dancing.

Repeat this several times, gradually increasing the length of time they hold or freeze.

Through yoga games, children learn to pay more attention to their breath, body, and surroundings. Practicing mindfulness helps to increase self-awareness by encouraging them to be aware and stay in the present moment.

Using a Mirror to Facilitate Self-Awareness: Have children practice looking in the mirror, describing their facial expressions in the mirror.

For 6-Year-Olds
Belly Breathing:
How to Do It: Have children lie down and place a small stuffed animal on their stomach. Ask them to take a deep breath through their nose and watch the stuffed animal rise, then slowly exhale through their mouth and watch it fall.

Benefit: Helps children focus on their breath and calm their minds.

Mindful Listening

How to Do It: Play a sound, such as a soft bell or chime, and ask children to listen carefully until they can no longer hear it. Encourage them to pay attention to any other sounds they hear around them.

Benefit: Increases focus and awareness of the present moment.

Body Scan

How to Do It: Guide your child through a body scan, asking them to focus on different parts of their body, starting with their toes and moving up to their head. Encourage them to notice every sensation throughout their body, from their toes to their head.

Benefit: Increases relaxation and body awareness.

Mindful Coloring

How to Do It: Provide coloring sheets and ask children to color slowly and carefully, paying attention to the colors and the movement of the crayons.

Benefit: Encourages focus and creativity while providing a calming activity.

Practice the Five Senses

How to Do It: Ask your child to identify and describe their five senses by asking them the following questions:

- Five things they can see.

- Four things they can touch.

- Three things they can hear.

- Two things they can smell.

- One thing they can taste.

Benefit: Helps children to be present in the moment through sensory awareness.

Mindful Walking

How to Do It: Take a slow walk with your children and encourage them to notice the sensations in their feet with each step, such as the coolness or wetness of the grass (and the sounds and sights around them (such as birdsong, the sound of a river).

Benefit: Integrates mindfulness into physical activity and promotes calmness and awareness.

Gratitude Practice
How to Do It: Ask children to think of three things they are grateful for each day and share them out loud with you or draw them.

Benefit: Promotes a positive mindset and appreciation for the world around them.

Incorporating these mindfulness practices into daily routines can help young children develop emotion regulation, focus, and a greater sense of calm and well-being. Remember to keep these practices short (maximum 5-10 minutes) and fun at first. Be patient and consistent, as young children may need guidance, encouragement, and encouragement to stay focused. and need more practice.

7- Simple Mindfulness Exercises Such as Abdominal Breathing and Mindful Listening for Self-Awareness

Here are some simple mindfulness exercises to enhance self-awareness for normal 2-6 years old children and children diagnosed with ADHD, boys and girls:

For Normal 2- to 6-Year-Olds

For Girls
Flying Butterflies: Have girls lie on their backs with a small stuffed animal on their stomachs. Instruct them to breathe deeply and slowly and watch as the stuffed animal rises and falls with each breath.

Fairytale Visualization: Guide the girls through a short visualization exercise using a fairy tale or their favorite story (such as Cinderella). Encourage them to imagine the sights and sounds of that fictional world with deep breathing, then imagine and feel themselves in that fictional space.

Rainbow Stretch: Using colorful ribbons or scarves, have girls move their hands while breathing deeply and slowly, and slowly move the ribbons to resemble a rainbow above their heads.

For Boys

Superhero Focus: Have boys choose their favorite superhero pose (such as Superman). Practice holding the superhero pose while breathing deeply and slowly, and have them imagine themselves gaining focus and strength like their favorite hero.

Animal Imitation: Create a "jungle" with stuffed animals representing different animals. Have boys move quietly through the jungle, imitating the movements and sounds of each animal they encounter.

Ninja Moves: Teach boys simple ninja-inspired moves like slow punches and kicks, and focus and balance. Pair each move with a deep breath to encourage focus and control. (Ninja exercise involves physical movement and exercises, body control skills, and a focus on precision and balance.)

Exercise for Both Boys and Girls

Mindful Coloring: Provide nature-themed sheets and crayons. Encourage children to color slowly and with concentration.

Musical Freeze: Play soothing music and ask children to dance or move freely around the room. When the music stops, they should freeze in a yoga pose or hold a gentle stretch until the music resumes.

Nature Sounds: Take children outside or use a nature sounds app. Ask them to close their eyes and listen quietly to different sounds, such as "birds chirping" or "leaves rustling." Discuss what they discovered later.

Breathing with a Stuffed Animal: Have children lie on their stomachs with a stuffed animal. Instruct them to watch the doll rise and fall as they breathe. This exercise helps them focus on their breathing and become aware of their bodies.

Five Senses Exploration: Guide children through a sensory exploration exercise. Ask them to name the following:

  - Five things they can see.

  - Four things they can touch.

  - Three things they can hear.

  - Two things they can smell.

  - One thing they can taste.

Feeling Check: Use emotion cards or faces to help children identify and label feelings. This exercise encourages children's emotional awareness and vocabulary development.

Implementation Tips

Respect Preferences: Allow children to choose activities that interest them and make them feel comfortable.

Encourage Exploration: Use topics and activities that stimulate children's curiosity and imagination.

Be Supportive: Provide positive reinforcement and create a safe space for children to freely express their thoughts and feelings during and after practice.

By adapting mindfulness exercises based on the interests and preferences of boys and girls separately, you can create a more engaging and effective mindfulness practice in the school environment (kindergarten, preschool) for each of them.

For Children Aged 2 to 6 Years with ADHD

Mindfulness exercises for children aged 2 to 6 with a diagnosis of ADHD should be designed to help them focus, regulate their emotions, and engage their senses in the exercises. Here are some specific exercises:

Balloon Breathing: Give each child a small balloon. Instruct them to breathe in and out slowly, inflating the balloon with each breath. This visual and tactile activity helps them focus on their breathing.

Sensory Exploration: Provide a sensory bucket with materials such as rice, beans, or sand. Encourage children to explore the different textures with their hands and focus on the feel of each. This exercise can be relaxing and the basis for more concentration and attention.

Movement Exercises: Incorporate short movement exercises throughout the day. Guide children in simple yoga stretches and slow deliberate movements (such as slow turtle movements) to help release excess energy.

For Girls with ADHD

Breathing with Butterflies: Present butterfly breathing images. Instruct girls to place a butterfly toy on their stomach and practice deep breathing. They can watch how the butterfly rises and falls with each breath.

Nature Walks: Take girls on guided nature walks. Encourage them to observe and draw the sights, sounds, and textures they encounter. This activity combines movement with mindfulness and sensory awareness.

Storytelling and Puppet Play: Use puppets to act out a simple story about mindfulness or emotions. Encourage girls to express their feelings and thoughts through storytelling using puppet movements. This activity promotes emotional awareness.

For Boys with ADHD

Superhero Focus Training: Consider mindfulness exercises as superhero training. Use superhero-themed visuals and guide boys through activities such as "Superhero Breathing" (deep breathing) or "Superhero Listening" (paying attention to specific sounds).

Construction Site: Provide a construction-themed site with building blocks or toy tools. Guide boys through mindful building activities, paying attention and focusing on each piece and how it fits together.

Animal Adventure: Lead boys in animal-themed yoga poses. Use fun animal names (e.g., lion pose, frog pose) and encourage them to move their bodies consciously and with control like those animals.

Implementation Tips

Interest-Friendly: Use topics and activities that align with children's interests and preferences to keep them engaged.

Provide Structured Mindfulness Practice: Keep mindfulness sessions structured with clear instructions and expectations, which can help children with ADHD stay focused.

Encourage Participation: Praise and encourage children for participating and trying new mindfulness exercises, and create a positive and supportive environment.

By incorporating these gender-specific (boys and girls) and ADHD-specific mindfulness exercises into your school-based (kindergarten, preschool) learning activities, you can help a variety of children develop mindfulness skills and respect their individual interests and needs.

Here are some examples of simple mindfulness exercises for young children for home and school that promote self-awareness, focus on abdominal breathing, and mindful listening:

For Home
Belly Breathing Exercise
1. Sit next to your child on the floor or a comfortable cushion.

2. Place one hand on your child's abdomen and the other on their chest.

3. Encourage them to breathe deeply and feel their abdomen rise and fall with each inhale and exhale.

4. As they breathe, say, "Inhale, belly goes up… exhale, belly goes down."

Listening Exercise Consciously
1. Choose a quiet environment with minimal distractions.

2. Play soothing music or nature sounds (e.g., rain, ocean waves).

3. Encourage your child to listen carefully to the sounds and notice how they make them feel.

4. Ask them to describe what they hear and how it makes them feel.

For School (Kindergarten, Preschool)
Abdominal breathing breaks include:

During transitions or breaks, take a few minutes to practice group abdominal breathing. (For example, when the drawing bell ends and the exercise bell starts.)

- Ask the children to sit comfortably with their eyes closed.

- Guide them through a few deep breaths, focusing on the rise and fall of their abdomens.

- Encourage them to notice how they feel after the exercise.

Mindful Listening Circles
- Gather the children in a circle for a mindful listening circle activity.

- Choose a simple sound (for example, a hand tapping on a table or a soft bell).

- Ask each child to take turns listening to the sound and focus on its rhythm and tone.

- Ask them to describe what they hear and how it makes them feel.

Tips for Implementation
- Keep the Exercises Short: Start with short exercises (2-3 minutes) and gradually increase the time as the children become more comfortable with the exercises.

- Make the Exercises Fun: Use fun and engaging language and use movements or games to make the exercises enjoyable for young children.

Be Patient: Children may have trouble focusing at first, but with consistent practice, these exercises will become easier to do.

Involve the Whole Family: Practice mindfulness exercises with your child at home to make it a fun and bonding experience for the family.

Remember to adapt mindfulness exercises to your child's developmental stage and age-appropriate attention span. By regularly incorporating these gender-specific (boys and girls) and ADHD-friendly mindfulness exercises into preschool activities, you can help children develop mindfulness, self-awareness, emotional understanding, and emotion regulation skills, thereby enhancing their social-emotional learning throughout life.

CHAPTER 4: SELF-REGULATION AND SELF-MANAGEMENT

1- EMOTION REGULATION

2- IMPULSIVITY CONTROL

3- ATTENTION MANAGEMENT

4- GOAL SETTING

5- TIME MANAGEMENT

6- INTRINSICALLY MOTIVATED ACTION (SPONTANEITY)

7- WORKING MEMORY

Self-Regulation

Definition
Self-regulation in children includes several key components:

- Emotion Regulation: Managing and responding to one's emotions in a healthy and socially acceptable way.

- Impulse Control: The ability to resist immediate reactions or temptations, allowing them to think before acting impulsively.

- Attention Management: Focusing and maintaining one's attention on tasks, despite distractions.

- Goal Setting: Setting and working toward personal goals with persistence and effort.

- Time Management: Effectively organizing time to complete tasks and responsibilities.

- Motivation: Finding the inner motivation to complete tasks and overcome challenges, even when they are not interesting to the individual.

These essential life skills help children better navigate daily challenges, interact positively with others, and achieve their personal and academic goals. Developing these skills in early childhood and preschool is very important and beneficial and can lead to better outcomes throughout their lives.

In the context of educating young children, self-regulation is a vital skill that helps children develop emotional intelligence, social skills, and academic readiness. Young children learn to independently regulate their emotions and expressions and adapt them to social expectations.

Some children, due to a lack of appropriate self-regulation skills, face emotional dysregulation, which means they often have difficulty managing their emotional reactions in various situations, such as:

1. Feeling emotions more intensely than they should.

2. Experiencing certain emotions for longer than they should.

3. Feeling certain emotions at inappropriate times.

4. Responding to emotions in extreme ways.

5. Having severe mood swings or explosive emotional changes.

Parents and teachers may often consider emotional dysregulation as a sign of ADHD, when in fact, these extreme, negative, and unhealthy emotional reactions are often the result of a lack of proper training in positive, self-regulatory skills at home and at school.

Emotional self-regulation helps children feel good about themselves. It reduces the shame and anxiety associated with uncontrollable emotions and helps them better cope and thrive in social settings and relationships with others.

Appropriate emotional self-regulation is an indicator of children's academic readiness. Children aged 2 to 6 who know how to regulate their emotions experience fewer emotional distractions. In academic settings, emotional self-regulation allows children to remain positive in the face of various academic challenges, which leads to optimal learning, higher grades, and improved standardized test scores.

Self-Regulation Strategies
Here are some examples of self-regulation strategies that can be used with young children. Help children practice the following exercises and activities:

Breathing Strategies
Balloon Breathing: Inhale and exhale through your mouth, like blowing up a balloon.

Deep Breathing: Take slow, deep breaths in through your nose and out through your mouth.

Breathing 4,7,8: Take slow, deep breaths (inhale for 4 seconds, hold for 7 seconds, exhale for 8 seconds).

Movement Strategies
Free Body Movement: Move your body freely to release your emotions."Jumping Up and Down!": Jump up and down repeatedly to release your energy.

Crawl: Move your body in slow movements like a "snake", crawl to calm down.

Visual Strategies

Stare: Stare at an object, such as a picture or a toy, to calm down.

Finger Painting: Paint with your finger to express your feelings and calm down.

Slow Coloring: Slowly color pictures to create a sense of calm.

Tactile Strategies

Play Dough: Play with play dough to release tension.

Fidget Toys: Use relaxing toys called "fidgets" to release energy, such as soft, flexible balls or fidget balls. Use for stress relief.

Sensory Bucket Fun: Play sensory exploration games with buckets filled with rice, beans, or sand.

Verbal Strategies

I Am Angry/Calm/Sad/Happy: Use simple language to identify and label emotions.

Feelings Chart: Create a chart of different emotions and have children point to their feelings.

Storytelling: Use stories to help children process and regulate emotions.

Other Strategies

To regulate and control your emotions:

Count to 10: Count slowly to 10 to calm down.

Hug Yourself: Hug yourself to feel relaxed.

Break: Walk away from the stressful activity or situation and get some distance.

Remember to adapt these strategies to your children's unique, needs and abilities, and encourage them to try different techniques until they find the one they like best.

Key factors affecting children's emotional self-regulation, for example, include:
1. Physical: Includes various genetic factors, temperament, and physical abilities of children.

2. Emotional: Includes children's personality traits, their exposure to various physical and psychological harms, and their ability to manage impulsive (impulsive) responses.

3. Cognitive: Categorizes and describes children's emotions. Includes the ability to focus and manage their distractions.

4. Social and Environmental: Includes interpersonal interactions, level of empathy, and recognition of values.

Young children (2 to 6 years old) are still learning to manage and regulate their emotions and behaviors, which can be challenging for them. Research has shown that with appropriate strategies, patience, and consistency, significantly more self-regulation components can be taught to normal young children and those diagnosed with ADHD. Of course, it is better to pay attention to this important point that for effective learning and the development of self-regulation skills, it is very important to match activities to the developmental level and individual needs of each child.

Appropriate self-regulation strategies that can be taught to children aged 2 to 6 (normal children and with ADHD) to help them develop healthy emotion regulation skills include:

1. Recognizing Emotions
- Labeling Emotions: "I feel angry/sad/happy."

- Recognizing Facial Expressions: "You look 'sad' when you 'frown'."

- Understanding Emotional Causes: "I feel sad because I miss my favorite toy."

2. Regulating Emotions
- Inhibiting (Stopping or Slowing Down) Emotions: "Before reacting quickly, take a deep breath."

- Moderating (Regulating) Emotions: "Count to 10 before responding with anger and frustration."

- Expressing Emotions in a Healthy Way: "I feel angry, so instead of hitting or throwing things, I'm going to stomp my feet."

3. Responding to Emotions

- Initiating Positive Actions: "Let's take a break and find a relaxing activity."

- Responding with Empathy: "You seem upset, would you like me to hug or hold you?"

- Building Emotional Resilience and Coping Strategies: "It's okay to feel sad sometimes, coping with stress makes us stronger. Together we can get through that difficult situation with patience, endurance, and perseverance."

1- Recognizing Emotions

Labeling Emotions

Labeling emotions are an essential skill for children's emotional development. There are several effective ways to teach 3- to 5-year-olds how to label their emotions:

- Modeling Emotions: Help children talk about their feelings and explain why they feel a certain way. For example, say, "I feel happy because we're going to the park!" or "I'm a little frustrated because I can't find my keys."

- Use Books and Stories: Read books that explore emotions. Discuss how the characters in the stories are feeling and why. This helps children understand different emotions and express themselves.

- Art, Music, and Movement: Encourage children to express their feelings through creative activities. Drawing, dancing, or singing can help them connect feelings with actions and movements.

- Identify Feelings: When your child experiences a feeling, name it. For example, say, "I see you're feeling 'sad' because your toy broke." This exercise helps them identify and label their feelings.

- Show Your Support and Understanding: Validate their feelings without judgment (even when you don't like the behavior). Say, "It's okay to feel angry" or "I understand why you're upset." This practice helps them feel seen and heard and feel more comfortable expressing themselves without fear of being judged.

Recognizing Facial Expressions

Teaching young children to recognize facial expressions is very important for their social-emotional development. Here are some effective strategies, for example:

- Use Pictures: Collect photos of people your child knows that show a range of facial expressions. Make flashcards with these pictures. Discuss the feelings associated with each expression and why they are expressed. You can also imitate a similar expression and play "guessing" games.

- Analyze Facial Features: Focus on specific features such as the eyebrows, mouth, eyes, nose, and forehead. Show how they change with different emotions. Encourage your child to practice them in front of a mirror.

- Observe Facial Expressions: Ask your child to notice the emotions in their facial muscles when they experience happiness, sadness, anger, etc. "Smiley face" exercises in front of a mirror can help them recognize these expressions in others.

- Point Out Changes: Highlight "neutral" faces of family members and friends. This helps children notice facial changes in expression.

- Watch Movies and TV: Identify facial expressions together with the sound off. Discuss the emotions they convey in the movie. (For example, ask your child about the facial expression of a person in a movie to guess what emotion it is expressing.)

- Apps: Let your child play apps that teach emotions and facial expressions in a game format.

- Encouragement of Questioning: Remind your child that it is okay to ask questions about people's feelings to better understand how others are feeling.

Understanding Emotional Causes

Teaching children aged 2 to 6 about the causes of emotions is essential for their emotional development. Here are some strategies to help children identify and express their feelings and emotions:

Storybook: Read a story that depicts a variety of emotions. Ask them open-ended questions about the story, such as: How do you think the character felt when...? Why do you think they felt that way? How would you feel if you in their position?

Talk: Discuss how our feelings can change depending on what is happening around us.

Feeling Charts: Use visual aids such as feeling charts or feelers to help children identify and express their feelings.

Modeling: Demonstrate healthy emotional expression and management. Be open about your feelings and share them with your child. This practice helps them learn how to label and understand their feelings.

Remember that emotional development is a complex process that begins in infancy and continues into adulthood. As children develop their sense of self, more complex emotions emerge, such as embarrassment, surprise, joy, embarrassment, shame, guilt, pride, and empathy. Creating a safe space for children to explore and express their emotions is crucial for their overall development.

2. Regulating Emotions

Controlling Emotions

Teaching children to control their emotions is an essential life skill that can benefit them in many ways. Here are some simple ways to teach young children to control their emotions:

- Deep Breathing: Encourage children to take deep breaths through their nose and out through their mouth. This exercise can help them calm down and regulate their breathing.

- Counting: Ask children to count to 10 or 20 before reacting hastily to any situation. This exercise can help them pause and think before acting.

- Distance: Teach children to distance themselves from a difficult or stressful situation and to take a break when they feel tired. This exercise can help them calm down and think more clearly.

- Talk: Encourage children to talk about their feelings with a trusted adult or friend. This exercise can help them process and manage their feelings.

- Drawing: Give children paper and crayons and ask them to draw how they feel. This exercise can help them express and release their feelings.

- Rest: Give children time to rest when they are feeling upset or tired. Sometimes taking a break and doing something relaxing can help them better manage and regulate their feelings.

- Use Positive Affirmations: To help them build self-confidence and manage their feelings, teach children positive affirmations like "I can do it." or "I am strong!"

- Use Visualization: Encourage children to imagine a happy place or scenario to help them feel calm.

- Practice Empathy: Encourage children to put themselves in someone else's shoes and understand how they might be feeling. This exercise can help them better manage their empathy and emotions.

- Offer Choices: Give children options like "Do you want to count to 10 or relax?" or "Do you want to draw or talk about your feelings?" This exercise can help them feel more in control of the situation and manage their emotions.

Remember, every child is unique, and what works for one child may not work for another. Be patient, adaptable, and creative in your approach to helping your child develop emotion regulation skills.

Explore Emotions

Teaching children aged 2 to 6 to explore emotions is essential for their emotional development. Here are some strategies and activities you can use:

- Mindfulness: Encourage children to notice how their feelings feel in their bodies. For example, if they are anxious, they may feel their heart beating faster, breathing faster.

- Exploring Thoughts: Help children identify the thoughts associated with their feelings. Thoughts significantly influence feelings, so discussing this connection can be valuable.

- Building Vocabulary: Introduce basic emotion words like happy, mad, sad, and afraid to young children. Older children can learn more complex terms like disappointed, frustrated, and nervous.

- Daily Routine: Make exploring emotions part of your routine. Ask children how they are feeling and validate their feelings. This practice helps them feel understood and supported.

- Use Characters: Talk about feelings by exploring how characters in books or TV shows are feeling. For example, pause while watching a movie and ask, "How do you think they are feeling right now?"

Remember, building a trusting relationship with children and explaining the purpose of these activities in a child-friendly way will yield better results and increase their willingness to participate with you.

Expressing Feelings in a Healthy Way

Teaching children aged 2 to 6 how to express their feelings in a healthy way is essential for their emotional development.

Here are some strategies you can use, for example:
- Identifying Feelings: Help children recognize and name their feelings. Use emotion picture cards or discuss characters in books or TV shows to explore different feelings.

- Normalizing Feelings: Let children know that all feelings are valid and natural. Share your feelings openly to model healthy expression.

- Basic Vocabulary: Teach basic emotion words like happy, angry, sad, and afraid. Older children can learn more complex terms like disappointed, frustrated, and nervous.

- Creative Expression: Encourage creative expression through art, music, or movement. This helps children process emotions and find healthy ways to express them.

- Calming Techniques: Introduce calming strategies like deep breathing or counting to help children regulate their emotions.

Remember, children are still developing self-control, so gently guide them as they learn to express their emotions in appropriate ways. Patience and understanding are key to your teaching success.

3. Responding to Emotions

Initiating Positive Actions
When teaching children aged 2 to 6 how to respond to emotions, consider the following positive actions:

For Feelings of Sadness

"It's okay to feel sad sometimes." - Validate their feelings and tell them that it is normal to feel upset.

"Let's take a deep breath together." - Practice deep breathing exercises to help them calm down.

"You are not alone, I am here to help you with this." - Provide a calming and reassuring presence and emotional support and companionship.

For Feelings of Anger

"I can see that you are really upset. Can you tell me more about what is bothering you?" - Actively listen and try to understand the root cause of their anger.

"It is okay to feel angry, but let's find a way to deal with it safely." - Teach them alternative ways to express anger, such as counting or resting.

"You are safe, and I am here to help you stay calm." - Creates reassurance and a sense of security.

Let's take a deep breath together and count to 10 before reacting. - Practice calming down before acting on feelings.

For Feelings of Fear

"You are safe, and I am here with you." - Builds confidence and a sense of security.

"What do you think will happen if you do this?" - Encourage them to think critically about the potential outcomes of their actions.

"Let's face our fears slowly and carefully." - Gradually expose them to the feared situation or object in a controlled environment.

"You are braver than you think, and I believe in you." - Build their confidence and self-esteem.

For Feelings of Anxiety

I know you're worried about your competition (like a painting competition), but we can practice (painting) together." - Offer reassurance and support.

"Let's break it down into smaller steps, one step at a time." - Help them feel more in control by breaking things down into manageable chunks.

"You're doing your best, and that's all anyone can do." - Encourage them to focus on their effort rather than perfection.

"Take a deep breath with me and let's visualize a positive outcome together." - Practice relaxation and positive visualization techniques together.

Remember, every child is unique, and what works for one child may not work for another. Be patient, adaptable, and creative in your approach to helping your child develop emotion regulation skills.

Respond with Empathy

Teaching children aged 2 to 6 how to respond to emotions with empathy is a valuable skill. Here are some strategies:

- Model Empathy: Show children how to empathize by acknowledging their feelings. Say things like, "I can see you're sad, but it's okay to feel that way sometimes."

- Use Emotional Words: Encourage children to express their feelings using words. For example, "I feel happy when I play with my friends."

- Read Books: Choose books that explore emotions and discuss the characters' feelings. Ask questions like, "How do you think this person is feeling?"

- Role-Play: Pretend play can help children practice empathy. Set up scenarios in which they take on different emotions and respond with empathy.

- Validate Feelings: Let children know that it's okay to feel a certain negative emotion in a situation. For example, say, "I know you're frustrated. It's okay. Let's work together to find a solution."

Remember, empathy helps build strong relationships and boosts emotional intelligence.

For Feelings of Sadness

"That sounds really hard. I can imagine how you must be feeling."

"I'm so sorry you're going through this. It must be really hard."

"You seem really upset. Can you tell me more about what's going on?"

For Feelings of Anger

"I can see why you'd be upset about this. It makes me angry too."

"I'm so sorry that this happened. It's not fair."

"You're really feeling sad right now, aren't you?"

For Feelings of Fear

"That sounds really scary. I can imagine how you must be feeling."

"I'm here with you, and we'll get through this together."

"You're really worried about this, aren't you?"

For Feelings of Anxiety

"I can see why you're feeling anxious about it. It's a big responsibility."

"You're doing the best you can, and that's something to be proud of."

"I'm here to help you work through this. We'll work through it together."

When responding with empathy, try to:
- Accept their Feelings: Show that you understand and recognize their feelings.

- Validate their Experience: Let them know that their feelings are normal and valid.

- Use Open-Ended Questions: Encourage them to talk more about their feelings and thoughts.

- Offer Support and Reassurance: Let them know that you're there to support and help them.

Remember, empathy means understanding and relating to other people's feelings, not fixing the problem or minimizing their feelings. By responding with empathy, you can help your child feel heard, validated, and understood, which can be incredibly powerful in building trust and strengthening your relationships.

Building Emotional Resilience and Coping Strategies
Resilience
Refers to the ability to withstand adversity, trauma, or stress. It is the ability to

cope with problems, adapt to changing circumstances, and maintain emotional well-being despite challenging circumstances. Resilience is not the absence of problems, but the ability to navigate them effectively.

Emotional resilience in children refers to their ability to:

- Manage: Control and regulate their emotions.

- Bounce Back: Recover from problems and upsets.

- Adjust: Adapt to changing circumstances.

- Coping: Deal with stress, anxiety, and adversity.

Emotional resilience is the ability to withstand challenges, stress, and adversity. By responding to emotions in a way that fosters emotional resilience, you can help young children develop this important life skill.

Strategies for Building Emotional Resilience in Children
1. Label and Validate Feelings
"You're feeling angry right now, aren't you?"

I can see that you're really upset.

2. Accept and Validate Feelings
It's okay to feel that way.

"Your feelings are normal."

3. Teach Emotion Regulation Techniques
- Deep breathing exercises.

- Count to ten.

- Visualize a happy place.

4. Encourage Communication
"What's the problem?" or "How did that make you feel?"

Listen actively and attentively.

5. Offer Choices and Encourage Problem-Solving
"Would you like to take a deep breath or count to 10?"

"What do you think we can do to solve this problem?"

6. Practice Empathy
"I know you're really upset. I'd feel the same way."

"I understand why you're feeling that way."

7. Model Emotion Regulation
- Express your feelings in a healthy way.

- Apologize when necessary.

- Show empathy and understanding towards others.

8. Cultivate a Growth Mindset
- Encourage effort and progress, not just success.

- Learn that mistakes are opportunities for growth.

- Praise perseverance and resilience.

By using these strategies, you can help young children develop emotional resilience that will benefit them throughout their lives.

Coping Strategies
Coping strategies refer to the process of managing and dealing with difficult or unpleasant emotions, situations, or experiences. It involves finding ways to cope and reduce stress, anxiety, or discomfort while maintaining emotional comfort. Coping is an essential skill for everyone, especially children, because it helps them navigate life's ups and downs with less damage and more resilience.

Emotional Coping Strategies for Children
Children use a variety of emotional coping strategies to manage their emotions, which can be divided into two main types: positive and negative coping strategies.

Positive coping strategies include:
- Problem-Focused Coping: The goal is to solve problems or find solutions to reduce stress.

- Emotion-Focused Coping: Expressing and processing feelings through talking, writing, or creative activities.

- Social Support Seeking: Reaching out to others for help and comfort.

- Self-Care: Engaging in self-care activities such as drawing, listening to music, or taking a warm bath.

- Mindfulness: Focusing on the present moment and letting go of worries about the past or future.

Negative coping strategies include:
- Inflexible: May lead to rigid thinking and behavior.

- Maladaptive: Can worsen mental health and relationships.

- Harmful: Can lead to physical and emotional harm.

- Unhealthy: Leads to poor overall mental and physical health.

Factors affecting children's coping strategies include:
- Age: Younger children may use more rudimentary coping strategies, while older children may develop more complex strategies.

- Temperature: Children's temperament can affect their coping styles, with some being more anxious or impulsive.

- Parental Modeling: Children learn coping strategies by observing their parents' coping strategies.

- Social Support: Children who have a strong social support network are more likely to develop positive coping strategies.

- Life Experiences: Traumatic events or stressful experiences can shape a child's coping strategies and emotional resilience.

Tips for parents and caregivers include:
- Model Healthy Coping Strategies: Model healthy coping strategies yourself.

- Teach Positive Coping Skills: Encourage children to use positive coping strategies.

- Validate Emotions: Acknowledge and validate children's feelings.

- Enhance Social Support: Encourage social connections and a strong support network.

- Monitor Progress: Monitor children's coping strategies and provide guidance as needed.

By understanding the different emotional coping strategies used by children, parents and caregivers can support them in developing healthy habits that promote their emotional resilience and overall well-being.

Level of Emotion Regulation Ability in Young Children
Levels of emotion regulation ability in children 2 to 6 years old include:

For 2-Year-Olds
Awareness and Expression: At this age, children begin to identify and express basic emotions such as happiness, sadness, and anger. However, their emotion regulation is minimal and is mainly driven by immediate needs and frustrations.

Behavior: Emotional outbursts and tantrums are common because they have limited ability to control their impulses and responses.

For 3-Year-Olds
Emerging Rules: Three-year-old children begin to develop a better understanding of their emotions and may use simple strategies to manage their emotions, such as seeking reassurance from a caregiver.

Behavior: They can follow simple rules and routines that help them manage their emotions. However, they still need significant support from adults to effectively regulate their emotions.

For 4-Year-Olds
Developing Skills: Four-year-old children become more adept at recognizing their own and others' emotions. They begin to understand cause and effect in emotional contexts and may use basic coping strategies.

Behavior: They can engage in cooperative play and begin to demonstrate self-control. They may use verbal expressions to communicate their feelings rather than physical outbursts.

For 5-Year-Olds

Advanced Awareness: Five-year-old children have a broader emotional vocabulary and can reflect on their feelings and actions. They begin to use more complex strategies for emotion regulation, such as deep breathing or counting to ten.

Behavior: They can better manage transitions between different activities and minor frustrations, and can follow more complex rules. They show greater empathy and understanding of the feelings of others.

For 6-Year-Olds

Increasing Regulation: Six-year-old children are capable of more advanced self-regulation. They can identify the triggers of their emotions and use a variety of coping strategies to manage their emotions.

Behavior: They are better at resolving conflicts, expressing empathy, and understanding the consequences of their actions. Their ability to self-reflect and make thoughtful decisions improves significantly.

These levels of emotion regulation ability reflect normal developmental milestones for children aged 2 to 6. Each child's development may be different, and providing supportive and ongoing guidance can help progress in emotion regulation skills.

Strategies to support emotion regulation in 2-year-olds include:

Regular Routines: Establish regular, predictable daily schedules to create a sense of security in a routine.

Pattern of Calm Behavior: Demonstrate calm and composed behavior in stressful situations.

Use Simple Words: Help children identify and label their feelings using simple words.

Comfort: Provide comforting objects, such as a favorite toy or soft blanket, to help soothe them.

Distraction Techniques: Direct attention to a different activity when they are upset.

Positive Reinforcement: Praise and reward calm behavior and successful attempts to control their emotions immediately.

Strengths
Curious: Eager to explore their environment and learn new things.

Quick Learner: Quick to learn new words, actions, and concepts.

Strong Bonds: Form close attachments with caregivers and family members.

Expressivity: Communicate their needs and wants, even with a limited vocabulary.

Imitation: They quickly learn new behaviors by imitating adults and older children.

Challenges
Limited Self-Control: They often have difficulty managing their impulses and emotions.

Temperament: They are prone to emotional outbursts when frustrated or tired.

Communication Barriers: Their limited vocabulary can lead to frustration when they are unable to express their needs.

Separation Anxiety: They experience distress and separation anxiety when separated from their primary caregivers and parents.

Routine Changes: They often fight and oppose environmental changes or changes to their usual routines, which leads to emotional distress.

Normal Behaviors
Temperament: Their frequent tantrums are a way to express frustration.

Curiosity: They are constantly exploring and testing boundaries with curiosity.

Imitation: They imitate the actions and speech of adults and peers.

Attachment: In attachment, they often seek their comfort and security by being strongly dependent on caregivers.

Parallel Play: Rather than engaging directly in play with other children, they often prefer to play alongside them in a parallel manner.

Strategies to support emotion regulation in 3-year-olds include:
1. Model Healthy Emotion Regulation: Children often learn from what they see, so model healthy emotion regulation yourself.

2. Label Emotions: Recognize and label your child's emotions to help them develop emotional awareness.

3. Teach Coping Strategies: Encourage your child to use coping strategies, such as deep breathing, counting, or talking about their feelings.

4. Provide Empathy and Comfort: When your child is upset, provide them with physical comfort and empathy as much as possible.

5. Provide a Predictable Routine: Set up a daily routine that is predictable and consistent to help reduce anxiety and uncertainty.

6. Encourage Communication: Encourage your child to express their feelings in simple language and listen carefully to what they say.

At age 4, children's emotion regulation skills continue to develop and improve. Here are some common features of emotion regulation in 4-year-olds:

Strengths
1. Better Emotional Awareness: Four-year-old children have a better understanding of their emotions and can identify and label more complex emotions, such as "jealousy" or "confused."

2. Improved Self-Awareness: They can recognize their feelings and describe them in simple sentences.

3. Increased Use of Coping Strategies: Four-year-old children may use more advanced coping strategies, such as talking about their feelings, drawing pictures, or using play to express their feelings.

4. Greater Ability to Control Impulsivity: They may have more control over their impulsivity and can pause and think before acting in some situations.

Challenges
1. Sometimes Impulsive: Four-year-old children may still struggle with controlling their impulsivity, especially in situations that trigger strong emotions.

2. Emotional Intensity: They can still experience strong emotions, but with better support they can regulate them.

3. Testing Boundaries: Four-year-old children may test personal boundaries and push limits to see how far they can go, which can lead to anger if others don't let them.

4. Difficulty with Change and Transition: They may still struggle with changing routines and tasks, especially if they are not informed in advance.

Normal Behaviors

1. Fewer Tantrums: Four-year-old children may have fewer tantrums than younger children, but they can still occur when they are frustrated.

2. More Whining and Crying: Children in this age may use whining or crying as a way to express their feelings and get attention.

3. Impatience: Four-year-old children may become impatient when they are waiting for something or when things are not going their way.

4. Separation Anxiety: They may become anxious or upset when separated from a parent, a trusted adult, or caregiver.

Strategies to support emotion regulation in 4-year-olds include:

1. Model Healthy Emotion Regulation: As children learn from what they see, continue to model healthy emotion regulation.

2. Encourage Communication: Encourage your child to express their feelings in simple language and encourage communication.

3. Teach Coping Strategies: Introduce more advanced coping strategies, such as problem-solving, deep breathing, or creative visualization.

4. Offer Choices: Offer choices to help your child feel more in control of the situation and reduce their frustration (e.g., "Do you want to wear the blue shirt or the red shirt?").

5. Encourage Empathy: Encourage your child to consider the feelings and perspectives of others, which can help them empathize and better regulate their own emotions.

6. Practice Problem-Solving Together: Work with your child to solve problems and come up with solutions that can help develop critical thinking skills and self-confidence.

At age 4, children's emotion regulation skills continue to improve and they may show more advanced abilities.

Here are some common characteristics of emotion regulation in 5-year-olds:
Strengths
1. Improved Emotional Awareness: Five-year-old children have a better understanding of their emotions and can identify and label more complex emotions such as "excitement," "calm," or "pride."

2. Increased Ability to Regulate Emotions: They can use a variety of strategies to regulate their emotions, such as taking deep breaths, counting to 10, or talking about their feelings.

3. Better Control of Impulsivity: Five-year-old children may have more control over their impulsivity and can think before they act in most situations.

4. Greater Empathy: They are more able to understand and consider the feelings and perspectives of others.

5. Problem-Solving Skills: They may be more able to think critically and come up with solutions to problems.

Challenges
1. Still Impulsive at Times: Five-year-old children may still struggle with controlling their impulsivity, especially in situations that trigger strong emotions.

2. Emotional Responsiveness: They may react quickly to situations without thinking fully, which can lead to emotional outbursts.

3. Testing Boundaries: Five-year-old children may continue to test personal boundaries and break boundaries set by parents and others, which can lead to power struggles or anger.

4. Difficulty with Transitions: They may still Struggle with changes in routine and tasks, especially if they are not informed in advance.

Normal Behaviors
1. Less Mood Swings: Five-year-old children may have fewer tantrums than

younger children, but they may still have mood swings when they are confused or frustrated.

2. More Arguing and Negotiating: Children this age may be better at arguing and negotiating as they learn to express their needs and wants.

3. Impatience: Five-year-old children may become easily irritated and impatient with others who do not accept their point of view.

4. Fear of Failure: They may become anxious or upset when they make mistakes or fail at something because of their fear of failure.

Strategies to support emotion regulation in 5-year-olds include:
Model Calm Behavior: Show how you stay calm in stressful situations so that children can imitate your behavior.

Teach Coping Strategies: Introduce techniques such as deep breathing, counting to ten, or using a quiet corner.

Use Positive Reinforcement: Reward positive behavior and successful attempts at emotional control and regulation with consistent praise and positive reinforcement.

Create Routines: Regular daily routines create a sense of security and predictability.

Talk about Feelings: Encourage children to talk about their feelings and help them identify and understand different feelings.

Read Books about Feelings: Use stories to illustrate different feelings and strategies for dealing with worry and emotional outbursts.

Problem-Solving Skills: Teach children to solve problems that cause frustration and increase their ability to manage emotions.

Strengths
Curiosity and Eagerness to Learn: They are eager to discover new things and learn.

Improved Communication Skills: They demonstrate a greater ability to verbally express their thoughts and feelings.

Empathy: They demonstrate greater understanding and concern for the feelings of others.

Independence: They demonstrate a growing ability to complete tasks and activities on their own.

Imagination: They demonstrate greater creativity when playing and engaging in imaginative play.

Challenges

Impulsivity: They may often act impulsively and rashly without thinking through the consequences of their behavior.

Emotional Outbursts: They may have difficulty managing strong emotions, sometimes leading to anger or meltdowns.

Social Interactions: They may find it difficult and sometimes challenging to maintain friendships and social interactions.

Concentration: They may have difficulty focusing on tasks for long periods of time, especially if the activity is not very interesting to them.

Frustration: Easily frustrated and sometimes angry when tasks are difficult or when they fail.

Normal Behaviors

Active Play: Often enjoys active play and physical activities with boundless energy.

Storytelling and Pretend Play: Engages in pretend play, imagination, and elaborate storytelling.

Friendships: Begins to form stronger friendships and cooperate with peers.

Seeks Independence: Shows a desire to do things independently and may also make their own opinions and choices.

Curiosity: Frequently asks many, sometimes repetitive, questions about the world around them and seeks to understand how things work.

Strategies to support emotion regulation in 6-year-olds include:

Teach Problem-Solving Skills: Encourage children to think about ways to solve problems before they react emotionally.

Model Healthy Emotional Responses: Show them appropriate ways to express emotions, control, and manage stress by modeling appropriate behavior.

Encourage Open Communication: Create an environment where children feel safe to talk about their feelings.

Use Role-Play: Practice different emotion-regulation scenarios and appropriate responses to help them use them in real-life situations.

Mindfulness and Relaxation Techniques: Teach simple mindfulness exercises, such as deep breathing or guided imagery.

Provide Clear Instructions: Help children understand what is expected of them and provide clear, concise instructions.

Positive Reinforcement: Encourage and praise children for using appropriate emotion-regulation strategies and behaviors.

Strengths
Increased Independence: They can complete more tasks on their own.

Improved Social Skills: They are better at making and maintaining friendships.

Curiosity and Eagerness to Learn: They are eager to learn new things and explore their interests.

Advanced Communication: They can often express their thoughts and feelings clearly.

Problem-Solving Skills: They are beginning to think critically and find appropriate solutions to problems and issues.

Challenges
Frustration with Failure: They become easily frustrated and discouraged when they do not succeed at tasks immediately.

Peer Pressure: They gradually feel the effects of peer pressure, which can lead to stress.

Balcony between Independence and Dependence: They both want to be independent and still need guidance and support from adults.

Emotion Regulation Skills: They learn the skills needed to manage intense emotions.

Attention Span: May still have trouble maintaining focus on tasks that are not very engaging.

Normal Behaviors
Approval-Seeking: Often seek approval from adults and peers.

Active Play: Enjoy physical activities and games and show high energy levels.

Interest in Rules: Begin to understand and follow rules and may also enforce rules when playing with peers.

Role-Playing and Imaginative Play: Engage in complex pretend play and enjoy creating stories.

Independence-Seeking: Show a strong desire to do things on their own, even if they still need help.

Emotion Regulation in Children Aged 2 to 6 Years with ADHD
There is a significant difference in the level of emotion regulation in young children diagnosed with ADHD compared to normally developing children. Research has consistently shown that these children have more difficulty regulating emotions than typically developing children. For example:

In 2-Year-Olds
Intensity of Emotions: Hyperactive 2-year-old children often experience emotions more deeply and intensely than typically developing children. This intensity of emotion can lead to frequent and exaggerated emotional outbursts.

Duration of Emotions: Different emotions may last longer for hyperactive children, making it harder for them to calm down and move on from an upsetting event.

Impulsivity: Due to impulsivity or impulsivity, hyperactive children may react immediately to their emotions without thinking about the consequences, leading to frequent tantrums and behavioral meltdowns.

Calming: They often have a harder time calming down and may need more support from their parents and caregivers to calm down.

Frustration Tolerance: ADHD children tend to have a lower frustration tolerance, meaning they become more frustrated and upset when things don't go according to plan.

Social Challenges: These children's emotional dysregulation can affect their social interactions, making it more difficult for them to form relationships and make friends.

In 3-Year-Olds
- Three-year-old children with ADHD may be more likely to exhibit anger and emotion dysregulation than normal children.

- They may have more difficulty understanding and labeling their emotions, leading to increased frustration and behavioral problems.

- They may be less able to regulate their emotions and behaviors, leading to increased impulsivity and hyperactivity.

In 4-Year-Olds
- They may still struggle with emotion regulation, but may be beginning to improve.

- They may still show more intense emotions and have a harder time calming down after an emotional upset than normal children.

- They may be more likely to engage in physical aggression or destructive behavior when frustrated or upset.

In 5-Year-Olds
- They may show similarities in emotion regulation to normal children, but may still experience more problems.

- They may be more prone to experiencing negative emotions such as anger, frustration, and anxiety and have a harder time managing these emotions.

It is important to note that these findings are general trends and that individual differences play an important role. Some children with ADHD may have better emotion regulation skills than other children without ADHD. In addition, some normal children may have more difficulty with emotion regulation due to other factors, such as temperament or environmental factors.

In 6-Year-Olds

Emotional Intensity: Compared to normal children, their emotions are often more intense and difficult to manage. Hyperactive children may have frequent and exaggerated emotional reactions.

Controlling Impulsivity: Impulsivity leads to frequent outbursts of emotion and difficulty delaying quick reactions.

Soothing: They have more difficulty self-soothing and may rely more on external supports to calm down.

Duration of Emotions: Their emotions may last longer, making it harder for them to get through an upsetting event.

Social Skills: They often have trouble understanding and understanding social cues such as tone of voice or body language and may react inappropriately in social situations, leading to challenges in making and maintaining friendships.

Frustration Tolerance: They have lower frustration tolerance, get upset easily and quickly when things don't go according to plan, and may have frequent emotional and behavioral meltdowns.

Strategies to Support Emotion Regulation for Children with ADHD
1. Emotional Labeling and Validation
   - Teach children to identify and label their feelings in simple language to make it easier for them to express.

   - Validate their feelings and acknowledge that being upset or frustrated sometimes happens and is okay.

2. Deep Breathing and Relaxation Techniques
   - Teach children deep breathing exercises such as "slow and deep inhales and exhales."

   - Encourage relaxation techniques such as progressive muscle relaxation, visualization or guided imagery.

3. Emotional Expression and Communication
   - Encourage children to express their feelings through drawing, writing or talking.

- Teach active listening skills, allowing children to process and express their feelings.

4. Problem-Solving and Coping Skills
- Teach problem-solving strategies such as breaking problems down into smaller steps or finding alternative solutions.

- Encourage children to think about how they can manage their feelings in different difficult situations.

5. Physical Activity and Exercise
- Encourage physical activity to help regulate emotions and relieve tension (such as running, jumping, yoga).

- Participate in physical activities together, which strengthens the parent-child bond and helps manage and reduce stress.

6. Sensory Integration Strategies
- Provide sensory experiences that help regulate emotions, such as fidget toys, weighted blankets, or swings.

- Use sensory materials (such as play dough or sand) for calming activities.

7. Teach Social Skills
- Teach social skills such as empathy, sharing, and cooperation.

- Use role-playing games with different social scenarios to practice emotion regulation in different contexts.

8. Parent-Child Interaction
- Use parent-child interaction techniques to strengthen parent-child relationships and emotion regulation skills.

9. Teach Emotion Self-Regulation Techniques
- Teach children to recognize and accept their thoughts, feelings, and bodily sensations.

- Introduce and demonstrate simple mindfulness and relaxation techniques, such as deep breathing, progressive muscle relaxation, and guided imagery. These exercises can help hyperactive children to calm their moments of emotional distress.

10. Consistency and Daily Routine

- Create a structured environment.

- Create a daily schedule with consistent expectations and boundaries.

- Use visual reminders and schedules to help children stay organized and focused.

11. Positive Reinforcement and Praise

- Provide positive reinforcement for emotion regulation efforts (for example, "I admire your regular practice of deep breathing. Well done!").

- Praise children for effectively dealing with frustration or upset.

- Praise and reward positive behaviors and efforts to regulate the emotions of hyperactive children. This encourages them to continue using these strategies and reinforces their progress.

12. Provide a Safe Space

- Create a quiet, designated place where hyperactive children can go and return to when they feel stressed. This space should be equipped with soothing items such as soft toys, books, or calming activities.

13. Emotional Vocabulary Training

- Help hyperactive children build a rich emotional vocabulary so they can better identify and express their feelings. This training can be done through discussion, reading books about feelings, and role-playing scenarios.

14. Professional Help and Collaboration

- Work with a child psychologist and educator to develop an individualized treatment plan for your child.

- Collaborate with teachers, caregivers, and other professionals to provide ongoing support for your child.

Trainability: Both normal and ADHD young children 2 to 6 years old can learn strategies for regulating their emotions. Techniques such as deep breathing, identifying feelings, and using calming activities can be helpful for all children.

2- Teaching Impulse Control Strategies

Impulse Control

Impulse is the tendency to act quickly without thinking. For example, children may blurt out something, or run across the street without looking both ways. Impulse is not the same as being rude or undisciplined. It is a pattern of behavior that begins in the brain.

Impulse control is the ability to resist impulsive responses to perform an action. It is an ability that develops in children over time. Factors that contribute to the development of impulse control are complex and include multiple domains, including biological, developmental, psychological, and cultural factors.

Impulse control strategies are techniques used to help children with ADHD and other children who struggle with impulsive behaviors manage impulses and regulate their emotions.

While young children may not be developmentally ready for all of these impulse management and emotion regulation strategies, some can certainly be taught to them in a way that is appropriate for their age and abilities. Such as:

- Counting: When they have the urge to act impulsively, start with simple counting activities like counting to 5 or 10 and gradually increase the numbers as they get older.

- Deep Breathing: Use simple breathing exercises, such as "inhale, hold your breath, exhale."

- Reward Systems: Provide a specific reward program to motivate children to demonstrate impulse control and responsible behavior (such as score sheets or tokens for shopping, going to the playground, and things that interest them).

- Toys: Provide toys like play dough or finger puppets to help them release excess energy, anxiety, and stress. Anxiety and stress can exacerbate impulsive behaviors.

- Physical Activity: Encourage physical activity (such as running, jumping, or dancing) during playtime.

- Acting: Act out different emotions (such as happy, sad, angry) and ask them to guess how you feel.

- Imitating: Have them take deep belly breaths while imitating you, like a stuffed animal character like a bear, while making the sound of "roar." Breathe like a bear (e.g., say, "Breathe like a bear" like me).

Adapting Impulsivity Management Strategies for Children Aged 2 to 6 Years with ADHD

- Keep the Training Short and Simple: Use short sentences and simple language to explain concepts and exercises.

- Use Visual Aids: Use pictures or visual aids to help understand strategies.

- Make the Training Fun: Incorporate games, songs, and game-based activities to make learning fun.

- Role-Playing: Use role-playing to demonstrate social skills and control impulsivity in a fun way.

- Practice Regularly: Practice these strategies regularly throughout the day.

- Remember to always supervise and adapt these activities to your preschooler's age and individual needs and abilities.

3- Teach Attention Management and Control Strategies

Attention Control

Definition
Attention management and control refers to the ability to focus on a specific task or activity while ignoring distractions. It is a critical cognitive skill that helps children manage and complete tasks effectively, make better decisions, and better achieve their goals.

Attention control is essential for children aged 2 to 6 because it helps them:
- Stay Focused: Complete tasks, such as puzzles, crafts, or games, without being easily distracted.

- Make Better Choices: Make informed decisions about what to do next and stay on track with their goals.

- Develop Social Skills: Pay attention to social cues, follow directions, and take turns with peers.

- Build Self-Regulation: Regulate emotions and behaviors by staying calm and focused.

Teaching Attention Control Strategies to Children Aged 2 to 6 Years

Visual Reminders: Use visual aids such as posters, charts, or pictures to remind them of strategies.

Simple Language: Use simple language and short sentences to explain strategies.

Role-Play: Demonstrate strategies through role-play, such as pretending to be a "focused friend" or "attention superhero."

Practice Regularly: Practice strategies during routines, such as circle time, transitions, or snack time.

Make It Fun: Incorporate games, songs, and play-based activities to make learning fun.

Attention Control Activities for Children 2 to 6 Years Old

- Focus on the Task: Encourage them to focus on a specific task or activity while ignoring distractions.

- One-Move Rule: Encourage them to finish one task before moving on to another.

- Listen with Your Eyes: Teach them to make eye contact while you are talking to them to help them stay focused.

- Take Deep Breaths: Encourage deep breathing exercises to help them relax and refocus.

- Use Pictures or Symbols: Provide pictures or symbols to help them stay on track by guiding them and looking at them.

Adapting Attention Control Training for Children 2 to 6 Years Old with a Diagnosis of ADHD

- Extra Support: Provide extra support and accommodations than normal children, such as extra time to complete tasks or using assistive technology.

- Visual Programs: Use visual programs to help them understand the daily routine and how to transition tasks with the help of pictures.

- Fidget Toys: Let them release their excess energy and anxiety with the help of fidget toys or other sensory tools.

- Break Tasks into Smaller Steps: Break complex tasks into smaller, manageable steps to help them stay focused.

- Positive Reinforcement: Provide positive reinforcement and praise for efforts made to improve attention control.

Remember to always consult a child psychologist or counselor before introducing new strategies, especially for children aged 2 to 6 with a diagnosis of ADHD.

4- Goal Setting

Goal setting involves helping children set personal goals and work hard to achieve them. This process teaches valuable skills such as planning, perseverance, and self-discipline. Goal setting involves the following steps:

1. Set a Goal: The child decides on a specific, achievable goal. For example, learning to ride a bike.

2. Break Down the Goal: The goal is broken down into smaller, more manageable steps. For example:

First learn to balance on a stationary bike. Then practice pedaling while supported.

Finally, try riding independently on training wheels before moving on to a two-wheeler.

3. Create a Plan: Create a plan for regularly practicing each step toward the goal. This may include daily practice sessions and encouragement from caregivers.

4. Perseverance and Emotion Regulation: The child is encouraged to continue practicing with persistence and perseverance even when faced with difficulties. Guide your child to keep trying by controlling negative emotions like frustration and discouragement, and celebrate small successes along the way. If they encounter obstacles, help them find new strategies to overcome them.

5. Think about Progress: Regularly reviewing progress toward a goal helps your child understand the importance of effort and perseverance in achieving their goals.

Example: Learning to ride a bike.
1. Set a Goal: "Your child wants to ride a bike independently."

2. Break the Goal:

Week 1: Practice balancing on a bike without pedaling.

Week 2: Pedal with the help of an adult holding the bike.

Week 3: Try pedaling with training wheels.

Week 4: Try riding without training wheels for short distances.

3. Create a Schedule: Schedule daily practice sessions in a safe, open area.

4. Persistence and Emotion Regulation: Encourage your child to persevere, even if they fall off the bike and feel discouraged. Adjust the goal-achievement plan as needed to help them make progress. Preschoolers often get frustrated or angry when they encounter obstacles in their path to achieving important goals. They need help and guidance in managing their emotions in such difficult situations. For example, they may need to be reminded to take deep breaths or to use a quiet space when they feel tired.

5. Reflect on Your Child's Progress: Discuss your child's progress at the end of each week, celebrating their efforts and any milestones they have achieved. For example, praise them for persevering and controlling their emotions, and for trying and practicing after a fall and taking a break to learn their target skill, in this example, riding a bike.

In general, as children aged 2 to 6 begin to set goals along with regulating their emotions and managing their emotions, they rely heavily on the support of parents, teachers, adults, and structured environments to practice and develop these skills. With consistent practice and guidance, they can gradually improve their ability to persist and persist in achieving goals and regulating their emotions. By engaging in goal setting, children learn that achieving goals requires effort, perseverance, and sometimes adapting emotion management strategies along the way. This skill is essential for their overall development and future success.

Appropriate Goal Setting Strategies for Children 2 to 6 Years Old with ADHD

For children aged 2 to 6 with a diagnosis of ADHD, appropriate teaching strategies for "goal setting" in self-management include:

- Simple, Clear Instructions: Break tasks into small, manageable steps and provide clear, concise instructions.

- Positive Reinforcement: Use praise and rewards to encourage progress and effort.

- Visual Aids: Use pictures or visual programs to help children understand and remember the steps.

- Control Impulsivity: Use modeling, positive reinforcement, simple routines, waiting practice, and visual cues to control impulsivity.

Example: Learning to ride a bike.

Clear Instructions: Teach your child to first balance on the bike, then pedal with support, and eventually ride independently.

Positive Reinforcement: Praise your child for small successes, such as maintaining balance for a few seconds or pedaling without support.

Visual Aids: Use a chart with pictures that show each step of the process to help your child better visualize and remember the process of continuing to practice cycling.

For example, when teaching a bike, you can use the following strategies:
- Visual Cues: Place cones or markers along the path that they must stop and wait before continuing, reinforcing the need to pause and think before acting.

- Waiting Practice: Create games where they have to wait for a signal (such as a clap or whistle) before they start pedaling, and encourage them to avoid hasty actions.

- Routine Practice: Practice routines that involve waiting, such as waiting at a stop sign or a green light, which can help them gradually learn and internalize the need for patience.

- Positive Reinforcement: Praise and reward them when they successfully wait or follow instructions correctly, and reinforce appropriate behavior.

- Modeling: Show them how to wait and control impulsivity, and provide a simple, clear example for them to follow so they can better follow.

These strategies help children aged 2 to 6 with ADHD stay more focused, understand the expectations of working toward a goal, and have confidence in their abilities to achieve it.

5- Time Management

Definition
The definition of time management in the context of self-regulation and social-emotional learning for children aged 2 to 6 refers to the ability to understand and effectively manage one's time to complete tasks and activities in a structured and timely manner. It includes several key components:

- Understanding Time: Helping children aged 2 to 6 understand basic concepts of time, such as knowing the difference between morning and afternoon, and understanding the duration of activities (e.g., story time).

- Planning: Teaching children to plan their actions and follow sequences, such as the steps involved in getting ready for school or getting ready for bedtime.

- Prioritizing Tasks: Encouraging children to prioritize tasks and activities, understanding which ones need to be done first (e.g., finishing their snack before playing).

- Following Routines: Creating and maintaining regular, consistent daily schedules to provide a predictable structure helps children know what to expect and when.

- Transition Management: Helping children move smoothly from one activity to another, reducing resistance to change and helping them adapt to change.

- Goal Setting: Encourage children to set simple, appropriate and achievable goals (e.g., completing a puzzle or cleaning up toys) and work towards achieving them within a specific time frame.

Teaching time management skills to children aged 2 to 6 years old builds the foundation for effective self-regulation and helps children develop the ability to manage their behaviors, emotions and activities in a structured and productive way.

Time management teaching strategies for normal 2 to 6 years old children include:

- Visual Schedules: Use visual schedules with pictures to help children understand the sequence of daily activities. This practice provides a clear structure and helps them know what to expect at the next steps in the future.

- Timers and Clocks: Introduce simple timers or clocks to help children understand the concept of time passing. Set a timer for specific activities, such as study time or room cleaning time.

- Routine Chart: Create routine charts that outline daily tasks like getting dressed, brushing your teeth, and putting on your school backpack. This encourages kids to follow sequential instructions and manage their time effectively.

- Task Breakdown: Break down tasks into smaller, manageable steps with specific time allocations (e.g., half an hour of drawing, half an hour of playing).

- Transition Cues: Use verbal or visual cues to transition between activities. For example, a gentle reminder five minutes before transition helps children prepare for the change.

- Goal Setting: Encourage children to set small, achievable goals, such as completing a puzzle or tidying up their play area. Praise and celebrate their achievements to reinforce the importance of time management in achieving their goals.

- Positive Reinforcement: Praise and reward children for completing tasks on time to encourage good time management habits.

Time Management Teaching Strategies for Children Aged 2 to 6 Years with ADHD

- Structured Routines: Create clear, consistent routines to provide a predictable framework. Hyperactive children benefit from knowing what to expect and when.

- Short, Manageable Tasks: Break activities into shorter, manageable tasks to prevent children from feeling overwhelmed. This practice helps maintain their attention and reduce impulsiveness.

- Clear, Simple Instructions: Provide concise, straightforward instructions to avoid overwhelming your child. For example, when guiding your child through a "watercolor painting" assignment, you could say, "Let's paint together, "one, two, three": "One, dip the brush in water. Two, dip the brush in paint. Three, draw the brush on the paper." This clear and simple instruction helps them understand the steps and stay focused better.

- Special Timers: Use special, attractive timers, such as colorful sand timers or digital timers with attractive images, to make the concept of time more tangible and appealing to hyperactive children.

- Calming Strategies: Use calming strategies, such as deep breathing exercises or creating a cozy, quiet corner to rest, to help hyperactive children regulate and strengthen their energy and focus before moving on to a new task.

- Positive Reinforcement: Provide immediate, positive reinforcement for completing tasks within the allotted time. This encourages children to stay on track and manage their time effectively.

- Flexible Time Breaks: Provide flexible time breaks to accommodate your child's need to move and rest. Short, frequent breaks can help hyperactive children better maintain their attention and focus and better control and manage their time to complete tasks.

The goal of teaching strategies to support children aged 2 to 6 to understand and manage time is to promote self-regulation and effective social-emotional learning.

6- Intrinsically Motivated Action (Spontaneity)

Intrinsically motivated action or spontaneity in self-regulation refers to the ability to act spontaneously, quickly and naturally, without forethought, while effectively managing motivations and emotions. It involves balancing impulsive, hasty actions with thoughtful decision-making to flexibly adapt to new situations.

Spontaneity is essential for young children because it helps them:
Develop Creativity: Think outside the box and come up with innovative solutions.

Improve Problem-Solving: Respond to unexpected situations with ease and flexibility.

Strengthen Social Skills: Participate in playful and interactive activities with others.

Show Self-Confidence: Be more confident in their abilities and decision-making.

Educational strategies for intrinsically motivated action (spontaneity) for normal 2 to 6 years old children include:

- Encourage Free Play: Allow children to explore unstructured playtime and decide what to do in the moment to foster natural spontaneity.

- Positive Reinforcement: Praise children for spontaneous actions that are appropriate and well-managed.

- Modeling: Demonstrate spontaneous but safe behaviors and show children how to act (e.g., demonstrate new imaginative play). For example, by modeling, show them:

- Responsiveness: Encourage them to think quickly, be ready to respond, and respond to situations without hesitation.

- Open-Mindedness: Teach them to be open and receptive to new ideas and perspectives.

- Risk-Taking: Encourage them to take calculated risks and try new things.

- Adaptability: Teach them to adapt to changes and unexpected situations.

- Accept Mistakes: Encourage them to see mistakes as opportunities to grow and learn.

Appropriate Teaching Strategies for Intrinsic Motivation (Spontaneity) for Children Aged 2 to 6 Years with a Diagnosis of ADHD
- Task Breakdown: Break complex tasks into smaller, manageable chunks to reduce frustration.

- Provide Order: Create a structured environment with order and order. Provide predictability to help them feel more comfortable with spontaneity.

- Sensory Toys: Allow fidget toys or other sensory tools to release excess energy while engaging in spontaneous activities.

- One-on-One Support: Provide one-on-one support and guidance during activities to help them develop spontaneity skills.

- Positive Reinforcement: Provide positive reinforcement and praise for efforts made to develop spontaneity skills.

- Immediate Feedback: Provide immediate feedback on spontaneous actions while effectively managing impulses and emotions to help them understand the consequences of doing anything.

- Structured Choices: Provide limited, structured choices to guide their spontaneous decisions, reduce their pressure and stress, and promote successful spontaneous actions.

- Guided Spontaneity: Create scenarios where children can practice spontaneous actions in a controlled environment under your supervision, and help them learn when and how to act.

These strategies help all young children, including those diagnosed with ADHD, learn balanced ways to be spontaneous and self-regulated. It should be noted, however, that teaching spontaneous, self-directed behaviors to children aged 2 to 6 can be more challenging, especially for children diagnosed with ADHD, due to their natural impulsivity. However, with consistent guidance, clear boundaries, and positive reinforcement, children can learn to balance spontaneity with safe, responsible actions. It is a process that requires patience and understanding, but it can be rewarding as children learn and develop better self-regulation and decision-making skills.

7- Working Memory

Definition
Working memory is a cognitive system that temporarily holds and controls information needed to perform complex tasks such as learning, reasoning, and comprehension. Working memory serves as a mental workspace where information is stored and managed in the short term.

For example, when a child is asked to remember a series of numbers while solving a math problem, he or she uses his or her working memory to hold the numbers and simultaneously process the solution. Working memory is essential for tasks that require concentration, planning, and problem-solving.

What Is the Relationship between Working Memory and Self-Regulation in the Social-Emotional Learning of 2 to 6 Years Old Children?

Working memory and self-regulation are closely linked in the social-emotional learning of young children aged 2 to 6 years. Here's how they relate:

The Foundation of Self-Regulation: Working memory is crucial for self-regulation because it allows children to retain and manipulate information, which is essential for controlling impulses and managing emotions.

Emotion Recognition: Working memory helps children recognize and understand their emotions, which is a key component of self-regulation.

Problem-Solving Skills: Improving working memory enables children to think through problems and find solutions, and helps with better self-regulation.

Social Interactions: Children with better working memory are more adept at navigating social interactions, which includes regulating their behavior and reactions in social settings.

Teaching Strategies to Strengthen Working Memory in Normal Children Aged 2 to 6 Years

At Home

Memory Games: Play games like "flash cards and find similar shapes" that help children remember the rules and cards. Cards with various pictures on them are played by matching similar cards.

Storytelling: Encourage children to tell interesting stories or events, which helps them practice remembering details.

Visualization Exercises: Ask children to visualize and describe scenes or objects, strengthening their ability to retain information in their minds.

Daily Routines: Create consistent routines to help children remember a sequence of tasks and reduce the cognitive burden of uncertain schedules.

Interactive Reading: Engage children who can read in reading activities so they can predict what will happen next and actively engage with the text to strengthen their working memory.

At School

Break Down Information: Break information into smaller, more manageable chunks to make it easier for children to remember.

Use Visual Aids: Use visual aids such as diagrams and pictures to support their working memory and comprehension.

Repetition and Practice: Ask children to review and practice what they have learned regularly to strengthen their working memory.

Interactive Activities: Use hands-on activities and group work to keep children engaged and help them recall information through active participation.

Positive Reinforcement: Praise and reward children immediately for remembering and correctly applying various information to increase their self-confidence and motivation.

These strategies can help normal children aged 2 to 6 years improve their working memory and support their cognitive development, social-emotional learning, and overall learning.

Specific Teaching Strategies to Strengthen Working Memory in Children with ADHD

At Home

Create Routines: Establish consistent daily routines to help children remember tasks and reduce cognitive load.

Use Visual Aids: Implement visual schedules, checklists, and charts to provide reminders and clear structure to enhance working memory.

Break Tasks into Small Steps: Simplify tasks by breaking them down into smaller, more manageable steps to make them easier to remember.

Interactive Play: Engage in memory-boosting games such as first and last names, matching or alphabet sorting games, and completing puzzles with children.

Positive Reinforcement: Give children immediate rewards for remembering tasks and following routines to encourage consistent effort.

At School

Written Instructions: Provide children with written instructions to supplement verbal instructions.

Use Cueing: Teach cueing to help children memorize and remember information and sentences with clues they create themselves. (For example, acronyms: putting the first letters of words together to memorize a complete sentence, or rhyming related words to create a poem.)

Interactive Lessons: Incorporate interactive and hands-on activities, such as poetry and song memorization contests, to keep children engaged and help strengthen memory.

Regular Reviews: Have children remember material better by frequently reviewing what they have already learned.

Visual Support: Teach children how to use visual aids, such as posters and charts, to reinforce key concepts and information.

These strategies can help children with ADHD improve their working memory and support their overall cognitive development and learning.

What Are the Benefits and Effects of Strengthening Working Memory on Self-Regulation and Social-Emotional Learning in Children Aged 2 to 6 Years with ADHD and Normal Children?

Strengthening working memory in children aged 2 to 6, including those with ADHD, can have significant benefits in both self-regulation and social-emotional learning. For example:

Benefits of Strengthening Working Memory

Improved Self-Regulation: Working memory is critical for self-regulation, which involves managing thoughts, feelings, and behaviors. Strengthened working memory helps children follow instructions, stay focused, and complete tasks.

Better Academic Performance: Children with stronger working memory perform better in academic areas such as reading comprehension, math, and problem solving.

Advanced Social Skills: Improving working memory can help children remember social rules, understand other people's perspectives, and respond more appropriately in social situations.

Impacts on Self-Regulation

Increased Attention Control: Strengthening working memory helps children maintain attention and resist distractions, which is essential for self-regulation.

Better Emotion Control: Children with improved working memory are better able to manage their emotions and impulses, leading to more effective self-regulation.

Enhanced Problem-Solving Skills: Working memory is linked to better problem-solving abilities and allows children to think through challenges and find solutions through experience.

Impact on Social-Emotional Learning

Improved Social Interactions: Children with stronger working memory are better able to perceive and remember social cues, leading to more positive and appropriate social interactions.

Enhanced Empathy: Working memory helps children remember and process information about how others are feeling, enhancing empathy and understanding.

Better Conflict Resolution: Improved working memory allows children to think through conflicts better and find appropriate solutions, strengthening their social-emotional skills.

Tips for Children with ADHD: Children with ADHD often struggle with working memory, which can affect their self-regulation and social-emotional learning. Appropriate and targeted educational interventions and strategies can help these children improve working memory, overall learning, and thus their overall development in life.

CHAPTER 5: SOCIAL AWARENESS

1- EMOTIONAL UNDERSTANDING

2- SOCIAL CUE RECOGNITION

3- EMPATHY

4- UNDERSTANDING OTHERS' PERSPECTIVES, PERSPECTIVE-TAKING

5- RESPECT FOR OTHERS

6- COLLABORATION

7- COMMUNICATION

8- CULTURAL AWARENESS

Social Awareness

Definition

Social awareness in early childhood, children's social-emotional learning is the ability to understand and empathize with others, recognizing social cues and different cultural norms. For example, a child aged 2 to 6 years old, who demonstrates social awareness may notice that a friend is sad and offer to comfort them, which shows empathy and understanding of other people's feelings and perspectives. and offer comfort, demonstrating empathy and understanding of the feelings and perspectives of others. This basic skill helps children build positive relationships and navigate social interactions effectively.

In the context of early childhood, child aged 2 to 6 years old education, social awareness is a vital skill that helps young children recognize and understand the differences of others. Build positive relationships with peers and adults and prepare them for future social interactions. Here are the key components of social awareness:

1. Emotional Understanding: The ability to recognize, understand, and interpret the feelings and needs of others.

2. Social Cue Recognition: The ability to pay attention to and interpret verbal and nonverbal cues in social interactions, such as facial expressions and body language.

3. Empathy: The ability to share the feelings of others and imagine what they are feeling. For example, recognizing when a friend is upset and trying to comfort them.

4. Perspective-Taking: Understanding that others may have different thoughts and feelings. This recognition helps children understand different perspectives.

5. Respect for others: Showing consideration and respect for the feelings, rights, and belongings of others.

6. Collaboration: The ability to work with others to achieve a common goal or outcome.

7. Communication: The ability to effectively express one's thoughts, feelings, and needs through verbal and nonverbal communication. Active listening is body language and facial expressions.

8. Cultural Awareness: The ability to understand and respect different cultures, customs, and traditions.

What Are the Benefits of Teaching Social Awareness to Young Children?

Teaching social awareness to children aged 2 to 6 years has many benefits:

Improved Empathy: Helps children understand and share the feelings of others and fosters kindness and compassion.

Better Relationships: Equips children with the skills to create positive interactions and build friendships.

Advanced Communication: Promotes effective verbal and nonverbal communication and helps with clearer expression and understanding.

Conflict Resolution: Teaches children how to resolve disagreements and find peaceful solutions.

Cultural Respect: Encourages respect for cultural diversity and helps children value the differences of others.

Positive Behavior: Reduces bullying and promotes appropriate, pro-social behaviors, helping to create a calmer, more harmonious classroom environment.

Overall, social awareness equips young children with essential skills for their emotional and social development and provides a strong foundation for their future interpersonal success.

The Relationship between Social Awareness and Emotional Understanding in Children Aged 2 to 6 Years

Social Awareness
Social awareness is the ability to perceive and respond to social cues and dynamics around them.

Development: For young children, social awareness includes recognizing the emotions of others, understanding social norms, and interpreting the context of social interactions.

Emotional Understanding

Emotional understanding is the ability to recognize and understand one's own and others' emotions.

Development: Emotional understanding includes identifying different emotions, understanding the causes and consequences of emotions, and being able to talk about different emotions.

How They Communicate?

Emotion Recognition

Social Awareness: Children begin to understand facial expressions, tone of voice, and body language as cues of others' emotions.

Emotional Understanding: They begin to associate these cues with specific emotions, for example, realizing that a frown indicates sadness or a smile indicates happiness.

Developing Empathy

Social Awareness: Through observing others, children learn to understand and consider how others are feeling in different situations.

Emotional Understanding: When children understand that others have feelings and perspectives that are different from their own, empathy develops. This understanding encourages compassionate responses in them.

Social Interactions

Social Awareness: Children learn social norms such as taking turns, sharing, and cooperating by observing how others behave and interact.

Emotional Understanding: They begin to understand the emotional impact of these social behaviors and recognize that acts of kindness make others feel good, while hurtful actions can make others sad or angry.

Communication Skills

Social Awareness: Effective communication involves being aware of others' responses and adjusting one's behavior based on those responses.

Emotional Understanding: Children learn to express their feelings appropriately and understand the emotional content of others' messages, improving their ability to navigate social interactions.

Conflict Resolution

Social Awareness: Recognizing when conflict is occurring and understanding the social context.

Emotional Understanding: Understanding the emotional triggers and responses involved in conflicts, which helps to find empathetic and effective solutions.

Impact on Social-Emotional Learning

Developing social awareness and emotional understanding is crucial for children's overall social-emotional learning. These skills help children form positive relationships, navigate social complexities, and develop a strong sense of empathy and emotional intelligence.

By strengthening both aspects, social awareness and emotional understanding, parents, caregivers, and teachers can help children develop their social and emotional skills. They can interact more successfully with others and regulate and manage their emotions effectively.

1- Emotional Understanding

Definition

Emotional understanding in social-emotional learning for children aged 2 to 6 is the ability to recognize, label, and understand one's own and others' emotions. For example, a child can recognize that they feel sad when their toy is taken without permission and understand that their friend might feel the same way in a similar situation. This basic skill helps children develop empathy and greater social-emotional understanding in social interactions.

Emotional understanding is an important component of social-emotional learning because it helps children develop empathy and refers to the following abilities that are gradually learned throughout a child's development:

Recognizing and Identifying Emotions: Accurately identifying one's own and others' emotions.

Understanding Emotional Causes: Identifying the reasons behind one's emotions, including one's own and others' emotions.

Emotional Cues: Identifying and understanding nonverbal emotional cues such as facial expressions, body language, and tone of voice that convey different emotions.

Empathy: Understanding how others feel and why they feel those emotions.

Teaching Emotional Understanding Strategies in Social-Emotional Learning for Normal 2 to 6 Years Old Children

- Emotion Cards: Use cards with different facial expressions and have children match them to the corresponding emotions.

- Storytelling: Use different stories to help children identify and understand emotions. Talk about the characters' emotions and why they might be feeling the way they are.

- Role-Playing: Involve children in role-playing scenarios to practice recognizing and responding to emotions.

- Emotion Labeling: Teach children to label emotions using simple vocabulary.

- Emotion Recognition: Encourage children to recognize and identify their own and others' emotions.

-Building Empathy: Teach children to understand and respond to the emotions of others by using phrases such as "I see you're feeling sad" or "I'm here for you."

- Social Skills: Encourage children to communicate effectively with peers and adults by using phrases such as "I'm feeling happy" or "I need help."

- Self-Awareness: Encourage children to think about their feelings and experiences.

Teaching Emotional Understanding Strategies in Social-Emotional Learning Suitable for Children Aged 2 to 6 Years with ADHD

- One-on-One Support: Provide one-on-one support and guidance during emotional understanding activities.

- Movement-Based Activities: Incorporate short, simple movement-based activities that help release excess energy while promoting emotional understanding.

- Visual Aids: Use visual aids such as emotion charts or colored sensors to help children identify and label emotions.

- Simple Instructions: Provide short, clear, concise, and straightforward instructions so as not to overwhelm the child.

- Positive Reinforcement: Provide immediate praise or rewards, however small, verbal and nonverbal, for identifying and expressing emotions correctly.

- Emotion Cards: Use cards with pictures or drawings that represent different emotions. Ask children to identify the emotions and talk about times when they or others might have felt them.

- Emotion Sorting: Sort objects or pictures into categories based on emotions (for example, paper masks of happy, sad, angry faces).

- Role-Playing: Participate in short, simple role-playing activities that involve emotional scenarios, such as sharing, taking turns, or dealing with frustration.

- Expressing Emotions: Ask children to act out different emotions without speaking and encourage others to identify the emotions expressed (like pantomime).

-Talking: Use simple conversation starters and discussions. For example, "How do you think your friend is feeling right now?" or "Why do you think your friend is upset right now?" Even if the child says, "I don't know why!" This exercise often encourages children to think about the feelings of others.

These educational activities, which are the foundation for optimal interpersonal communication, help children aged 2 to 6 learn and develop emotional understanding strategies that are essential for their social-emotional development and overall well-being throughout their lives in many different situations.

2- Recognizing Social Cues

Definition
The definition of "Social Cue Recognition" in children aged 2 to 6 refers to the ability to understand and interpret social cues such as facial expressions, body language, and tone of voice. For example, a child who sees a peer frowning and realizes that the peer is sad is recognizing social cues. This skill helps children improve in social interactions and respond appropriately to the feelings and behaviors of others.

Strategies for Teaching Social Cue Recognition in Children Aged 2 to 6 Years
- Interactive Stories: Read books that focus on children's emotions and social

interactions, then discuss the verbal and nonverbal signs of emotions and the characters' behavior with the children.

- Emotional Games: Play games such as "Riddles, Pantomimes" in which children display signs of different emotions in the form of nonverbal movements and others guess them.

- Facial Expression Matching: Use cards and masks with different facial expressions and ask children to match them with the corresponding emotions. Example: Choose and match the card that says "Happy feeling" with the "Smiling mask".

Appropriate Teaching Strategies for Recognizing Social Cues in Children Aged 2 to 6 Years with ADHD

- Visual Support: Use visual aids such as color charts with pictures of facial and body expressions to help children identify and interpret social cues.

- Role-Playing: Have children participate in simple role-playing games and activities that involve practicing social scenarios and recognizing social cues.

- Step-by-Step Guidance: Provide clear, simple steps to help children understand and respond to social cues (such as "looking at people's faces to see if they are happy or sad," for example, if someone is "frowning," they do not look "happy").

- These strategies can help all children aged 2 to 6, including those with ADHD, develop the ability to recognize and respond appropriately to social cues, and strengthen their social interactions and relationships.

3- Empathy

Definition

The definition of empathy in the context of social-emotional learning for children aged 2 to 6 is the ability to understand and share the feelings, needs, and perspectives of others and to relate to them. This skill involves recognizing a situation where another person is happy, sad, angry, or scared and being able to respond to those feelings in an appropriate, caring, and supportive way. For example, a child who shows empathy will try to calm and cheer up a classmate when he notices them crying. This skill helps build strong, positive relationships and fosters a supportive and inclusive environment.

Teaching empathy to children aged 2 to 6 is essential for several reasons:
- Socio-Emotional Development: Empathy helps children develop emotional intelligence, understanding, and compassion for others.

- Conflict Resolution: Empathy can help resolve conflicts and allow children to understand each other's perspectives and feelings.

- Emotion Regulation: Empathy can help children regulate and moderate their own emotions by recognizing and validating the feelings of others.

- Building Relationships: Empathy fosters strong relationships by creating a sense of connection and understanding between people.

Strategies for Teaching Empathy to Children Aged 2 to 6 Years
- Model Empathy: Demonstrate empathetic behavior yourself, such as comforting a friend who is upset. Children learn by observing adults.

- Storytelling: Use books and stories that feature empathetic characters. Discuss the characters' feelings and actions. Read stories that depict characters experiencing different emotions (e.g., feeling left out, afraid). Ask children to imagine how they would feel in that situation and what they would say to make the character feel better.

- Role-Playing: Encourage children to role-play different scenarios so they can practice empathy (such as playing the role of a hiker helping a friend who has fallen or jokingly calming a friend who is crying).

-Role Reversal: Act out scenarios in which children take turns being the "actor" and the "observer." This helps them develop perspective-taking skills and understand how others are feeling.

- Perception Games: Play games like "What would you do if you were him?" or "How would you feel if you were him?" in which children imagine themselves in different situations and respond accordingly.

- Active Listening: Encourage children to listen carefully to others as they share their feelings. Ask open-ended questions like, "How did that make you feel?" or "What was going through your mind?"

- Reflective Listening: Reflective listening involves repeating what you have heard from the other person while also validating their feelings. This helps children develop empathy by understanding the feelings of others.

- Compassion Cards: Make cards with different scenarios (e.g., a friend is feeling sad) and have children write or draw a supportive message (e.g., "I'm sorry you're feeling sad").

Appropriate Teaching Strategies for Teaching Empathy to Children Aged 2 to 6 Years with ADHD

Keep Empathy Training Short and Simple: Use shorter scenarios and stories, as children with ADHD may have shorter attention spans.

- Visual Supports: Use animated images and videos to show different emotions and empathetic behaviors, and help them understand empathy through visual cues.

- Consistent Routines: Create routines that include appropriate opportunities to discuss and practice empathy.

- Positive Reinforcement: Offer praise and rewards when hyperactive children demonstrate empathetic behavior, and reinforce appropriate actions and empathy, no matter how small.

- Simplified Role-Play: Keep role-play activities short and focused, so hyperactive children can more easily engage in the activity without getting bored.

- Interactive Games: Use games that foster empathy and social skills, such as activities where children must help each other achieve a common goal.

These strategies help all children, including those with ADHD, develop empathy and stronger, more supportive relationships with their peers.

- Incorporate Movement into Your Education: Children diagnosed with ADHD often benefit from physical activity. Incorporate movement-based activities into your teaching that promote empathy (such as acting out scenarios or role-playing).

- Use Regular Repetition: To reinforce empathy skills and encourage practice, repeat lessons regularly without long breaks.

- Be Flexible: Be prepared to adjust strategies based on the individual needs of each child.

By implementing these strategies, you can help preschoolers develop empathy, understanding, and compassion for others, setting them up for success in social-emotional development and relationships throughout their lives.

4- Understanding others' Perspectives, Perspective-Taking

Definition

The definition of understanding others' perspectives, perspective-taking in the context of social-emotional learning for children aged 2 to 6 years is the ability to understand and consider the perspectives, thoughts, and feelings of others. This skill involves recognizing that others may have different experiences and reactions to the same situation than we do, and in fact, trying to see things from their perspective. For example, a young child who practices perspective-taking is somewhat able to understand why his friend doesn't want to share his toy with him. For example, he may guess that his friend doesn't give him his toy because he feels possessive or is afraid of breaking or losing it. Perspective-taking is a key component of empathy and helps children have a deeper understanding of others. This skill helps children improve their own communication by feeling empathy, understanding and considering the perspectives, thoughts and feelings of others, and navigate social relationships more effectively throughout life.

Teaching children aged 2 to 6 to understand the perspectives of others is essential for several reasons:

- Socio-Emotional Development: Perspective-taking helps children develop emotional intelligence, understanding and compassion for others.

- Conflict Resolution: Perspective-taking can help resolve conflicts and allows children to understand each other's perspectives and find common ground.

- Communication: Perspective-taking fosters and improves strong relationships by encouraging children to actively listen and respond thoughtfully, creating a sense of connection and understanding between people.

Perspective-Taking and Understanding other People's Perspectives for Children Aged 2 to 6 Years

- Role-Playing: Use role-playing to act out scenarios in which children take on different roles (e.g., friend, teacher, parent). This helps them develop perspective-taking skills and understand different perspectives.

-Role-Reversing: Act out scenarios in which children take turns being the "actor" and the "spectator." This helps them develop perspective-taking skills and understand how others are feeling.

- Think Aloud: Encourage children to think aloud about a situation from different perspectives (e.g., "What do you think would happen if...?"). For example, the child might ask themselves out loud: What if I make fun of my friend's drawing? So what if my friend makes fun of my drawing?

- Perspective Games: Play games like "How would I feel if I were you?" in which children imagine themselves in different situations and respond accordingly.

- Storytelling: Read stories that depict characters experiencing different perspectives (e.g., a friend who feels left out). Ask children to imagine how they would feel in that situation.

- Hot Seat: Have children sit in a "hot seat" game, for example, where they are the center of attention and their peers ask them questions from different perspectives (e.g., "How would you feel if your friends made fun of you?"). Regularly ask children how they would feel in different situations to encourage them to think about other people's perspectives.

- Perspective Pantomimes: Ask children to act out scenarios from different perspectives without talking (e.g., happy, sad, angry). Ask your peers to guess their perspective.

- Reflective Listening: Reflective listening involves repeating what you have heard from the other person while also validating their perspective. This practice helps children develop empathy and understanding.

Appropriate Strategies for Teaching Understanding others' Perspectives, Perspective-Taking to Children Aged 2 to 6 Years with ADHD

- Keep Perspective-Taking Training Short and Simple: Use shorter scenarios and stories, as children with ADHD may have shorter attention spans.

- Structured Role-Play: Use short, structured role-play activities that are simple and engaging and help hyperactive children focus while practicing perspective-taking.

- Use Visual Aids: Visual aids such as pictures or videos can help illustrate emotional expressions and scenarios.

- Visual Stories: Use visual stories with pictures to illustrate different perspectives and make it easier for hyperactive children to understand.

- Immediate Feedback: When children successfully understand the perspective and attitude of others in a situation with appropriate and positive behavior, provide immediate feedback and praise.

- Interactive Games: Play interactive games with children that involve taking turns and considering the opinions of others. Keeping the activities dynamic and engaging is important and essential to help maintain the focus and attention of hyperactive children.

- Incorporate Movement into Your Teaching: ADHD children often benefit from physical activity. Include movement-based activities that promote perspective-taking. Such as:

- Use Repetition: To reinforce perspective-taking skills and encourage practice, repeat lessons regularly without long breaks.

- Be Flexible: Be consistent and flexible, and be prepared to adjust instructional strategies based on each child's individual needs.

These strategies can help all children aged 2 to 6, including those with ADHD, strengthen their ability to see things from other people's perspectives and increase their empathy and social skills, leading to improved social-emotional development, stronger relationships, and better conflict resolution skills throughout their lives.

5- Respect for others

Definition

The definition of respect for others in social-emotional learning for children aged 2 to 6 years includes recognizing and valuing the feelings, rights, and needs of others. This skill includes showing kindness, listening, sharing, and understanding that everyone deserves to be treated with dignity and consideration. For example, a child who knows this skill may wait their turn to speak or share toys willingly and understand the importance of fairness and empathy in interactions. This essential life skill helps children build positive relationships and a supportive community.

Strategies for teaching respect for others to children aged 2 to 6 years include:

- Modeling: Model respectful behaviors, such as "listening carefully" and using "polite language," so that children can learn this skill better by example and observation.

- Storytelling: Read books that emphasize the importance of respect and discuss with them the respectful or disrespectful behaviors of the characters in the story.

-Role-Playing: Engage children in role-playing scenarios in which they practice respectful behaviors such as "listening attentively" and using "polite language."

- Positive Reinforcement: Praise and encourage children when they show respect for others with positive behavior, and reinforce their positive behavior with verbal and nonverbal rewards and rewards.

-Teach Etiquette: Introduce basic family and social etiquette such as saying "please" and "thank you," and explain why these phrases are important.

Appropriate Strategies for Teaching Respect for others to Children 2 to 6 Years Old with ADHD

- Structured Role-Play: Use short, focused role-play activities to practice respectful behaviors to ensure that the child remains engaged in the activity.

- Clear Expectations: Set clear, consistent rules for children's respectful behavior and remind them of these rules frequently.

- Visual Reminders: Use visual aids, such as posters and charts, to demonstrate respectful behaviors and reinforce learning.

- Immediate Feedback: When hyperactive children demonstrate respectful behaviors, provide them with immediate, specific feedback and help them better understand the impact of their actions.

- Calming Strategies: Help children learn how to remain calm and respectful while maintaining respectful behaviors. Teach and encourage techniques for managing energy and impulsive emotions, such as counting numbers or deep breathing.

6- Collaboration

Definition
The definition of collaboration in the context of social-emotional learning for children aged 2 to 6 years is the understanding and ability to work with others toward a common goal or purpose. This skill includes sharing resources, taking turns, listening to others, and participating appropriately and cooperatively in group activities. For example, a 2- to 6-year-old child with cooperation skills helps a classmate build a block tower together, taking turns adding pieces, and working together in a coordinated manner.

This skill is a critical social-emotional skill for growing and developing strong relationships, promoting teamwork, and creating a supportive environment essential to fostering positive social interactions in 2- to 6-year-olds.

Teaching cooperation to 2- to 6-year-olds is essential for several reasons:

- Developing Social-Emotional Skills: Cooperation helps children develop social-emotional skills such as empathy, communication, and problem-solving.

- Teamwork: Cooperation promotes teamwork and collaboration, which are essential for solving problems and achieving shared goals.

- Conflict Resolution: Collaboration helps resolve conflicts by encouraging children to find mutually beneficial solutions.

- Relationship Building: Collaboration fosters the creation and maintenance of strong relationships by building a sense of mutual trust and respect.

Strategies for Teaching Cooperation to Normal 2 to 6 Years Old Children
- Group Projects: Engage children in group activities (such as building a puzzle together) that require sharing ideas and working towards a common goal.

- Sharing Activities: Engage children in activities that involve sharing resources, such as art projects or building blocks.

- Role-Playing: Use role-playing to act out scenarios in which children take on different roles (e.g., teacher-student, friend-friend). This helps them develop cooperation skills and understand different perspectives.

- Problem-Solving: Give children problems that require them to work together to solve, such as cleaning up toys or planning a pretend play scenario.

- Stories: Read stories that depict characters working together to achieve a common goal (e.g., a team of animals working together to build a shelter).

- Pantomime Shows: Ask children to act out cooperative activity scenarios that require cooperation (e.g., lifting a heavy object together) in the form of nonverbal pantomimes.

- Coaching: Pair older or more experienced children with younger or less experienced children to encourage coaching and cooperation.

- Choice-Based Activities: Offer choices that require cooperation, such as "Do you want to build a bridge or a castle?" This encourages children to work together toward a common goal.

- Turn-Taking Games: To teach cooperation, play games that require patience and participation (such as board games or simple ball games).

- Modeling Cooperative Behavior: By modeling cooperative behavior yourself, children can learn better by example and observation.

- Praise and Rewards: When children demonstrate cooperative behavior, reinforce the value of their work with small rewards and small rewards.

Teaching Strategies for Teaching Cooperation to Children Aged 2 to 6 Years with ADHD
- Short, Structured Activities: Use short, structured group activities to keep hyperactive children engaged in the activity without getting bored or confused (such as building a tower with blocks in a small group).

- Clear Instructions: Provide clear, simple instructions for cooperative tasks to ensure that children clearly understand what is expected of them.

- Positive Reinforcement: Give immediate praise and rewards for each cooperative behavior, helping children with ADHD understand the benefits of working together and see the consequences.

- Visual Aids: Use visual aids such as charts or pictures to explain cooperation in collaborative activities and show the steps for completing group tasks.

- Incorporate Movement into Activities: Incorporate movement-based activities into activities that promote cooperation.

- Use Regular Repetition: Repeat lessons regularly to reinforce cooperation skills and encourage practice.

- Be Flexible: Be prepared to adjust strategies based on each child's individual needs.

These strategies can help all children aged 2 to 6, including those with ADHD, learn the importance of and practice cooperation, build strong social skills, and have positive interactions in life.

7- Communication

Definition
The definition of communication in social-emotional learning for children aged 2 to 6 is the ability to express thoughts, feelings, and needs clearly and effectively while listening to and understanding others. This skill involves using verbal and nonverbal methods such as speaking, gestures, facial expressions, and body language to interact with peers and adults. For example, a 2- to 6-year-old who demonstrates good communication skills may use words for things like asking for help, sharing ideas in group activities, and asking for help. This essential and fundamental life skill helps 2- to 6-year-olds build better relationships, resolve conflicts, and participate meaningfully in social interactions.

Teaching relationship building skills to 2- to 6-year-olds is essential for several reasons:
- Socio-Emotional Development: Relationship building helps children learn and develop social-emotional skills such as empathy, communication, and conflict resolution.

- Trust and Respect: Strong relationships foster trust and respect between people and create a positive and supportive environment.

- Emotional Intelligence: Building appropriate and positive relationships helps children develop emotional intelligence by understanding the feelings and needs of others.

- Academic Success: Strong relationships can positively impact children's academic performance by providing support and motivation.

Strategies for Teaching Communication to Children Aged 2 to 6 Years
- Interactive Storytelling: Encourage children to tell stories or read aloud and strengthen their ability to express themselves and listen to others.

- Group Discussions: Set up "friendship circle" times where children can sit in a circle and take turns sharing their thoughts, listening to their peers, and having an active group.

- Visual Aids: Use pictures and symbols to support verbal instructions and strengthen children's understanding and communication.

- Encouraging Questions: Create an environment where children feel comfortable asking questions and expressing their curiosity.

- Positive Interactions: Engage in positive interactions with children, such as playing or talking.

- Active Listening: Practice active listening by focusing on the speaker and responding thoughtfully.

- Emotional Validation: Validate children's feelings by acknowledging them and offering support.

- Role-playing: Use role-playing to act out scenarios that require relationship building (e.g., sharing toys or helping others).

- Pairing: Pair children with peers for activities that foster bonding and cooperation.

- Individual Instruction Time: Spend one-on-one time with each child to build personal relationships and strengthen bonds and relationships.

- Sensory Play: Engage in sensory play activities, such as art projects, with children that strengthen bonds and relationships.

- Family Involvement: Encourage family involvement by inviting parents to participate in relationship-building and bonding activities or school events.

Appropriate Communication Teaching Strategies for Children 2 to 6 Years Old with ADHD
- Short, Focused Activities: Use short, simple, and engaging communication activities to capture the attention of hyperactive children.

- Visual Supports: Use visual aids such as flashcards or picture programs to help children understand and stick to verbal instructions.

- Positive Reinforcement: Provide immediate praise and rewards for effective communication and consistently reinforce their efforts.

- Structured Routines: Create clear, predictable routines that provide specific opportunities for communication and help hyperactive children feel secure and focused.

- Interactive Play: Include games that reinforce turn-taking and verbal interactions, making communication fun and engaging for hyperactive children.

- Incorporate Movement into Your Teaching: Hyperactive children often benefit from physical activity. Incorporate movement-based activities into your teaching that strengthen bonding.

- Be Flexible: Be prepared to adjust strategies based on each child's individual needs.

- Positive Reinforcement: Offer rewards and immediate positive reinforcement to show appreciation and praise for the efforts of hyperactive children to build relationships.

These strategies help all children aged 2 to 6, including those who are hyperactive, learn and develop strong communication skills that lead to improved social-emotional development, trust, respect, and academic success throughout their lives.

8- Cultural Awareness

Definition
The definition of cultural awareness in the context of social-emotional learning for children aged 2 to 6 includes being open-minded, curious, and understanding, valuing, and respecting diverse cultural backgrounds, practices, and perspectives. This skill includes recognizing and respecting differences in the languages, values, and traditions and backgrounds of different peers and others. For example, a child who is culturally aware may celebrate holidays that are culturally appropriate with their classmates or show curiosity and respect for different customs and traditions.

This essential and important skill helps children develop a broader understanding of the world around them throughout their lives in different situations and places with empathy and respect. Cultural awareness helps individuals develop empathy, tolerance, and understanding toward people from different backgrounds.

Teaching cultural awareness to children aged 2 to 6 years is essential for several reasons:
- Creating an Inclusive Environment: Cultural awareness helps create an inclusive environment with a broader range of social acceptance where all children feel valued and respected.

- Enhances Empathy: Understanding different cultures encourages empathy and compassion for others.

- Builds Understanding: Cultural awareness helps children to understand and appreciate the diversity of cultures, traditions, and backgrounds.

--Prepares for Global Citizenship: Cultural awareness prepares children for the increasing globalization in which children will interact more widely with people from different backgrounds on a global scale.

Strategies for Teaching Cultural Awareness to Children Aged 2 to 6 Years
- Cultural Exchange: Includes activities that introduce and respectfully celebrate different cultures (such as cooking international foods or creating crafts from around the world).

- Sensory Exploration: To better understand cultural differences, provide children with different textures, smells, tastes, and sounds from different cultures (such as Japanese sticky rice or Indian spices) to foster a sense of cultural exploration.

- Art Projects: Encourage children to participate in art projects that reflect different cultures (for example, painting a mandala from India or creating African-inspired masks).

- Storybooks: Read books that introduce diverse characters and cultures. Then talk and discuss the stories and what they learned with children.

- Role-Play: Use role-play to act out scenarios that demonstrate cultural differences (for example, wearing traditional clothing or attending a celebration).

- Cultural Display: Encourage children to share and display aspects of their cultural background (such as traditional clothing, music, or holidays).

- Classroom Decorations: Decorate the classroom with colorful posters, multicultural flags, to create an inclusive multicultural environment.

- Speech: Invite parents or community members from different cultural backgrounds to talk about their traditions and customs in simple language for children.

- Family Involvement: Encourage family involvement by inviting parents to share their cultural heritage with the class.

Suitable Strategies for Teaching Cultural Awareness to Children Aged 2 to 6 Years with ADHD

- Interactive Learning: Use hands-on activities and movement-based or sensory exploration games, such as making traditional crafts or playing cultural games, to keep ADHD children engaged in the activity.

- Break Down Complex Concepts: Break complex concepts into smaller, more manageable chunks to help ADHD children understand and process cultural information.

- Offer Choices: Offer ADHD children choices that promote cultural exploration (for example, choosing a traditional food to try or a cultural art craft to make).

- Short, Engaging Stories: Read short, simple stories to ADHD children that clearly illustrate cultural diversity, and make sure they are interesting and easy for them to follow.

- Visual Aids: Use pictures, videos, and interactive displays to teach about different cultures to make learning more dynamic and engaging for ADHD children.

- Daily Routines: Integrate cultural awareness activities into ADHD children's daily routines to provide a predictable structure for their understanding.

- Role-Playing: Engage hyperactive children in simple role-playing activities to act out different cultural scenarios and help them learn through active participation in the group.

General Strategies for Teaching Cultural Awareness to Children Aged 2 to 6 Years

- Modeling: Demonstrate empathy, respectful communication, and cooperation in your interactions with children and others.

- Prompt Questions: Foster cultural curiosity by encouraging children to ask questions about different cultures, feelings, and perspectives.

- Positive Reinforcement: Praise and appreciate children's efforts to understand feelings, express empathy, and cooperate with others.

Consistency and Repetition: Repeat and reinforce social awareness concepts through daily routines, activities, and discussions to help children gradually internalize these skills.

By incorporating these strategies, games, and educational exercises into the activities of children aged 2 to 6, parents and educators can help children learn and gradually develop cultural awareness skills. Practicing this ability fosters empathy, understanding others' perspectives, cooperation, effective communication, and an appreciation for cultural diversity from an early age, which will be useful in building strong relationships and navigating social situations throughout children's lives.

CHAPTER 6: COMMUNICATION SKILLS

1- DEVELOPMENTAL LEVELS OF COMMUNICATION SKILLS FOR CHILDREN 2 TO 6 YEARS OLD

2- ENCOURAGING OPEN-ENDED QUESTIONS AND ACTIVE LISTENING

3- PRACTICING "I" STATEMENTS AND POLITE CONVERSATION

4- TEACHING "NO"

5- APPROPRIATE INTERACTIONS BETWEEN GIRLS AND BOYS

6- TEACHING SHARING AND TURN-TAKING

7- CONFLICT RESOLUTION

8- BULLYING

9- LYING

Communication Skills

Definition

The definition of communication skills in social-emotional learning for children aged 2 to 6 includes the ability to effectively express thoughts, feelings, and needs, as well as to listen and understand others. This skill involves using words, gestures, facial expressions, and body language to interact with peers and adults. For example, a 2- to 6-year-old child with appropriate communication skills may use words to ask for help, share a story, or recognize and express the feelings of friends through words. Developing these skills is essential for building relationships, resolving conflicts, and participating meaningfully in social interactions.

In other words, communication skills are the ability to convey and understand messages, ideas, and feelings through verbal and nonverbal means. Effective communication includes:

- Verbal Communication: The use of words, phrases, and sentences to convey meaning and intent.

- Nonverbal Communication: The use of facial expressions, gestures, and body language, tone of voice, to convey meaning and intent.

- Active Listening: Paying attention to others, understanding their perspectives, and responding thoughtfully and appropriately to them.

Teaching communication skills to children aged 2 to 6 is vital for several reasons:

- Building Relationships: Effective communication helps children build strong relationships with peers and adults.

- Boosting Self-Confidence: Good communication skills increase self-confidence and help children feel more secure.

- Improving Problem-Solving: Communication skills help resolve conflicts and find solutions to problems.

- Boosting Learning: Clear communication helps children better understand and retain information.

1- Developmental Level of Communication Skills for Children Aged 2 to 6 Years

What is the normal developmental level of communication skills for children aged 2 to 6 Years?

For 2-Year-Olds
Vocabulary Growth: Children usually have a vocabulary of about 50 to 100 words and begin to combine two words to form simple sentences, such as "I want water" or "Mommy, come."

Understanding Directions: They can follow simple directions and understand basic concepts such as "big" and "small."

Expressing Needs and Feelings: Begin to express their needs and feelings through words, gestures, and facial expressions.

For 3-Year-Olds
Sentence Formation: Able to form three- to four-word sentences, such as "I want water" or "Mommy is home."

Asking Questions: Begin to ask questions, often beginning with "what," "where," and "why."

Storytelling: Can tell simple stories or describe past events in limited detail.

For 4-Year-Olds
Complex Sentences: Use more complex sentences with correct grammar, such as "I played in the park with my friend."

Conversation Skills: Participate in two-person or group conversations and understand the concept of turn-taking.

Understanding and Using Concepts: Begin to understand and use time-related concepts such as "yesterday," "today," and "tomorrow."

For 5-Year-Olds
Detailed Explanations: Can give detailed explanations and tell stories with more coherence and detail.

Understanding Abstract Ideas: Begin to understand more abstract concepts and use language to express thoughts and ideas.

Social Communication: Know the rules of polite conversation, such as saying "please" and "thank you," and can negotiate and compromise in social situations.

For 6-Year-Olds

Narrative Skills: Can tell more complex stories with a clear beginning, middle, and end that the audience can understand, including more complex details.

Understanding and Expressing Emotions: Use language to describe feelings and better understand the feelings of others.

Advanced Vocabulary: There is a significant growth in vocabulary and vocabulary. They begin to understand and use more complex words and appropriate grammatical structures in communication.

Timely and appropriate reinforcement of these natural stages of communication development for children 2 to 6 years old, leads to significant growth in children's communication skills from ages 2 to 6 and creates a strong foundation for their future academic and social success.

Strategies for Teaching Communication Skills for Normal Children Aged 2 to 6 Years

- Mirror Reflection: Repeat and imitate children's facial expressions and body language to encourage nonverbal communication, such as reflecting an image in a "mirror".

- In this game, two people stand facing each other, one is the leader, the other is the "mirror". The leader begins to make simple movements by moving only from the waist up. The "mirror" exactly repeats the leader's movements, just like a mirror.

- Ask Open-Ended Questions: Encourage critical thinking by asking open-ended questions (e.g., "What do you think would happen if...").

- Practice Active Listening: Model active listening by listening to children's responses and thoughtful responses.

- Free-Form Pretend Play: Encourage children to bring materials from home and play pretend freely and creatively. This practice reduces the pressure of formal learning for children 2 to 6 years old and, with greater ease, strengthens creativity and the verbal expression and active listening skills necessary for effective communication.

- Interactive Storytelling: Engage children in storytelling activities so they can create and tell stories to promote their creativity and use of language and rhetoric.

- Peer Conversations: Provide opportunities for children to have structured conversations with peers and help them take turns and practice active listening.

- Music and Songs: Use fun songs and rhymes, poems and children's songs to reinforce language skills while encouraging participation and repetition to help them learn better.

- Visual Support: Use pictures, diagrams and visual aids to support verbal instructions, helping them understand communication and learn better.

Communication Skills Teaching Strategies for Children Aged 2 to 6 Years with ADHD

- Short, Focused Activities: Keep communication skills training short and simple. Implement short, engaging communication exercises, such as quick games or short storytelling sessions, to keep your child's attention and interest.

- Visual Aids: Use visual aids, such as flashcards, digital boards, and other visual aids to support memory and organization.

- Offer Choices: Offer choices (e.g., "Do you want to talk about this or that?") to help children feel in control and comfortable communicating.

- Use Nonverbal Cues: Use nonverbal cues, such as gestures or facial expressions, to reinforce verbal communication.

- Encourage Independence: Encourage your child to express themselves appropriately and independently without interruption.

- By implementing these strategies, you can help preschoolers develop effective communication skills, enabling them to confidently express themselves and build strong relationships with others.

- Structured Routines: Create predictable routines that include opportunities for communication, providing a stable and consistent environment with minimal distractions for children with ADHD to practice skills.

- Immediate Feedback: Provide consistent and immediate positive reinforcement for effective communication, helping children with ADHD understand and repeat the appropriate communication behaviors they are looking for.

These strategies can help all children aged 2 to 6 years, including those with ADHD, develop strong communication skills that are essential for building relationships and participating effectively in social interactions.

2- Encourage Open-Ended Questions and Active Listening

Open-Ended Questions

Open-ended questions and active listening are vital communication skills for children aged 2 to 6. By teaching these skills, you can foster a culture of respectful communication, promote problem solving, and help children build strong relationships.

Open-ended questions are questions that encourage children to think critically, share their thoughts, and explore their ideas. They begin with what is called an "open" word, such as: What?, How?, Why?, When?, Where?, Who?

The Importance of Teaching Open-Ended Questions

Encourages Critical Thinking: Open-ended questions encourage critical thinking and problem solving by encouraging children aged 2 to 6 to consider multiple perspectives.

Critical thinking is the ability to analyze and evaluate available information or different situations to solve a problem or make reasoned judgments. Children typically begin to develop critical thinking skills around the ages of 3 to 4. At this stage, they begin to ask more questions, explore cause and effect, and engage in problem-solving activities. As they grow, these skills become more advanced and complex.

Example of Critical Thinking for 2- to 6-Year-Olds: Imagine a 4-year-old has a puzzle to solve. He looks at all the pieces and thinks about how they fit together to form and complete the picture, then tries different combinations to see which one pair together and match the picture. In essence, he is using critical thinking to figure out the best way to complete his puzzle.

An example of an open-ended question for 2- to 6-year-olds that fosters critical thinking and problem-solving might be:

"What do you think will happen if we plant a seed in the ground and take care of it?"

This question encourages children to think about the process of planting, growing, and caring for it, and encourages them to explore different possibilities and explore the natural world. This exercise allows them to express their thoughts, anticipate appropriate solutions to problems, and consider multiple perspectives.

- Develops Creativity: Open-ended questions allow children to express their creativity and imagination.

- Develops Vocabulary: Open-ended questions help children develop their vocabulary and language skills.

- Builds Confidence: Open-ended questions help children become more confident in their abilities and opinions.

Active Listening

Active listening is the process of fully focusing on and understanding the message being conveyed by another person. Signs of active listening in children include:

Unrelenting Attention: Focuses on the speaker and avoids distractions.

Maintains Eye Contact: Makes eye contact with the speaker to show that they are engaged with the speaker's message.

Nods and Gestures: Uses nonverbal cues such as nods and gestures to show interest.

Asking Clarifying Questions: Asks open-ended questions to ensure understanding and to clarify any doubts.

Why teach open-ended questions and active listening to preschoolers?

Teaching open-ended questions and active listening to preschoolers is essential because it helps children:

- Develop Social Skills: Learn and develop social skills such as cooperation, empathy, and conflict resolution.

- Enhance Emotional Intelligence: Develop emotional intelligence by encouraging them to understand and manage their emotions.

- Promote Problem-Solving: Develop problem-solving skills by encouraging them to think critically and explore different solutions.

Strategies for Teaching Open-Ended Questions and Active Listening to Normal Children Aged 2 to 6 Years

- Model: Model open-ended questions and active listening yourself to show children what it looks like.

- Role-Play: Participate in role-play activities with children that involve open-ended questions and active listening.

- Encourage Turn-Taking: Encourage children to take turns talking and listening to each other.

- Use Visual Aids: Use visual aids such as pictures or puppets through play to help children understand the concept of open-ended questions and active listening.

- Practice with Everyday Situations: Practice open-ended questions and active listening in everyday situations, such as sharing toys or resolving conflicts with others.

Open-Ended Questions and Active Listening Training for Children Aged 2 to 6 Years with ADHD

- Keep Open-Ended Questions and Active Listening Training Short: Keep open-ended questions short and concise for hyperactive children who may have shorter attention spans.

- Use Visual Reminders: Use visual reminders or pictures to help hyperactive children remember the concept of open-ended questions and active listening.

- Enhance Independence: Encourage independence by giving hyperactive children opportunities to practice open-ended questions and active listening with peers or adults.

- Use Educational Technology: Use appropriate educational technology and media, such as videos or interactive games, to teach open-ended questions and active listening in a fun and engaging way.

- By teaching open-ended questions and active listening strategies, you can help children aged 2 to 6 develop essential communication skills that will serve them well throughout their lives.

3- Practice "I" Statements and Polite Conversation

Practicing "I" statements and polite conversation are vital communication skills for children aged 2 to 6 years. By teaching these skills, you can help children express their feelings, needs, and wants in a respectful and effective way.

What Are "I" Statements?
"I" statements are statements that begin with the word "I" and express the speaker's thoughts, feelings, or needs. For example:

I am happy. I am sad. I want to play. I need help.

Why Are "I" Statements Important?
Expressing Feelings: "I" statements help children express their feelings and emotions in a healthy way.

- Develop Empathy: By using "I" statements, children learn to consider the feelings of others and develop empathy.

- Build Self-Confidence: Practicing "I" statements helps children feel more confident in expressing themselves.

What Is Polite Conversation?
Polite conversation involves using respectful language and tone to communicate with others. It includes:

- Saying Please and Thank You: Using polite phrases like "please" and "thank you" to show appreciation and respect.

- Asking Permission: Asking permission before doing something, such as "May I…" and "Or would you allow me to…"

- Showing Interest: Showing genuine interest in others by asking questions and actively listening.

- Apologizing: Expressing apology and regret when something goes wrong or when someone is hurt, using phrases like "excuse me" or "I'm sorry."

Why Is Polite Conversation Important?

- Develops Social Skills: Polite conversation helps children develop social skills such as cooperation, empathy, and conflict resolution.

- Promotes Respect: Polite conversation encourages respect for the feelings, opinions, and personal space of others.

-Strengthens Relationships: Practicing polite conversation helps children build strong, positive relationships with others.

Strategies for Teaching "I" Statements and Polite Conversation to Children Aged 2 to 6 Years

- Model Yourself: Model "I" statements and polite conversation yourself to show children what it looks like.

- Role-Play: Participate in role-play activities that involve practicing "I" statements and polite conversation.

- Use Visual Aids: Use visual aids, such as pictures or dolls, to help children understand the concept of practicing "I" statements and polite conversation.

- Encourage Turn-Taking: Encourage children to take turns speaking and listening to each other during conversations.

- Practice with Everyday Situations: Practice practicing "I" statements and polite conversation with everyday situations, such as sharing toys or asking for help.

Additional Tips for Teaching "I" Statements and Polite Conversation to Children 2 to 6 Years Old with ADHD

- Keep "I" Statements and Polite Conversation Practice Simple: Keep the language simple and concise for hyperactive children who may have shorter attention spans.

- Use Visual Reminders: Use visual reminders or pictures to help children remember the concept of practicing "I" statements and polite conversation.

- Encourage Independence: Encourage independence by giving hyperactive children opportunities to practice "I" statements and polite conversation with peers or adults.

- Use Technology: Use technology, such as videos or interactive games, to teach "I" statements and polite conversation in a fun and engaging way for hyperactive children.

- By teaching "I" statements and polite conversation strategies, you can help children 2 to 6 years old develop essential communication skills that will serve them throughout their lives.

4- Teaching Children to Say "No"

Teaching children to say "no" is an essential life skill that helps them set and maintain healthy boundaries and assertiveness. By effectively teaching children to say "no," you can help them build self-confidence and independence.

Why Is Saying "No" Important?
Teaching preschoolers to say "no" is vital for several reasons:

Personal Boundaries: It helps children understand and establish their own boundaries and ensures that they feel safe and respected in different situations.

Promotes Assertiveness: Saying "no" allows children to practice assertiveness, which helps them express their needs and wants.

Self-Advocacy: It enables children to express their preferences and needs, which is essential for their self-esteem and confidence.

- Safety: Enables children to avoid unsafe or uncomfortable situations and contributes to their overall well-being.

- Respect for others: Learning to say "no" appropriately helps children respect their opinions when others do the same, and fosters mutual respect and understanding in social interactions.

- Builds Self-Confidence: Saying "no" can help children feel more confident in their abilities and decisions because it helps children value themselves more.

- Enhances Independence: Saying "no" encourages children to make their own choices and take responsibility for their actions when making decisions.

Strategies for Teaching to Say "No" to Normal Children Aged 2 to 6 Years

- Model: Model your own saying "no" so that children see what it looks like and feels like.

- Use Simple Language: Use simple language to explain the concept of saying "no," such as "When we don't want something, we say "no.""

- Role-Play: Participate in role-playing activities that involve saying "no," such as refusing a toy or turning down an invitation.

- Practice with Everyday Situations: Practice saying "no" with children in everyday situations, such as turning down a snack or a friend's request.

- Encourage Empathy: Encourage children to consider the feelings of others when saying "no," such as "I know you want to play with you, but I'm tired right now."

Additional Tips for Teaching "No" Appropriately for Children Aged 2 to 6 Years with ADHD

- Keep "No" Short and Simple: Keep the language short and simple for hyperactive children who may have shorter attention spans.

- Use Visual Reminders: Use visual reminders or images to help hyperactive children remember the concept of saying "no."

- Encourage Independence: Encourage independence by giving your child with ADHD opportunities to practice saying "no" with peers or adults.

- Use Technology: Use technology, such as videos or interactive games, to teach saying "no" in a fun and engaging way for your child with ADHD.

Tips for Parents, Caregivers, and Teachers

- Validate Feelings: Validate your child's feelings when saying "no," such as "You feel upset because you really wanted that toy."

- Alternative Suggestions: Offer alternatives when your child says "no" (such as suggesting a different activity or toy).

- Praise Assertiveness: When your child says "no" firmly, praise them, such as using a firm but gentle tone.

By teaching children to say "no" effectively, you can help them develop healthy boundaries, assertiveness, and self-confidence. Remember to model it yourself, use simple language, and practice with everyday situations to make this vital and fundamental life skill a fun and engaging learning experience.

Teaching this skill of saying "no" helps children have a strong sense of self, better understand their social environments, and better adapt to different people throughout life by maintaining their own and others' boundaries.

5- Appropriate Interactions between Girls and Boys

Why is teaching appropriate interactions between girls and boys important in the social-emotional learning of children aged 2 to 6 years?

Teaching appropriate interactions between boys and girls aged 2 to 6 years is vital for several reasons:

- Respect and Equality: Helps children understand and practice respect for all genders, promotes equality, and reduces gender bias.

- Healthy Relationships: Early lessons in appropriate interactions set the stage for healthy, respectful relationships later in life.

- Social Skills: Enhances children's social skills by teaching them how to interact positively and inclusively with peers of all genders.

- Conflict Resolution: By encouraging respectful interactions, it can help children learn how to constructively manage differences and conflicts.

- Empathy and Understanding: Fosters empathy and understanding, allowing children to respect and value different perspectives and experiences.

In general, these lessons contribute to a more inclusive and respectful social environment and contribute to the social and emotional development of children. Therefore, teaching communication skills from an early age in children aged 2 to 6, both normal and with ADHD, is essential, vital, and valuable in order to create and strengthen positive communication channels and appropriate and healthy interactions between girls and boys in order to reduce social and emotional harm and appropriate and healthy interactions between girls and boys in the family and society.

There are several important communication strategies and activities in appropriate interactions between girls and boys that parents and teachers should consider:

- Verbal Communication: Encourage children, especially boys, to use verbal communication to express their thoughts, feelings, and needs. Because verbal communication is often a weak point in communication for boys, and this weakness can be overcome through practice by speaking in simple sentences.

- Eye Contact: Teach children to maintain eye contact calmly and respectfully while interacting with their peers, while maintaining personal boundaries, which helps build trust and better understanding of each other.

- Listening: Teach boys and girls to listen carefully to others, including their peers. Listening carefully helps build good relationships and prevent misunderstandings between boys and girls. Girls often like to be heard carefully and, unlike most boys, are very important to them.

- Emotion Regulation: Help boys and girls recognize, understand, and manage their emotions appropriately when communicating verbally and nonverbally with another boy or girl. Do not speak impulsively and quickly when there is a problem, disagreement or conflict. Do not react emotionally with aggression. Gradually learn to control your emotions and various positive or negative feelings in relationships with peers by learning to identify and label your feelings, take deep breaths and use relaxation strategies. Encourage them to think critically and find appropriate solutions to communication problems. This exercise helps develop social skills and build their self-confidence.

- Circle: Use children's circle to encourage group discussions, role-playing and the development of social skills between boys and girls.

- Drama: Incorporate drama into the curriculum to encourage children to practice social skills, empathy and appropriate communication with the opposite sex.

- Storytelling: Use storytelling to teach social skills such as maintaining personal boundaries, taking turns, sharing and cooperating between girls and boys.

- Role-Playing: Set up role-playing scenarios that children can use to Encourage the practice of social skills, such as sharing toys, maintaining personal boundaries, or resolving conflict between girls and boys.

- Visual Reminders: Use visual reminders such as pictures or posters that are interesting and understandable to preschoolers to reinforce skills and expectations (such as respect, privacy, turn-taking).

Appropriate Communication Skills Training for ADHD-Diagnosed Girls and Boys

- Visual Schedules: Use visual schedules or charts to help hyperactive girls and boys stay organized and focused during activities.

- Breaking Down Complex Tasks: When teaching communication skills to hyperactive girls and boys, break down complex tasks or instructions into smaller, more manageable steps to help hyperactive girls and boys understand and complete the tasks more easily.

- Positive Reinforcement: Use positive reinforcement techniques such as colored labels, reward tokens, or verbal praise to encourage appropriate behavior and communication skills among hyperactive girls and boys.

- Movement Breaks: Provide regular, supervised movement breaks to help girls and boys communicate appropriately. Provide hyperactive boys with opportunities to release excess energy and refocus on learning communication skills.

- Appropriate Space: For hyperactive boys and girls, create a space for their movement and restlessness by providing additional support or modifications during children's activities.

Tips for Teachers at School (Kindergarten, Preschool)

- Be Patient: Be patient with girls and boys who may be struggling with social communication skills or have difficulty following instructions.

- Use Visual Aids: Use visual aids, such as pictures or colorful digital boards, to help girls and boys who are inattentive and distracted to understand instructions or communication skills concepts.

- Encourage Participation: Include all girls and boys, including those who may be shy or struggling with social communication skills, in supervised group activities and praise and encourage them for participating and interacting with others.

- Model Appropriate Behavior: Model appropriate behavior among girls and boys by demonstrating positive communication skills and appropriate social behaviors with the opposite sex yourself.

- Foster a Positive Communication Environment: Create a positive environment for girls and boys to learn social communication skills with the opposite sex by promoting a sense of safety, respect, and trust between girls and boys.

Some Tips for Parents to Foster Healthy and Positive Sibling Relationships
Here are some tips for parents to encourage positive sibling interactions:

- Praise and Appreciate their Efforts: Praise your children when they show kindness, empathy, and respect toward each other. Appreciate their efforts to get along and resolve conflicts peacefully.

- Encourage Sharing and Turn-Taking: Encourage your children to share toys with their siblings, let them take turns, and be willing to compromise. This can gradually help build trust and cooperation between them.

- Enhance a Sense of Teamwork: Encourage your children to work together on projects or tasks, such as puzzles, games, or daily chores, with their siblings without conflict. This practice can help them develop teamwork skills and cooperation with the opposite sex.

- Create Opportunities to Bond: Plan activities like playing games, watching movies together, or going on trips that allow your children to interact positively with their siblings.

- Encourage Open Communication: Encourage your children to express their feelings and needs to each other. Actively listen and help them find solutions to conflicts with their siblings.

- Model Positive and Appropriate Behavior: Model positive and appropriate relationships with your partner or other family members to show your children what healthy relationships look like.

- Teach Empathy and Understanding: Teach your children to put themselves in their siblings' shoes and understand their perspective. Encourage them to be kind and compassionate to each other and to support and encourage each other appropriately in different situations, both in your presence and when they are not present, with consideration, kindness, and respect, and always make each other feel good and comfortable with empathy.

- Encourage Appreciation: Encourage your children to appreciate the positive things they do for their siblings.

- Enhance Responsibility: Encourage your children to take responsibility for their actions and the impact they have on their siblings, and try to make each other happy by apologizing and making amends.

- Celebrate Milestones: Encourage and celebrate each child's milestones and achievements, including achievements in positive relationships with their siblings.

- Keep Calm: When a sibling conflict arises, stay calm and avoid taking sides. Instead, encourage your children to resolve the conflict peacefully without fighting.

Strategies for Encouraging Positive Interactions

- Create a Positive Atmosphere: Create a positive atmosphere at home by being calm, patient, and respectful of your children.

- Use Positive Language: Use positive language when talking to your children, avoid constant criticism or negativity.

- Encourage Positive Body Language: Encourage positive body language such as smiling, polite verbal and nonverbal tone without sarcasm.

- Teach Conflict Resolution Skills: Teach your children how to resolve conflicts with their siblings in a peaceful, respectful, and fair manner.

- Create Equal Opportunity: Provide opportunities to communicate separately with each of your sons or daughters to better strengthen your bond with each of them. (For example, don't be jealous of your one-sided attention to your sibling.)

- Show Affection: Show affection to both your children, boys and girls, equally, which can help them feel loved and valued. And teach them about the importance and necessity of sibling affection by expressing affection.

- Set Clear Boundaries: Set clear rules and boundaries for appropriate behavior between siblings, such as no insults, no hitting or name-calling, and respecting each other's privacy.

Additional Tips for Parents of Children with ADHD

- Provide Extra Support: Provide appropriate support and accommodations for your hyperactive child who may have difficulty with social skills or following rules, by providing equal love and attention to both boys and girls.

- Use Visual Reminders: Use visual reminders or charts to help your hyperactive child remember rules and expectations.

- Suggested Choices: Give your hyperactive child choices throughout the day to help them feel in control and autonomous.

Remember that every family is unique, and what works for one family may not work for another. Be patient, accommodating, and flexible, and work with each of your children to create a positive sibling relationship at home. By implementing these communication skills and strategies, you can promote healthy interactions between your daughters and sons. To gradually empower them in this social-emotional skill, which is one of the most important foundational life skills, from an early age, and help reduce their social and emotional vulnerabilities at different stages of life.

Some Important Tips for Teaching Appropriate Interactions between Girls and Boys to Protect Each other's Privacy

Teaching your children to respect each other's privacy is an important part of helping them develop a positive and healthy sibling relationship. Here are some tips on how to teach them to protect each other's privacy, including:

- Share the Importance of Privacy: Explain to your children that everyone needs their own space and time and that it's important to respect each other's boundaries. You could say something like, "Just as you like to have your own space sometimes, your sibling needs it too. We need to respect each other's privacy."

- Set Boundaries: When it comes to invading each other's privacy, establish clear boundaries about what is and is not okay. For example, you could say, "It's not okay if you rummage through your sibling's room or read their personal things without permission or take their toys without permission."

- Encourage Respect for Personal Belongings: Teach your children to respect each other's personal belongings, such as toys, clothes, and personal items. You could say, "Do you remember how you feel when someone touches or takes your favorite toy without permission? This goes for your sibling too. Let's make a pact not to touch each other's things without permission and to be respectful." For example, praise your son when he observes appropriate behavior, such as asking permission before taking his sister's toy.

- Model Respectful Behavior: Children learn by observing, so model respectful behavior for them yourself. When you're at home, show respect for each other's privacy by knocking before entering a room, or asking permission before looking at something that belongs to the other person.

- Role-Play Scenarios: Practice different scenarios with your son or daughter, such as someone entering their room without permission or taking their drawing book without permission. This can help them understand the importance of respecting each other's privacy.

- Encourage Respectful, Clear Communication: Encourage your children to talk to each other calmly, respectfully, clearly, and openly when they need time or space to be alone. You could say, "Whenever you want to be alone or play alone, just tell your sibling calmly and clearly without insulting, screaming, or crying."

- Create a Safe, Respectful Environment: Make sure your home is a safe, respectful environment where everyone feels comfortable sharing their thoughts and feelings about each other without fear of judgment or punishment.

By following these tips, you can help your children develop a sense of respect for each other's privacy and create and maintain a positive, healthy sibling relationship by respecting each other's personal boundaries.

6- Learning to Share and Take Turns

Definition

The definition of sharing is that children willingly allow others to use or enjoy their toys, materials, or play space. This sharing is about understanding and practicing fairness and generosity in children's social interactions. For example, a child sharing their crayons with others during art class helps build shared play and friendships.

The definition of turn-taking is the ability for children to wait their turn in activities or conversations. With this skill, children learn patience and respect for the participation of others and understand the concept of fairness and equal participation. For example, being patient and patient in waiting for their turn to play on the swing or to speak during a group discussion helps foster effective communication and collaboration.

Both sharing and turn-taking skills are essential in building healthy social interactions and relationships.

By teaching strategies for sharing and turn-taking, you can help young children develop skills essential for future success.

Why Is Sharing and Taking Turns Important?
- Develops Social Skills: Sharing and taking turns help children develop social skills such as cooperation, empathy, and conflict resolution.

- Strengthens Friendship: Sharing and taking turns fosters friendship and a sense of belonging.

- Encourages Patience: Practicing sharing and taking turns helps children develop patience, tolerance, and understanding.

- Develops Emotional Intelligence: Sharing and taking turns helps children understand and manage their own and others' emotions.

Signs of high and developed emotional intelligence in children include abilities such as:

Recognize Nonverbal Cues: Recognize nonverbal cues by showing empathy and sympathy.

Emotional intelligence is the ability to manage your own emotions and understand the emotions of those around you. It has five key elements: self-awareness, self-regulation, motivation, empathy, and social skills. Young children's emotional intelligence is gradually strengthened and developed by teaching the components of social-emotional learning skills.

Strategies for Teaching Sharing and Turn-Taking to Normal 2 to 6 Years Old Children
- Modeling: Model by sharing your own or others' items.

- Role-Playing: Practice role-playing scenarios in which children take turns using items or toys.

- Visual Reminders: Use visual reminders or pictures to help children remember the concept of sharing and turn-taking.

- Encouraging Communication: Encourage children to express their needs and wants during shared activities.

- Encouraging Empathy: Encourage your child to consider the feelings of others during shared activities.

- Praise Effort: Praise children for their efforts at sharing and taking turns, even if they struggle at first.

Appropriate Sharing and Turn-Taking Instructions for Children Aged 2 to 6 Years with ADHD

- Keep the Instruction Simple: Keep the activity simple and focus on one toy or object to avoid overwhelming hyperactive children.

- Use Appropriate Visual Aids: Use appropriate visual aids, such as pictures or colorful symbols that are noticeable to children with ADHD, to help them remember the concept of sharing and taking turns.

- Offer Choices: Offer choices during sharing activities, such as "Do you want to play with the red ball or the blue ball?"

- Rotate Toys: Rotate toys or objects regularly between children to keep children engaged in your learning and prevent them from getting bored.

- Use Music: Use catchy, upbeat music or songs to engage children with ADHD, as they often respond better to activities with rhythm and melody.

- Use Movement: Incorporate movement or action into the activity to help children with ADHD stay focused.

- Use Educational Technology: Use technology, such as educational apps or games, to teach sharing and turn-taking in a fun and engaging way to engage hyperactive children.

By teaching sharing and turn-taking strategies, you can help children aged 2 to 6 years develop essential social skills, build strong relationships, and foster a sense of community. Remember to keep teaching sharing and turn-taking simple, use visual reminders, and praise efforts to make it a fun and engaging learning experience.

7- Conflict Resolution

Definition of Conflict
Conflict in children aged 2 to 6 usually refers to disagreements, arguments, and verbal and nonverbal conflict that arise during interactions with peers. This can occur, for example, when sharing toys, taking turns, or having different opinions about how to play.

Common Causes
- Developmental Stages: Children aged 2 to 6 are still developing social skills, emotion regulation, and empathy. They may not yet fully understand the perspective of others.

- Limited Communication Skills: Children aged 2 to 6 may have difficulty expressing their feelings or wants verbally, which can lead to misunderstandings or frustration.

- Rivalry: Children aged 2 to 6 often want "just the same toy" that their sibling or classmate has taken, which can lead to conflict over ownership of the toy or position in play.

Parents and teachers may ask themselves, "Shouldn't conflict between children and siblings, or friends and classmates at a young age be completely unnecessary and a sign of poor parenting and neglect on the part of the child's parents? Or is it not? Conflict is part of the development of human interactions and shouldn't it be completely prevented?"

In order to answer these questions, we must say that the existence of conflict between children, including siblings, friends and young school classmates (kindergarten, preschool) is a natural and part of human interactions and development. And even in the best possible educational conditions, conflicts arise between children and cannot necessarily be due solely to the wrong educational style of parents. Here are some key points regarding this issue:

1. Developmental Stage

Social Learning: Conflict among children aged 2 to 6 is a natural part of social development. Conflict helps children learn how to express their feelings, negotiate and understand the perspectives of others.

Emotion Regulation: Through conflict, children practice managing their emotions (such as frustration, anger), which is essential for their emotional development.

2. Conflict as a Learning Opportunity

Problem-Solving: Conflicts encourage children to think creatively so that they can resolve differences and strengthen critical thinking and adaptability.

Development of Social Skills: Negotiating and compromising during conflicts helps children develop important social skills such as empathy, cooperation and communication.

3. Guidance and Support

Adult Mediation: While conflicts are natural, adult intervention is often essential to guide children towards healthy conflict resolution strategies. Teaching them how to express their feelings, the importance of listening to each other and how to find solutions can significantly increase their social competence.

Creating a Safe Environment: Adults can help create a safe environment where children feel comfortable resolving conflicts constructively rather than resorting to negative behaviors such as aggression or rejection.

A safe environment for children is one that is physically and emotionally safe, where children feel protected from harm by others in urgent situations and can freely express their feelings without fear of negative consequences, judgment or judgement.

4. Preventing Harmful Negative Behavior

Recognize Patterns: Not all conflicts and fighting are beneficial. It is essential to distinguish between normal disagreements and harmful patterns, such as bullying. Negative behavior should be addressed promptly to protect the emotional and physical health of all children involved.

Privacy: Teaching children about privacy and respecting others can help prevent conflicts from escalating into more serious issues and conflicts.

In short, conflicts among children aged 2 to 6 are a normal and essential part of their social development and interaction. However, providing guidance and support for adults to help children navigate these conflicts in a healthy and constructive way is crucial. Rather than preventing all conflict, the focus should be on teaching children how to resolve conflicts effectively and equipping them with the tools they need for positive interactions throughout their lives.

Definition of Conflict Resolution

In the context of social-emotional learning for children aged 2 to 6, it refers to the ability to navigate and resolve conflicts in a constructive and peaceful manner. This skill includes:

- Understanding Emotions: Recognizing and expressing the feelings of oneself and others involved in the conflict.

- Effective Communication: Using words to express needs and feelings rather than resorting to physical actions or verbal and nonverbal violence.

- Listening Skills: Considering the perspectives of others involved in a conflict.

- Problem-Solving: Working together to find a solution that is acceptable to both parties involved in a disagreement.

For example, a 2- to 6-year-old child practicing conflict resolution skills might say, "I feel upset when you take my toy without asking. Can we take turns playing with it?" This approach to conflict resolution fosters respectful interactions and helps children learn and develop the social skills necessary to navigate relationships.

General Steps for Resolving Conflicts Peacefully

To help children aged 2 to 6, explain in simple language the general steps and ask them to take when facing conflict and conflict with others.

- Stay Calm: Remain calm and composed when conflict arises. This is not easy to learn. It takes practice and effort in different situations. It often helps to reduce tension and prevent it from escalating.

- Communicate: Communicate clearly and respectfully with the other person involved in the conflict.

- Identify the Problem: Identify the issue or problem causing the conflict and try to understand the other person's perspective.

- Active Listening: Actively listening to the other person's concerns and respond thoughtfully.

- Find a Solution: Work together to find a solution that meets both parties' needs.

- Compromise: Be willing to compromise and find a middle ground.

- Apologize: Apologize when necessary and forgive when possible.

- Working Together to Improve: Work together to maintain a positive relationship.

- Ask for Help: Try to ask for help and guidance from the adults around you.

Teaching Conflict-Resolution Strategies in Communication Skills for Children Aged 2 to 6 Years

- Role-Playing: Engage children in role-playing scenarios, opportunities for them to play and practice conflict resolution, such as sharing toys or taking turns.

- Storytelling: Use stories that highlight conflict resolution in the story and discuss the actions and feelings of characters during disagreements.

- Expressing Feelings: Encourage children to express their feelings using words and teach them how to listen to the feelings of others.

- Problem-Solving Steps: Introduce simple steps to problem-solving (such as: first, identifying the problem, second, thinking about solutions, and third, agreeing on a solution).

-Guided Conversations: Provide guided conversation settings where children can talk freely about conflicts they have experienced and how they resolved them, with your guidance and open-ended questions.

Teaching Conflict-Resolution Strategies in Communication Skills for Children Aged 2 to 6 Years with ADHD

- Structured Role-Playing: Use simple, structured, and brief role-playing activities to maintain attention and focus on specific conflict scenarios.

- Visual Aids: Use visual aids, such as diagrams or color pictures, to illustrate the conflict-resolution steps and make concepts easier to understand.

- Immediate Feedback: Provide immediate feedback and positive reinforcement for effective use of conflict-resolution skills.

- Calming Techniques: Teach and encourage calming strategies, such as deep breathing or a quiet corner, to help manage emotions before resolving conflict.

- Interactive Games: Combine interactive games that involve teamwork and cooperation and provide opportunities to practice conflict resolution in a play environment.

Here are some examples of interactive games that can help young children practice conflict-resolution skills:
- Building: Use plastic building blocks to create a shared play area. Children need to communicate and work together to decide which blocks to use and where to place them. If a disagreement arises, they can practice resolving it by discussing and compromising.

- Give Me the Problem: Children sit in a circle, then one of them starts the conflict-resolution game by saying, for example, "I want to play with the red car, but my friend wants the same red car. What should we do with this problem now?" The next child in the circle offers a solution, and then the next child offers his or her solution. This continues until several solutions have been discussed. This game helps children see multiple ways to resolve a conflict and find the most appropriate solution to resolve a conflict or disagreement.

- Puppet Play: Use puppets to role-play common conflicts that children may encounter, such as sharing toys or taking turns. After the puppet show, discuss with the children how the puppets resolved the conflict and encourage them to suggest other ways to resolve the conflict.

- Emotional Role-Playing: Children take turns acting out different emotions related to the conflict, such as frustration or sadness. Others guess how they are feeling and suggest ways to help or resolve the situation, promoting empathy and problem-solving.

- Team Challenges: Set up small group challenges, such as Curious Explorers or Obstacle Course, in which children must work together to successfully find a hidden object, such as a ball, or a common goal, such as a team race. Throughout the activity, guide them to communicate effectively and resolve disagreements, emphasizing teamwork and cooperation.

- These games make learning about conflict-resolution fun and engaging. engaging while providing hands-on opportunities for children to practice these essential skills.

These strategies support all children aged 2 to 6, including those with ADHD, in developing effective conflict-resolution skills, fostering peaceful and constructive social interactions.

Tips for Parents, Caregivers, and Teachers
- Model Healthy Conflict Resolution: Model healthy conflict resolution yourself at home and handle conflicts calmly and respectfully.

- Encourage Communication: Encourage your child to express their feelings and needs when they have conflicts at home.

- Praise Effort: Praise your child's efforts to resolve conflicts, even if they don't succeed at first.

- Enhance Empathy: Encourage your child to consider the feelings of others when they have conflicts at home.

By teaching conflict-resolution strategies, you can help children aged 2 to 6 develop essential social skills, manage emotions effectively, and build strong relationships. Remember to keep conflict-resolution teaching simple, use visual aids, and praise effort to make it a fun and engaging learning experience.

8- Bullying

Definition of Bullying
Bullying is a type of aggressive behavior in which a child intentionally and repeatedly hurts or upsets another child. Bullying can take the form of physical contact, words, or more subtle actions. Often, a child bully uses their physical strength, knowledge, or popularity to control or hurt others, and the behavior is repeated or has the potential to happen more than once. Teachers often note that pushing and teasing, making faces (pretending) are very common in early childhood. In some cases, classroom bullies may even isolate another child from the social group by not playing with them or refusing to share their toys.

Types of Bullying

- Physical Bullying: The use of physical force by hitting, tripping, kicking, pushing, or hitting.

- Emotional Verbal Bullying: Written or oral communication that uses cruel, insulting words to disrespect or belittle a child's appearance, ethnicity, or make fun of a child's disability.

- Relational Bullying: The harming of relationships between two friends in various ways, such as giving treats or toys to only one of them and causing conflict between them or preventing one or more students from interacting with others.

Common Causes of Bullying

Bullying behavior among children aged 2 to 6 can be caused by a variety of factors that affect their social interactions and emotional development. Here are some common reasons:

1. Developmental Stage

Limited Social Skills: Children aged 2 to 6 are still learning how to communicate effectively, share, and manage their emotions. When they can't verbalize their feelings or resolve conflicts, they may resort to aggressive behavior.

Lack of Empathy: At this age, children may not fully understand the impact of their actions on others. They may not recognize empathy and recognize when their behavior is hurtful.

2. Modeling Behavior

The Influence of Role Models: Children may imitate aggressive behaviors they observe in others, such as siblings, peers, or adults. If they witness bullying or aggressive behavior at home or in the media, they may adopt similar behaviors and repeat them in the same way.

Peer Influence: Children often look to their peers for social cues. If a child sees that engaging in certain behaviors (such as violence) will give them social power or status among their peers, they may engage in bullying to prove themselves or be accepted.

3. Desire for Control or Power

Social Hierarchy: As children aged 2 to 6 begin to form social groups, some may seek to establish dominance or control over others to gain status, which can lead to bullying behavior.

Insecurity: Children who feel insecure about their social status may bully others to boost their status or reduce their feelings of vulnerability.

4. Frustration or Emotional Dysregulation

Expression of Anger or Frustration: Children aged 2 to 6 may engage in bullying as a way to express feelings of frustration, anger, or hopelessness if they lack the skills to deal with those feelings appropriately.

Stressful Environments: Changes in the home or school environment (such as family issues, changes in routines, or exposure to conflict) can lead to increased anxiety and outbursts of negative and aggressive behaviors, including bullying.

5. Attention Seeking

Appreciation Seeking: Some children may resort to bullying as a way to get attention from peers or adults, even if that attention is received through negative behavior and actions.

Testing Boundaries and Privacy: Children aged 2 to 6 often test social boundaries and privacy and may use bullying behavior to see how far they can go in their interactions with others.

An Example to Better Understand the Boundary and Privacy Test Situation

During a group play session, a 2- to 6-year-old boy decides to take a toy from another child, a "girl," without permission. He knows that sharing is an important rule and that he should not do so without permission, but at this particular moment, he is curious to see what will happen if he takes the toy without the owner's permission and consent, and how the girl will react.

Boundary and Privacy Test

A 2- to 6-year-old boy is testing the boundaries of acceptable behavior and privacy. He wants to see if the girl will respond positively or negatively to his misbehavior. When the girl reacts by crying and screaming, the 2- to 6-year-old boy may feel "boyish" power or control even at that moment.

Possible Outcomes

Negative Response: If the 2- to 6-year-old boy takes the toy without permission by repeatedly using other people's toys, the other children may either avoid him or respond with their own aggressive behavior, which can lead to a cycle of conflict.

Learning Opportunity: On the other hand, if an adult intervenes in a timely manner with tact and calmness and explains why sharing with the owner's consent is important, how the girl feels when her toys are taken without her consent, and why we should respect the privacy of others, the boy can learn about empathy and positive socially acceptable interactions with girls and other children.

Outcome

In this example, the 2- to 6-year-old (that "boy") is not necessarily trying to be mean or mean. He is testing boundaries and testing social norms. If this behavior is not addressed properly, this experimental behavior can become a pattern of bullying for him. Caregivers or teachers can use this opportunity to teach about setting boundaries, privacy, sharing, and respecting others' feelings, and help children learn more appropriate ways to interact with their peers.

6. Lack of Social Skills

Challenges in Social Interaction: Children who have difficulty understanding social cues or engaging in cooperative play may resort to bullying as a maladaptive and negative strategy for interacting with their peers.

Difficulty Sharing, Taking Turns: If children feel their needs are not being met in group settings, a lack of appropriate social skills can lead to frustration and aggressive behaviors.

7. Cultural and Environmental Factors

Norms Social and Cultural: Cultural attitudes toward aggression and competition can influence children's behavior. In environments where aggressive behavior is tolerated or even encouraged, children may be more likely to engage in bullying.

Lack of Supervision: Inadequate adult supervision during play can lead to situations where children's uncontrolled bullying behavior is reinforced and expressed.

Teaching Coping Strategies to Children Aged 2 to 6 Years

Effectively dealing with bullying in children requires a joint effort by parents at home and teachers at school (kindergarten, preschool). Both can play vital roles in equipping children aged 2-6 years and children with ADHD with the strategies and skills needed to cope with bullying.

Tips for Parents and Teachers

Tips for parents at home include:

- Comfortable Communication: Create an environment where children feel safe to discuss their feelings and experiences. Encourage them to share stories about their day, including any conflicts or bullying they have encountered.

- Empathy Training: Talk to them about their own feelings and those of others. Discuss how bullying can affect others emotionally. Use storytelling, stories, or role-playing scenarios to illustrate these concepts.

- Role-Playing: How to react and respond appropriately to potential situations Practice bullying at home. Role-play different scenarios to help them practice how to respond appropriately and assertively.

- Encourage Positive Friendships: Help children build a network of supportive friends. Encourage them to spend time with peers who show kindness and stand up to bullying so that they have a source of support when bullying occurs.

- Model Positive Behavior: Be respectful in your interactions with others. Children are more likely to imitate and repeat behaviors modeled by their parents.

- Teaching Assertiveness: Teach children to express their feelings assertively and to express their opinions confidently. Teach them phrases they can use to express their discomfort, such as "Wait. I don't like that at all."

- Setting Boundaries: Help children understand the importance of boundaries and how to communicate them. Teach them to recognize when and who is allowed to cross those boundaries and how to respond.

Teaching young children to recognize boundaries is essential for their safety and well-being. Here is a practical example:

Example Activity: "Personal space bubble."

Introduction: Begin by explaining the concept of personal space to children. Describe the concept of personal space as an invisible "bubble" around each person that makes them feel comfortable and safe.

Demonstration: Use a hula hoop or create a circle on the floor with colored yarn to represent a hypothetical personal space bubble. Show children how to stand inside the bubble.

Discussion: Talk about different scenarios in which a person might enter this bubble. For example:

- Parents or caregivers can enter the bubble to hug or help them.

- Teachers may come closer to help them with school activities.

- Friends can come closer during play, but only if they feel comfortable.

Role-Play: Act out different situations with children, for example:

- A teacher needs to help them tie their shoelaces. Ask them how they feel and if it's okay for the teacher to enter their bubble?

- A friend wants to play with their toy. Discuss whether they feel comfortable and what to do if they don't.

- A stranger tries to approach them. Emphasize the importance of firmly saying "no," backing away, and telling a trusted adult.

- Practice Responses: Teach them phrases they can use to express their boundaries, such as:

    "Please don't come forward!", "No, I don't like it.", "I have to ask my parents first."

- Reinforcement: Regularly review the concept of personal space and practice responses with children through games, stories, and discussions. Praise children when they correctly express their boundaries.

Key Points
- Emphasize that it is always okay to say "no" if they feel uncomfortable.

- Make sure children understand and know why and how to ask for help if necessary, and who they can trust and talk to if they feel others have crossed their boundaries.

- Create a supportive environment where children feel safe to express their feelings and concerns.

- Through engaging activities and consistent reinforcement, children aged 2 to 6 can learn to effectively recognize and protect their personal boundaries.

- Control and Monitor Media Use: Be aware of the media (e.g., TV, tablet, phone), networks, and online computer games your child uses. Talk to your child about bullying or conflict on these media and make sure they understand acceptable behavior so they are less likely to engage in bullying behavior.

- Seek Professional Help if Needed: If your child is experiencing significant distress from bullying, seek the support of a counselor or therapist who can provide and teach additional coping strategies.

Tips for Teachers at School (Kindergarten, Preschool)

- Create a Safe Classroom Environment: Create a classroom atmosphere of respect, empathy, and cooperation. Explain clearly and simply to children that bullying is unacceptable and that all children deserve to feel safe.

- Educate about Bullying: Talk to students in simple language about what bullying is, how it affects others, and why it matters, and use age-appropriate discussions, books, animations, and videos to reinforce these ideas.

- Encourage Bystander Intervention: Teach children the role of "active bystanders" and empower them to know what to do when they see bullying. Encourage them to support peers who are being bullied and not just be passive bystanders.

- Provide Ways to Ask for Help: Make sure students know how to report bullying and can do so without fear of retaliation, and who to ask for help from and how quickly. If possible, create a safe, anonymous reporting system for asking for help and guidance. For example:

- Suggestion Box: Place a safe, accessible suggestion box in a common location (such as the school office or near the entrance) so that students can anonymously submit bullying reports. This allows children to share their concerns without fear of being identified.

- Support Resource: Designate a staff member (such as a counselor, teacher, or administrator) who is specifically trained to handle bullying reports. Make sure students know who this person is and how to reach them.

- Implement Conflict-Resolution Strategies: Teach conflict-resolution skills as part of the curriculum. Use role-playing and modeling to demonstrate how to resolve conflicts amicably.

Differentiated Educational Support for Children Aged 2 to 6 Years with a Diagnosis of ADHD

Be aware of the unique challenges that hyperactive children may face (such as being impulsive or inattentive, or having difficulty recognizing and understanding social cues). Provide additional support and guidance tailored to their needs.

- Regular Monitoring: Regularly check in with students to gauge their feelings about the school's social interaction environment and any potential bullying they may encounter. This can help establish a good line of communication with students.

- Partnering with Parents: Maintain good communication with parents about their children's social interactions. Share concerns and practical strategies for reducing bullying with parents so that they can consistently support their behavior at home.

- Praise Understanding Cultural Differences: Organize activities that promote understanding of cultural differences. This can help reduce prejudice and encourage acceptance of differences and reduce bullying among students.

- Professional Development: Attend teacher training classes to learn how to manage bullying in children and promote social-emotional learning. This professional development helps educators become aware of best practices for managing bullying in children and promoting social-emotional learning.

Teaching children aged 2 to 6 how to deal with bullying can be done in simple, actionable steps. Here is a practical and understandable guide for young children to follow when dealing with bullying, whether at home with siblings or at school with classmates.

Step-by-Step How to Deal with Bullying

1. Stay Calm and Confident
What to Do: Take a deep breath and stand up.

Why: It will help you feel brave and strong.

2. Tell Them to Stop
What and How to Say: Use firm words! Say firmly: "Please stop!" or "I said no! I don't like that!"

Why: Sometimes, bullies don't realize they are hurting your feelings, and telling them you are can help them understand.

3. Walk Away
What to Do: If they don't stop, go to a safe place (like the teacher's desk or another room in the house).

Reason: This distancing can help you avoid more hurtful behavior and gives you time to ask for help and feel better from your parents, teachers, friends, and family.

4. Find a Trusted Adult
What to Do: Look for a teacher at school or a parent at home. Tell them what's happening.

Reason: Adults can help stop the bullying and keep you safe and secure.

5. Talk to a Friend
What to Do: Share what's happening with a friend you trust.

Reason: Friends can support you and may even help you talk things out.

6. Practice Assertiveness
What to Do: If someone is treating you badly, practice what you have to say. Use phrases like "That's not nice at all!" or "I don't like that at all!"

Reason: The more you practice, the more comfortable you'll feel with saying those phrases when necessary.

7. Tell Them How You Feel
What to Do: If you feel safe, tell the bully how they make you feel. For example, "It makes me so sad when you say that."

Reason: Sharing your feelings can sometimes help the other person stop bullying.

8. Be Kind to Yourself
What to Do: Do something fun or relaxing, like drawing or playing your favorite game, after you've been away from the bully.

Reason: It's important to feel good again and not let other people's bullying take away your happiness.

Additional Tips for Parents

- Reinforce Learning: Discuss these steps with your child regularly and ask them to share their experiences with you, so they feel comfortable using these strategies in real-life situations.

- Use Role-Play: Create scenarios at home so they can practice these steps without any pressure.

- Encourage Open Dialogue: Make it clear that they can always talk to you about problems they are facing.

By providing clear and simple steps that young children can understand and remember, you can empower your child to effectively handle bullying situations both at home and at school and be less likely to be hurt emotionally, psychologically, or physically.

Addressing bullying is a multi-faceted approach that includes strengthening communication, teaching empathy and assertiveness, appropriately handling conflict, and creating safe, supportive environments both at home and at school. By collaborating and implementing these strategies, parents and teachers can significantly equip children, regardless of their developmental characteristics, to effectively and constructively manage critical situations of bullying and how to appropriately deal with and resolve conflicts. So that they can better and more powerfully stay away from the physical and psychological harm and trauma caused by childhood bullying throughout their lives.

9- Lying

Definition of a Lie

A lie is the intentional provision of false information or deception to others, involving statements or the creation of impressions that are not true, often with the intent to mislead others.

Types of Lies in Children Aged 2 to 6 Years

Fantasy Lies

Explanation: These lies are often part of imaginative play. Young children, especially children aged 2 to 4, often blur the line between reality and fantasy.

Example: A child may claim to have a pet dragon or that he is a superhero.

Avoidance Lies
Explanation: Lies told to avoid punishment or negative consequences for their actions.

Example: A child may deny spilling a glass of water on the floor to avoid being blamed.

Exaggerated Lies
Explanation: Children may exaggerate facts to make stories more interesting or simply to get attention.

Example: A child may say that he got his "big doll" as a gift when he was much younger.

Social Lies
Explanation: Lies told to fit in with peers or to avoid hurting other people's feelings.

Example: A child may pretend not to care about a toy they really like because their friend likes it.

Lit to Test Boundaries
Explanation: Sometimes children tell lies to test the boundaries and abilities of others.

Example: A child may claim to have brushed their teeth to see if their parents will notice that they have lied!

Coverage Lies
Explanation: Lies told to cover up a mistake or avoid embarrassment.

Example: A child may say that they have never broken a very small toy to avoid embarrassment.

Understanding the types of lies children tell can help caregivers, parents, and teachers address the underlying motivations for children's lying and guide them toward truthfulness and honesty in a supportive and constructive manner, remaining calm and nonviolent.

Common Causes of Lying in Children 2 to 6 Years Old
In 2-Year-Olds
Imaginative Play: At this age, children often blend the boundaries between reality and fantasy. They may not intend to deceive, but they often engage in imaginative, fantasy play.

Exploring Language: They experiment with language and storytelling without a clear understanding of lying.

In 3-Year-Olds
Avoiding Punishment: Children begin to lie to avoid the consequences of their actions, even if they do not fully understand the concept of lying.

Testing Boundaries: They begin to test the limits set by their caregivers, parents, and teachers to identify and understand the reactions to their actions.

In 4-Year-Olds
Autonomy Seeking: Children seek greater independence and may lie to exert control over their environment.

Attention Seeking: They may use lying as a means to get attention from adults or peers.

In 5-Year-Olds
Social Acceptance: Children lie to fit in with their peers or to be accepted into games or social groups.

Understanding Social Rules: As they better understand social rules, they may lie to avoid the consequences of breaking them, or to see what they can get away with.

In 6-Year-Olds
Protecting Self-Esteem: Lying can be a way to protect their self-esteem, especially if they feel embarrassed or insecure.

Sophisticated Social Interactions: At this age, children become more skilled at lying to navigate complex social situations and avoid conflict or punishment.

Differences in Boys and Girls
Boys: They may lie more to avoid punishment, test forbidden boundaries, or to be more controlling and dominant in social situations. They may also engage in exaggerated storytelling to get attention from others.

Girls: They may lie to protect their feelings, maintain social harmony, and avoid further conflict. They may also use lying as a way to build or maintain friendships.

While the motivations for lying can be similar in boys and girls, the social contexts and specific behaviors toward them may differ due to different social, cultural, and expectations patterns.

By understanding these common causes and differences, parents, caregivers, and teachers can better assess lying behavior and guide children toward honesty in a supportive and constructive manner.

Methods for Teaching about Lying to Children Aged 2 to 6 Years
At Home

Model Honest Behavior: Children learn by observing adults. Model honesty consistently in your own behavior and explain the value of honesty.

Create a Safe Environment: Make sure your child feels safe to tell the truth by avoiding harsh punishments for mistakes. Emphasize that truthfulness and honesty are valuable, even when it is difficult to tell the truth.

Use Stories and Books: Read age-appropriate books that introduce the importance of honesty and the consequences of lying. Talk and discuss the stories and characters with your child to further reinforce the book's teaching message that honesty is valuable.

Reinforce Honesty: Praise honest behavior with positive reinforcement. Praise your child consistently and immediately when they tell the truth, even if it involves admitting a mistake.

Role-Play: Engage in role-play activities with your child in which you and your child act out roles such as being honest and lying. This activity helps children practice the consequences of being honest and lying in a safe environment with you.

Explain the Consequences of Lying: Gently explain the consequences of lying, such as losing the trust of others, in simple, clear language. Use examples that children can understand, based on their age.

Consistency in Enforcing Rules: Be consistent and firm in enforcing rules and expectations about being honest and truthful. Explain what you expect clearly and simply, and deal with the consequences of lying in a non-violent and fair manner.

Building Empathy: Teach empathy by helping your child understand how lying can hurt others. Discuss their feelings and encourage them to think about how their actions affect those around them.

At School (Kindergarten, Preschool)

Classroom Discussions: Incorporate discussions about honesty and truthfulness into the curriculum. Use interesting and fun stories, scenarios, and discussions to help children better understand the importance of being honest.

Create a Trusting Environment: Create a classroom environment where children feel comfortable and safe to express themselves honestly without fear of punishment or harsh ridicule.

Peer Role Models: Encourage older students to model honest behavior for younger children. Peer influence can go a long way in promoting positive behaviors.

Interactive Activities: Use games and activities that promote honesty, such as group projects where children must work together and rely on each other's honest contributions.

Positive Reinforcement: Recognize and reward honest behavior in the classroom immediately. Acknowledging and praising honesty can encourage more of the same behavior.

Conflict-Resolution Training: Teach children how to resolve conflicts honestly and constructively. Role-playing and conflict resolution exercises can help children practice honesty in challenging situations.

Visual Aids and Reminders: Display posters and visual aids that demonstrate the importance of honesty. Use catchy reminders and children's slogans to reinforce the message of truthfulness throughout the day.

Incorporate Social-Emotional Learning Programs: Implement social-emotional learning programs that focus on character building, including truthfulness and honesty. These programs can provide structured lessons on social skills and ethical behavior for children.

By using these methods at home and at school, parents, caregivers, and teachers can effectively manage and eliminate lying in children aged 2 to 6 and promote a culture of truthfulness, honesty, and trust.

Teaching Children with ADHD How to Manage Lying

Teaching children with ADHD to manage lying requires understanding their unique challenges and tailoring strategies to their needs. Here are some effective approaches for both home and school settings:

At Home

Clear, Consistent Rules: Set clear rules about honesty and enforce them consistently. Children with ADHD benefit from knowing exactly what is expected of them.

Positive Reinforcement: Praise and reward honest behavior. Use an immediate, consistent reward system to encourage honesty (such as using a label or small rewards for telling the truth).

Role-Play: Engage in role-playing activities where you and your child take on roles such as the truth-teller and the liar. This practice helps them practice appropriate responses in a safe environment.

Break Down Instructions: Provide instructions in small, manageable steps. Children with ADHD may struggle with multi-step instructions, so breaking them down can be helpful.

Use Visual Aids: Create visual reminders about the importance of honesty. Posters or charts can be helpful as reminders.

Teach Empathy: Help your child understand how lying affects others. Talk about different feelings and encourage them to think about how their actions affect others.

Set a Timer: Use a timer to help your child stay consistent with tasks and move slowly from one activity to the next. This practice can reduce impulsive, hasty behaviors to avoid lying.

At School

Create a Routine: Create a structured daily routine with clear expectations. Consistency in the daily schedule helps children with ADHD feel calm and secure and understand what is expected of them.

Behavior Modification: Use respectful behavior modification to address lying without provoking a behavioral outburst. To avoid embarrassment, bring up the issue calmly and privately with your child.

Positive Reinforcement: Recognize and reward honest behavior in the classroom. Praise and positive reinforcement can encourage continued honesty.

Break Down Instructions: Provide instructions in small, manageable steps. They may find it difficult to follow and understand complex explanations.

Peer Role Models: Encourage older students to model honest behavior. Peer influence can be helpful in promoting positive behaviors.

Interactive Activities: Use games and activities that promote honesty and cooperation. Group projects and role-play can help children practice honesty in a social context.

Visual Reminders: Display posters and visual aids that highlight the importance of honesty. These reminders can help reinforce the message throughout the day.

Mindfulness and Self-Regulation: Teach mindfulness and self-regulation techniques to help children manage impatience, impulsivity, and improve emotional understanding and reduce lying.

Using these methods, parents, caregivers, and teachers can effectively address lying in children with ADHD and foster and promote a culture of honesty and trust in them.

CHAPTER 7: RESPONSIBLE DECISION-MAKING

1- IMPORTANT POINTS IN TEACHING RESPONSIBLE DECISION-MAKING

2- WHY IS RESPONSIBLE DECISION-MAKING IMPORTANT?

3- STRATEGIES FOR TEACHING THE COMPONENTS OF RESPONSIBLE DECISION-MAKING FOR NORMAL CHILDREN 2 TO 6 YEARS OLD

4- STRATEGIES FOR TEACHING RESPONSIBLE DECISION-MAKING FOR CHILDREN 2 TO 6 YEARS OLD WITH ADHD

Responsible Decision-Making

Responsible decision-making is a vital skill that helps individuals make informed, thoughtful, and reflective choices. Responsible decision-making is the process of making choices in which an individual considers the consequences of those choices for themselves and others, which involves considering the pros and cons of a situation, weighing available and possible options, and making a thoughtful choice based on that evaluation.

Responsible decision-making in the context of social-emotional learning for children aged 2 to 6 years includes the ability to make choices that are ethical, safe, and consider the impact on themselves and others. Components of responsible decision-making include:

Recognizing Problems: Recognizing that a problem exists and identifying it and recognizing when a decision needs to be made.

Generating Alternatives: Thinking about different ways to solve a problem or to make decision.

Evaluating Consequences: Considering the potential outcomes of each alternative, including its impact on themselves and others.

Choosing: Choosing the best option based on evaluating the consequences of making decision is the process of choosing a solution to a problem.

Reflecting on Decisions: Reviewing a decision after making it to learn from the experience and understand its impact.

Here are two examples of poor decision-making and responsible decision-making in similar situations for a 2- to 6-year-old child:

At School (Kindergarten, Preschool)
Situation: A child is playing with play dough in the school playroom.

Wrong Decision
The child decides to pour all the play dough on the floor and then tries to mix it with water, making a huge mess. The child does not consider the consequences of his actions and does not think about how he will clean up the mess afterwards.

If only the teacher would stop the child from making the mistake and help the child clean up the mess that is distracting him from other activities and tasks, the child would learn that making a mistake is okay and that someone else will be there to fix the problem for him.

If a child learns that it is okay and someone else will clean it up for him, he may continue to make the mess without thinking about the consequences of that bad decision and action. This can create a "behavioral pattern" in which the child expects others to take responsibility for his or her wrong decisions and actions

1- Important Points in Teaching Responsible Decision-Making

- Set Clear Expectations: Let your child know that it's okay to make a mess, but they should take responsibility for cleaning it up.

- Model Responsible Behavior: "Show" your child how to clean up after themselves and their surroundings, and encourage them to do the same.

- Provide Support: Help and guide them when needed, but gradually give your child more independence in cleaning.

- Praise Responsible Behavior: Praise and commend your child when they try to clean up after themselves and take responsibility for their actions.

By setting clear expectations, modeling responsible behavior, and providing support and praise for responsible behavior, your child can learn that making a mess is not acceptable and that they should take responsibility for cleaning it up.

Here's an example of how the conversation might go:
Teacher: "I see you made a big mess! Who do you think should clean it up?"

Child: "I don't know… maybe you?"

Teacher: "No, it's your job to clean it up because you made a mess. It's not my job, but let's work together to clean up this mess. Let me show you how we can clean it up and then you can do it yourself next time."

By having this conversation, the teacher teaches the child that making a mess is not acceptable and that they need to take responsibility for their actions.

Responsible Decision-Making

The child thinks about what they want to do with the play dough and decides to use it to create a specific shape or design.

The child remembers that they don't want to make a mess and decides to work on a table or surface where they can easily clean up any spills.

The child considers how they can use the play dough in a way that won't cause problems for others or the environment.

The teacher notices the child's responsible behavior and praises and encourages them for making good choices, which encourages the child to continue making responsible decisions.

At Home
Wrong Decision-Making

A child decides to paint and scribble on the wall without asking permission, thinking it's okay because "everyone else does it."

The child doesn't think about how his or her actions might affect others, such as making his or her parents upset or angry or damaging the house.

If only the parents would stop the child's misbehavior and clean up the mess that causes stress and frustration, the child will learn that it's okay to break the rules and be inconsiderate of others at home.

A parent may want to punish the child for this, but while the child may learn a lesson about not asking permission, simply stopping the misbehavior may be incomplete. Punishment is not necessarily the best approach, as it can lead to negative feelings and even more disobedience. Instead, it is essential to address the situation in a way that allows the child to learn what they did wrong, why it was wrong, and how to do better next time and make better decisions about what they want to do.

Here is an example of how to handle the situation:
Parent: "I see you decided to paint on the wall without asking permission. Can you tell me why you did it?"

Child: "I thought it was okay because everyone else does it!"

Parent: "I know you may have seen other people paint on the walls before, but that doesn't mean you have permission to do it. Painting on the walls is not allowed because it damages our property and can cause a lot of trouble. It also shows disrespect for our parents, our home, and the family members who live here."

Child: "Excuse me…"

Parent: "I know you're sorry, but what can we do to fix this mess?"

Child: "Help me clean it up?"

Parent: "Yes, let's work together to clean up the coloring and scribbling. And next time, before you start coloring and scribbling, ask permission first, okay?"

By having this conversation, parents: Acknowledge the Child's Point of View: Parents validate the child's feelings and thoughts and show that they understand where they are coming from (because they thought it was okay if everyone else did it).

Explain the Rules: Parents clearly explain why coloring on the wall is not allowed, focusing on the consequences and outcome of the action rather than just saying "no".

Encourage Responsibility: Parents encourage the child to take responsibility for their actions and help them come up with a plan to fix the mess.

Set Clear Expectations: Parents create a clear expectation for what should happen next time, (permission must be sought before coloring).

This approach helps the child understand that their actions and decisions have consequences and that they should respect others and their property. It also teaches them problem-solving skills and encourages them to think critically about their actions.

Remember be careful, the goal is not to punish the child, but to teach valuable lessons and help him develop good habits and decision-making skills.

Responsible Decision-Making

The child asks permission from the parent before coloring.
For example, to use washable markers or to paint on the wall paper that the parent has posted for him. Or not to paint on the wall at all inside the house

and to paint or draw outside on a special part of the wall that the parent has designated for him.

The child thinks about how his work might affect his parents and others and decides, for example, to paint or draw on a piece of paper or in his notebook instead of on the wall. The child considers how he can use his creativity in a way that respects others and their property.

The parent encourages and praises the child for his good choices, which encourages the child to continue making responsible decisions.

In both the "Smearing Play Dough" and "Scribble on the Wall" scenarios, the child learns how to be a responsible decision-maker, considering the potential consequences of his or her actions, considering others, and making choices that are respectful and considerate.

2- Why Is Responsible Decision-Making Important?

- Develops Critical Thinking Skills: Responsible decision-making helps children develop critical thinking skills, problem-solving skills.

- Builds Self-Confidence: When children make responsible decisions, they feel more confident in their ability to make good choices.

- Teach Empathy: Responsible decision-making encourages children to consider the feelings and needs of others with empathy.

- Helps Build Character: Responsible decision-making is a fundamental and valuable life skill that helps children develop positive and pro-social character traits such as honesty, respect, and kindness.

3- Strategies for Teaching the Components of Responsible Decision-Making for Normal Young Children

- Problem-Identification Activities: Use simple, everyday scenarios to help children recognize when a decision needs to be made. For example, "It's time to clean up. What should we do with our toys?"

- Choice Games: Play games where children choose between different activities or objects and discuss the consequences of each choice.

- Story-Based Learning: Read stories where characters face decisions, pausing in between to discuss the characters' choices and the possible consequences.

- Role-Playing: Engage children in role-playing exercises to practice making decisions in different situations, such as sharing toys or resolving a dispute with a friend.

- Open-Ended Questions: After making decisions, ask reflective open-ended questions: "How did this choice make you feel?" and "What might you do differently next time?"

4- Strategies for Teaching Responsible Decision-Making for Children 2 to 6 Years Old with ADHD

- Visual Aids: Use visual aids such as decision-making charts or picture programs to help hyperactive children understand the decision-making steps and follow along with the picture if needed.

- Structured Routines: Create clear, structured routines that include decision-making steps and provide a predictable framework that can help increase hyperactive children's focus.

- Short, Engaging Activities: Implement short, engaging activities that require decision-making, making sure the tasks are manageable and maintain the hyperactive child's interest.

- Positive Reinforcement: When hyperactive children make thoughtful decisions, provide immediate, positive feedback and reinforce appropriate behavior.

- Educational Technology: Use interactive apps or games designed to teach decision-making skills to make learning responsible decision-making fun, engaging, and engaging for children with ADHD.

- Calming Techniques: Teach calming techniques, such as deep breathing or using a quiet space, and practice helping children better control and manage their impulsiveness before making any decisions.

These strategies help all children aged 2 to 6, including those with ADHD, learn and develop the basic skills of responsible decision-making that are essential for their social and emotional development throughout their lives.

CHAPTER 8: CREATING A SUPPORTIVE SOCIAL-EMOTIONAL LEARNING ENVIRONMENT

1- THE IMPORTANCE OF A NURTURING AND INCLUSIVE ENVIRONMENT FOR SOCIAL-EMOTIONAL LEARNING

2- IMPORTANT TIPS FOR CREATING A NURTURING AND INCLUSIVE ENVIRONMENT

3- TIPS FOR CREATING A SUPPORTIVE SOCIAL-EMOTIONAL LEARNING ENVIRONMENT AT HOME AND IN THE CLASSROOM

Supportive Social-Emotional Learning Environment

What is a supportive social-emotional learning environment? Why is a supportive social-emotional learning environment necessary and essential for children's academic success and empowerment in life?

A supportive social-emotional learning environment for children aged 2 to 6 is an environment in which children feel safe, respected and valued. It includes:

- Emotional Safety: Creating a space in which children feel emotionally safe and can express their feelings without fear of judgment or ridicule.

- Positive Relationships: An environment conducive to building and nurturing strong and caring relationships between children, teachers and caregivers, while promoting mutual trust and respect.

- Inclusivity: An environment that is open to children's cultural differences, where every child feels accepted, regardless of their background, abilities or differences, and is welcoming to all children regardless of their background, culture, language or abilities. It can often be said that an inclusive environment ensures that every child feels valued and respected, regardless of their background or abilities.

- Empathy and Understanding: A calm and supportive environment that encourages empathy and understanding among children, helping them to recognize and respond to the feelings of others.

- Opportunities for Social Interaction: Children have many opportunities to engage in social interactions, role-play, and group activities that promote social skills and emotional intelligence.

- Social-Emotional Skills Instruction: Explicit instruction and modeling of social-emotional skills are integrated into daily programs and activities.

- Flexibility and Adaptability: The environment is flexible and adaptable to meet the diverse needs of children, including those with special or exceptional needs.

- Open Communication: Children are encouraged to express their thoughts, feelings, and needs through open communication channels.

- Emphasis on Mistakes and Failures: Mistakes and failures are viewed as opportunities for growth, learning, and improvement, rather than punishment or shame.

- Adult-to-Child Ratio: An adult-to-child ratio is desirable to ensure personal attention, support, and guidance for each child.

In a supportive social-emotional learning environment:

- Children develop a sense of belonging and connection with peers and adults.

- They are motivated to learn and participate in activities that promote social-emotional development.

- They develop essential life skills such as self-awareness, self-regulation, empathy, and problem-solving.

- They become more resilient and better equipped to deal `with challenges and setbacks.

1- The Importance of a Nurturing and Inclusive Supportive Environment for Social-Emotional Learning

A supportive and inclusive environment plays an important role in fostering social-emotional learning among children. Here are some of the factors that make such an environment important, including:

1. Emotional Safety and Trust
Emotional Safety: A nurturing and inclusive environment enhances the sense of security that is essential for children to feel comfortable expressing their feelings and thoughts.

Trust: Inclusion strengthens children's trust among peers and adults, encouraging open communication and a willingness to share feelings and experiences without fear of judgment.

2. Respect for Cultural Diversity and Differences
Inclusion: Accepting diversity helps children understand and respect differences in backgrounds, cultures, abilities, and perspectives.

Empathy: Exposure to diverse experiences encourages empathy and understanding of the feelings and experiences of others, and promotes a sense of community and belonging.

3. Development of Social Skills

Collaboration: An inclusive environment provides opportunities for children to collaborate with peers from diverse backgrounds and learn to work together toward common goals.

Conflict Resolution: Children learn how to respectfully and constructively overcome differences and conflicts, and strengthen and develop communication, negotiation, and compromise skills.

4. Emotion Regulation and Well-Being

Supportive Relationships: Strengthening relationships with peers and adults helps children better manage stress in relationships, regulate their emotions, and develop resilience when faced with challenges.

Positive Role Models: Inclusive environments often include a variety of positive role models (same age or older) who practically show children how to express healthy emotions and cope with them. And children have the opportunity to learn from observation.

5. Academic and Life Success

More Opportunities for Learning: Research shows that a nurturing and inclusive environment for social-emotional learning contributes to academic achievement, positive behavior, and long-term success in school and life by providing more opportunities for learning in childhood.

Adaptation: Children who experience inclusive and nurturing environments are better equipped to adapt to changes and challenges in their academic and personal lives.

2- Important Tips for Creating a Nurturing and Inclusive Environment

Promote Respect and Acceptance: Encourage respect for individual differences and cultural diversity through discussions, activities, and inclusive practices.

Create Volunteer Groups: Create opportunities for collaboration, teamwork, and shared experiences among children and families by forming volunteer groups to strengthen children's sense of social belonging.

Promote Positive Behaviors: Adults play an important role in modeling positive behaviors such as empathy, kindness, and inclusive behavior in their interactions with children and each other. Young children learn best by observing and repeating positive behaviors.

Support Children: Provide support and encouragement to meet children's social and emotional needs in a variety of ways that are appropriate to each child's age and characteristics, and ensure that each child feels valued and supported in their growth and development.

In short, a nurturing and inclusive environment creates a foundation in which children feel safe, valued, and supported in their social-emotional development. It empowers them with the skills necessary to navigate relationships, understand emotions, and contribute positively to their communities, now and in the future.

By creating a supportive social-emotional learning environment, educators can help children develop the skills they need to thrive academically, socially, and emotionally throughout their lives.

3- Tips for Creating a Supportive Social-Emotional Learning Environment at Home and in the Classroom

At Home and in the Classroom

Creating a supportive social-emotional learning environment at home or in the classroom is essential for promoting well-being, productivity, and positive interactions between children and adults. Here are some tips to help you achieve this goal at home and in the classroom:

Tips for Home
- Routines: Establish predictable daily schedules for wake-up, mealtimes, playtime, and bedtime. Consistency helps children feel secure and reduces anxiety.

- Designate Calm Spaces: Create a cozy nook or area where children can relax with soft pillows, blankets, and books.

- Limit Noise and Distractions: Reduce background noise during activities such as homework or playtime. Use soft music to create a calm environment.

- Encourage Open Communication: Create a space where children feel comfortable expressing their feelings and concerns. Actively listen to what they have to say and validate their feelings.

- Promote Order: Keep toys, books, and play equipment organized to minimize clutter. Teach children to tidy up their surroundings as part of their daily routine.

- Incorporate Nature and Greenery into Your Home: Bring elements of nature into your home with plants or natural decorations. Exposure to green spaces has been shown to calm and reduce stress in children.

- Practice Mindfulness and Relaxation Techniques: Teach children simple mindfulness exercises, such as deep breathing or guided relaxation, to help them manage their emotions and promote calm.

Classroom Tips

- Create a Welcoming Environment: Arrange classroom tables and chairs to create open spaces and comfortable seating areas. Use warm colors and decorations that promote a sense of calm and belonging.

- Create Clear Expectations: Set clear rules and expectations for children's behavior, and reinforce positive behavior with praise and encouragement.

- Use Visual Aids: Display schedules, routines, and visual cues to help children understand transitions and expectations throughout the day.

- Provide Sensory Toys: Sensory toys are items that are specifically designed to stimulate one or more of a child's senses. Provide sensory toys, such as "stress balls" or "sensory buckets," to help children learn to regulate their emotions and focus.

- Sensory buckets are containers filled with materials that provide sensory stimulation for children. They are usually made up of a base material such as rice, sand, or water. Then, various objects or tools are added for children to explore, manipulate, and play with.

- Encourage Group Play: Plan activities that encourage teamwork and cooperation among children. Teach conflict resolution skills and model positive social interactions.

- Provide Quiet Activities: Provide quiet corners with books, puzzles, or art materials where children can engage in calming activities independently or in small groups.

- Celebrate Successes and Efforts: Recognize and praise children's achievements and efforts with praise, labels, or classroom celebrations to reinforce positive behavior and create a supportive environment.

By implementing these tips, both at home and in the classroom, you can create a calm and pleasant supportive social-emotional learning environment that promotes positive behavior in children 2 to 6 years old and gradually enhances and enhances the overall learning experience in various social, cognitive, and emotional areas throughout their lives, supporting their social-emotional health and development.

CHAPTER 9: THE ROLE OF GAMES AND EDUCATIONAL TASKS IN SOCIAL-EMOTIONAL LEARNING

1- THE ROLE OF GAMES AND EDUCATIONAL TASKS IN CHILDREN'S SOCIAL-EMOTIONAL LEARNING AT HOME

2- THE ROLE OF GAMES AND EDUCATIONAL TASKS IN CHILDREN'S SOCIAL-EMOTIONAL LEARNING AT SCHOOL

Definition of Games and Educational Tasks in Social-Emotional Learning

Games and tasks in the area of social-emotional learning are activities that are designed to be both enjoyable and educational for most children aged 2 to 6, helping them to strengthen and develop important social and emotional skills. These games and tasks can include cooperative games, role-playing, problem-solving tasks, and other interactive activities that encourage children to learn through play.

The Role of Games and Tasks in Social-Emotional Learning for Children Aged 2 to 6 Years

Encourage Collaboration: Games that require teamwork teach children how to work together, share responsibilities, and support each other in achieving a common goal. This helps build cooperation skills and foster a sense of community.

Develop Communication Skills: Educational tasks often involve verbal interactions, listening, and expressing ideas. Through these activities, children learn to communicate effectively, express their thoughts, and understand others.

Strengthening Emotion Regulation: Games that involve turn-taking, waiting, and frustration management help children practice self-control and emotion regulation. They learn to manage their emotions in a socially acceptable way.

Promoting Empathy and Understanding: Role-playing games and storytelling allow children to put themselves in the shoes of others and foster empathy and understanding of different perspectives and feelings.

Building Self-Confidence: Successfully completing tasks and games increases children's self-confidence and self-esteem. They feel proud of their achievements and are encouraged to take on new challenges.

Problem-Solving Skills: Many educational tasks involve puzzles or challenges that require critical thinking and problem-solving. These activities help children develop cognitive skills and the ability to think strategically.

Creating a Positive Learning Environment: Educational games and tasks make learning fun and engaging, creating a positive and supportive environment in which children are more willing to participate and take risks in their learning.

1. Fun Games and Appropriate Assignments to Teach and Reinforce Social-Emotional Learning at Home and at School

Fun games play an important role in teaching and reinforcing social-emotional learning skills both at home and at school. Here are some key reasons why fun games are important for social-emotional learning:

The Importance of Fun Games for Social-Emotional Learning Engagement and Motivation

At Home: Fun games capture children's interest and motivation, make learning enjoyable, and encourage active participation.

At School: Games create a dynamic, interactive learning environment that engages students and fosters enthusiasm for developing social and emotional skills.

Skill Development through Play

At Home: Games provide opportunities for children to practice and strengthen social-emotional learning skills such as empathy, communication, and teamwork in a calm and supportive environment.

At School: Through structured play, students can develop skills such as problem-solving, conflict resolution, and emotion regulation that are essential for social interactions and academic success.

Emotion Regulation

At Home: Fun games can help children manage emotions by providing a safe space to express feelings, learn coping strategies, and understand the impact of their actions on others.

At School: Games promote self-awareness and mindfulness, and teach students to recognize their emotions and respond appropriately in social situations.

Building Positive Relationships

At Home: Playing games together strengthens bonds between family members, promotes positive communication, and fosters a sense of belonging and support.

At School: Games encourage cooperation and collaboration among peers, fostering positive relationships, empathy, and respect for diversity.

Practical Application of Skills

At Home: Fun games allow children to apply the social-emotional learning skills they have learned in real-life scenarios, increasing their ability to navigate social challenges and make responsible decisions.

At School: Games provide a structured platform and foundation for students to practice social-emotional learning skills in a controlled environment, preparing them for interactions inside and outside the classroom.

Positive Learning Environment

At Home: Incorporating games into daily routines creates a positive atmosphere in which learning social-emotional learning skills becomes natural and enjoyable.

At School: Fun games contribute to a classroom environment where students feel valued, respected, and encouraged to grow socially and emotionally.

1- Fun Games to Teach and Reinforce Social-Emotional Learning at Home

Here are some fun games and simple daily tasks that can help teach and reinforce social-emotional learning skills for boys and girls with ADHD, suitable for parent-child play and interaction with siblings or peers:

At Home
Parent-Child Play

Emotional Moods
Objective: Practice recognizing and expressing emotions.

How to Play: Show your emotions (e.g., happy, sad, surprised) using facial expressions and gestures. The other person guesses the feeling and discusses the situations that trigger those feelings.

Feelings Entry Board
Goal: To encourage open communication about feelings.

How to Play: Create a feelings board with different emotion shapes (happy, sad, angry, etc.) and ask each other to point out how they are feeling. Talk and discuss the reasons for those feelings and ways to manage them with the children.

Emotional Story Time
Goal: To explore empathy and understanding other people's perspectives.

How to Play: Read an emotional story together and talk about the characters' feelings and actions. Ask questions like "How do you think they felt?" or "What would you do if you were there in that situation?"

Mindful Breathing or Yoga Poses
Goal: To promote calmness and mindfulness.

How to Play: Practice simple breathing exercises or yoga poses suitable for children together. Focus on deep breathing and relaxation techniques to manage emotions and reduce stress.

Gratitude Notebook
Goal: To foster gratitude and positive thinking.

How to Play: Provide a gratitude journal where you write down something you are grateful for each day. Share the items with each other and discuss why those things are meaningful to your child.

At Home
Child playing with siblings or friends of the same age:

Lego Building Blocks (Cube Toys)
Goal: To strengthen teamwork and communication skills.

How to Play: Use plastic building blocks, Legos, or other construction toys to work together on a shared project. Discuss and debate roles, share ideas, and problem-solve together.

Empathy Game
Goal: To practice empathy and perspective-taking.

How to Play: Role-play different scenarios in which one person pretends to be "sad or needy." Encourage others to respond with empathy and supportive actions.

Sharing and Turn-Taking
Goal: To strengthen sharing and patience.

How to Play: Play games or activities that require turn-taking, such as board games, card games, or outdoor activities. Emphasize encouraging and celebrating each other's successes.

Nature Explorer
Goal: To enhance observation skills and appreciation for nature.

How to Play: Make a list of items to find create outdoors (e.g., a red leaf, a flat rock). Work together to find and collect each item while talking and discussing with children.

Problem-Solving Challenges
Goal: Develop critical thinking and conflict resolution skills.

How to Play: Set up challenges or puzzles that require teamwork, such as building a bridge with limited materials or finding a way out of a pretend "tangle."

Teaching Tips for Fun Games to Reinforce Social and Emotional Learning Appropriate for Children 2 to 6 Years Old with ADHD
- Short, Varied Activities: Keep activities short and switch between tasks to maintain engagement.

- Clear Instructions: Provide clear, step-by-step instructions and model the activity before you begin.

- Movement Breaks: Consider movement breaks to release excess energy and refocus.

- Positive Reinforcement: Praise and encourage effort and participation.

By integrating these fun games and daily tasks into interactions at home and with peers, you can effectively teach and reinforce social and emotional learning skills in a playful and engaging way, which is beneficial for normal and ADHD children alike.

2. Fun Games to Teach and Strengthen Social-Emotional Learning at School (Kindergarten, Preschool)

Here are some fun games and simple daily tasks that can help teach and strengthen children's social-emotional learning skills, especially in the school setting:

At School
Boys' Classroom
Emotion Detective
Objective: To recognize and understand emotions in oneself and others.

How to Play: Use flashcards or pictures of facial expressions that show different emotions (happy, sad, angry, etc.). Ask students to identify their emotions and discuss what might be causing them to feel that way.

Team Building Activities
Objective: To promote cooperation and teamwork.

Example:
Spaghetti Tower: Give boys materials or food (e.g., Lego, spaghetti) to build the tallest tower together.

Obstacle Course: Set up an indoor obstacle course and challenge teams and encourage communication and problem-solving.

Sharing Circle
Goal: Encourage communication and listening skills.

How to Play: Set aside a specific time each day when the boys can sit in a circle and take turns sharing something about themselves or their feelings. Use a "talking stick or object" to facilitate turn-taking and respectful listening. Only the person holding the speaker's stick (such as a stick or crayon) or object (such as a Lego piece) is allowed to speak. In this game, everyone gets a chance to express themselves without interruption. While someone else is speaking, others are expected to listen attentively without interrupting or making side comments. This practice reinforces active listening and shows respect for the speaker.

Role-Play Scenarios
Goal: Practice empathy and conflict resolution.

Example:
Conflict Resolution: Act out stories and role-play scenarios in which boys encounter conflict (e.g., sharing toys, resolving disagreements).

Helping others: Create role-play situations in which students can help a friend who is upset or in need of support.

Mindfulness Activities
Goal: Promote self-awareness and calm.

Example:
Conscious Breathing: Have boys practice simple inhale-exhale breathing exercises or guide them through guided imagery to help them relax and focus. Guided imagery is a relaxation technique that involves using your imagination to create calming mental images. This could be a peaceful beach or a cool, shady spot in the woods. Use your senses (such as sight, sound, touch, smell) and your imagination. For example, imagine waves gently lapping on the shore or light shining through the leaves of trees.

When children imagine themselves in a peaceful or positive scenario, their bodies and minds begin to relax, which often leads to reduced muscle tension, slower breathing, and an overall sense of calm and increased self-awareness.

Nature Walks: Take short walks outside where boys can observe nature and think about their surroundings.

At School (Kindergarten, Preschool)
Girls' Classroom
Feelings Notebook
Goal: Encourage self-reflection and emotional awareness.

How to Play: Provide girls with notebooks or journals where they can write or draw their feelings each day. Encourage them to share their thoughts in group discussions.

Shared Art Projects
Goal: Foster creativity and teamwork.

Example:
Group Mural Painting: On work together on a large mural or collage that represents the classroom or a topic related to their learning.

Storybook Illustration: Create images for a story they read together, focusing on expressing feelings through art.

Empathy Games
Goal: Practice understanding other people's perspectives.

Example:
Understanding other People's Perspectives, Perspective-Taking: Pair girls together and ask them to talk about how they feel in pairs in different situations presented to them.

Role- Switching: Ask girls to switch roles in a conflict scenario to better understand each other's feelings and perspectives.

Gratitude Circle
Goal: Promote gratitude and positive thinking.

How to Play: Sit in a circle and take turns sharing something they are grateful for that day. Discuss why those things are important and how they feel.

Feeling Sorting Activities
Goal: Categorize and understand different feelings.

Example:
Emotion Cards: Sort emotion cards into categories such as "happy," "sad," or "angry." Discuss what each emotion feels like and when they might experience it.

Teaching Tips for Fun Games to Reinforce Social-Emotional Learning for Children Aged 2 to 6 Years with ADHD
  - Engaging Activities: To maintain attention, choose activities that are interactive, hands-on, and varied.

  - Structured Routines: Establish clear routines and expectations to provide consistency and reduce children's anxiety.

  - Movement Breaks: Provide short movement breaks between activities to release children's energy and refocus attention.

  - Positive Reinforcement: Praise and encourage children for their participation and effort in social-emotional learning activities.

By incorporating these fun games and daily tasks into boys' and girls' classrooms, teachers and educators can effectively teach and reinforce social-emotional learning skills in a supportive and engaging way that benefits all students, including children with ADHD.

In summary, fun games are effective in teaching and reinforcing young children's social-emotional learning at home and at school because they engage children in practice, promote skill development through play, support emotion regulation, build better relationships, provide practical application of skills, and foster a positive learning environment. By integrating games into social-emotional learning instruction, teachers, educators, and parents can effectively nurture children's social and emotional development and prepare them for lifelong academic success.

CHAPTER 10: THE ROLE OF MUSIC IN TEACHING AND ENHANCING SOCIAL-EMOTIONAL LEARNING

1- In the Normal Child Development, What Is the Level of Understanding of Listening to Music or Learning to Play Music in Children Aged 2 to 6 Years?

2- How Does Music Affect the Social and Emotional Development of Children Aged 2 to 6 Years?

3- Gender Considerations for Girls and Boys in Learning Music

4- Sample Participatory Music Making Activity for Children Aged 2 to 6 Years

5- Challenges of Participating in Music Classes for Children Aged 2 to 6 with ADHD

6- Ways to Encourage Children to Learn Music and Play an Instrument

1- In the Normal Growth and Development of Children, What Is the Level of Understanding of Listening to Music or Learning to Play Music in Children Aged 2 to 6 Years?

In the normal child development, children's level of understanding gradually changes. In general, children between the ages of 2 and 6 often begin to recognize and respond to familiar sounds, enjoy simple melodies and rhythms, and begin to identify different sounds. Gradually, they become interested in and prefer certain types of music, can recognize different happy or sad rhythms, and begin to sing and dance along to happy songs.

They can gradually follow more complex rhythms and melodies, and begin to understand and classify different types of sounds and genres of music.

Understanding and Learning Music in Children between the Ages of 2 and 6 Years

In 2-Year-Olds
Listening to Music: Enjoy simple songs and nursery rhymes. They may begin to recognize and respond to familiar songs by clapping, dancing, or humming.

Playing Music: Can experiment with simple musical instruments such as shakers and drums and produce basic rhythms and sounds.

In 3-Year-Olds
Listening to Music: Show a greater interest in different types of music and can memorize and sing parts of familiar songs. They often enjoy moving and dancing to music.

Playing Music: Can use simpler instruments purposefully, such as beating rhythms on drums or playing the xylophone. They are beginning to develop a sense of rhythm and time.

In 4-Year-Olds
Listening to Music: Able to recognize and differentiate between different genres and rhythms of music. They can sing whole songs and begin to understand lyrics.

Playing Music: Begin to imitate melodies and rhythms they hear. They can follow basic patterns and begin to play simple songs on instruments such as keyboards or recorders.

In 5-Year-Olds

Listening to Music: Develop a deeper understanding of music and can express preferences for specific songs or genres. They understand the themes of songs and can discuss them.

Playing Music: Demonstrate better coordination and can play simple melodies on instruments. They may begin lessons in more structured music activities, such as learning basic notes on the piano.

In 6-Year-Olds

Listening to Music: Have a more accurate musical ear, recognize different instruments and musical elements in songs. They can follow along with more complex lyrics and rhythms.

Playing Music: Able to learn to read simple musical notes and play short pieces on instruments such as the piano or violin. They can participate in group music activities and demonstrate better timing and cooperation.

This development highlights the growing understanding and ability to listen to and play music as children develop from ages 2 to 6, laying the foundation for a lifelong appreciation and potential mastery of music.

2- How Does Music Affect Social-Emotional Development?

The role of music in the social-emotional development of normal 2- to 6-year-old children:

Music plays an important role in the social-emotional development of young children by increasing their ability to understand and express emotions, build social connections, and develop a sense of identity. Music plays a role in a variety of social-emotional skills, including:

- Emotional Self-Awareness and Expression: Music provides a way for children to express their feelings. It allows them to express their feelings and experiences nonverbally. Singing, playing an instrument, or nonverbal body movements with music allow them to express feelings that they may not yet have specific words to express. Activities such as improvising music or creating their own songs can encourage children to express themselves and their self-awareness.

- Communication Skills Development: Music activities often involve verbal interactions that help children better understand and learn to express themselves and others.

- Emotional Understanding: Listening to different types of music can help children recognize and understand different emotions. Songs with different tempos and moods teach children to recognize how music makes them feel happy, calm, and enhance their emotional literacy.

- Social Skills: Music activities often involve group participation, which provides opportunities for children to develop social skills such as cooperation, communication, and empathy through group activities. Singing, dancing, or playing instruments together can foster a sense of community and teamwork.

- Emotional Self-Regulation: Children's engagement with music can help them develop self-regulation skills. Activities such as clapping to the beat or following and repeating the rhythm of music require attention and control, which is important for controlling and managing their emotions and behavior.

- Cultural Awareness: Music exposes children to different cultures and traditions. It fosters attention and respect for cultural diversity and acceptance of differences in the attitudes of others. Learning songs in different contexts helps children understand and care about cultural differences.

- Cognitive Development: Music activities involve introducing and teaching patterns, sequences, and rhythms that enhance important cognitive skills such as memory, attention, and problem-solving. These cognitive skills are closely linked to children's social-emotional development.

- Boosting Self-Confidence: Successful participation in music activities can increase children's self-confidence and self-esteem. Performing music, even in a small group, in front of others, even in a simple way, helps children feel and develop a sense of accomplishment and pride.

Incorporating music into young children's daily routines provides a holistic approach to their social-emotional development and makes learning enjoyable and effective.

Of course, the question may arise: what does "the effect of a holistic approach to music" mean?

In fact, when we say that music provides a holistic approach to the social-emotional development of young children, we mean that music supports multiple aspects of a child's development simultaneously. Rather than focusing on one developmental area, music helps develop emotional, social, cognitive, and cultural skills all at once. This all-round development greatly helps children develop in a holistic way, strengthening and enhancing their overall well-being and their ability to interact effectively with the world around them throughout their lives from different perspectives.

The Role of Music in Social-Emotional Learning in Children 2 to 6 Years Old with a Diagnosis of ADHD

Music has a positive role in the social-emotional learning of both 2- to 6-year-olds with and without ADHD, but the effects of music may be more pronounced in 2- to 6-year-olds with ADHD due to the unique challenges they face in learning.

For 2- to 6-year-olds with ADHD, music can be beneficial in several ways:

- Motivation: Music can be a motivating factor. Hyperactive children may be more willing and motivated to participate in activities that incorporate live music and help them collaborate, empathize, and communicate with their peers in fun and engaging ways. This leads to greater motivation to participate in learning activities and strengthens their social-emotional skills.

- Improved Focus and Attention: The rhythmic and melodic elements of music can help these children improve their focus and maintain their attention better. Playing music or participating in various musical activities can increase their ability to focus.

- Strengthen Organizational Skills: Maintaining structure and following instructions is often difficult for children with ADHD due to attention deficits, poor concentration, and distractions. Music can provide a structured framework that can help children with ADHD develop their organizational skills by strengthening their attention and focus. For example, learning to play a song involves following a sequence of notes, which can become a habit of better organization.

- Encourage Physical Activity: Music can be a fun way for children with ADHD to get physical activity, which is essential for managing their energy levels and improving their overall well-being.

- Enhance Emotional Expression: Music provides an outlet for these children to express their feelings in a healthy way. Music can help them identify and manage their emotions through activities such as singing or playing an instrument.

- Support Social Skills: Group music activities can help hyperactive children develop social skills such as taking turns, listening, and cooperating with others.

- Controlling Impulsivity: Listening to or playing calming music can have a calming effect and help reduce hyperactivity and impulsivity. On the other hand, musical activities that require structured cues and rhythms can help children practice timing and control. Structured music requires children to wait for the right moment to play an instrument or sing. This waiting practice can help them control and regulate their impulsivity by fostering patience and self-regulation.

Incorporating music into social-emotional learning activities can provide enjoyable and effective opportunities to practice and reinforce various social-emotional learning skills and offer a holistic approach to the development and well-being of normal and hyperactive preschoolers.

- Turn-Taking: Musical games often involve turn-taking, which can help hyperactive children to wait. and learn the social skill of waiting for their turn. This activity helps build relationships by fostering cooperative play.

- Routine and Structure: Incorporating music into daily routines can create a sense of order and predictability. Routine songs can help hyperactive children feel more secure and understand what is likely to happen. Familiar songs and rhythms can create a stable environment for learning.

- Cultural Awareness and Empathy: Through music from different cultures, hyperactive children can learn about the diversity and differences of others and develop empathy. This activity expands their understanding of different perspectives and makes it easier and more accepting of others.

- Emotional Self-Regulation: Music can help hyperactive children learn coping strategies to manage stress and emotions. For example, soothing music can teach them techniques to soothe themselves when they are upset.

- Building Self-Esteem: Participating in music activities can increase self-confidence. Participation in musical activities, whether individually or in groups, helps children with ADHD experience a sense of achievement and pride in their abilities.

- Language Development: Music strengthens language skills through poetry and singing and helps children with ADHD communicate and grow their vocabulary. This activity is essential for developing the verbal skills needed in their social interactions.

- Creativity and Imagination: Music encourages creative thinking and imagination in children with ADHD. Children learn to think outside the box, which can increase their problem-solving skills and emotional understanding.

- Group Cohesion and a Sense of Social Belonging: Musical activities strengthen group cohesion and bonds between peers and promote a sense of social belonging in most of them. Children learn to support each other and contribute to society in positive ways.

3- Gender Considerations for Girls and Boys in Learning Music

While music can be beneficial for all children aged 2 to 6, it is essential to recognize and celebrate individual differences, including interests and learning styles. Girls and boys can benefit equally from music activities, although they may differ somewhat in their priorities and participation. Encouraging positive group activities can promote teamwork and respect for boundaries between girls and boys in communication and different perspectives.

When discussing gender considerations in the context of using music to teach preschoolers social-emotional skills, it is helpful to recognize the subtle differences in how boys and girls interact with music and express emotions. Here are some key points about gender considerations:

1. Cultural Influences and Stereotypes
Gender Norms: Traditional cultural norms can influence the "self-expression" of boys and girls. For example, boys may be encouraged to be more serious, such as hearing from childhood, "A man doesn't cry!", while girls may be encouraged to express their feelings openly, such as "Cry easy!" These norms can affect their comfort level in participating in musical activities.

Stereotypes in Music Preferences: Boys and girls may gravitate toward different types of music based on social preferences. Educators should be aware of these stereotypes and offer a variety of musical genres to appeal to all children.

2. Participation and Fun

Different Interests: Boys and girls may show different interests in music-related activities. While some boys may enjoy rhythmic drumming, girls may prefer singing or dancing. Providing a diverse range of options can ensure that all children feel involved and entertained.

Group Dynamics: Boys and girls may have different ways of interacting with each other. Musical activities can promote collaborative play and support the development of positive relationships between the sexes.

3. Encouraged Expression

Emotional Expression: Boys may need more encouragement to express emotions through music, as they may feel pressure from society to conform to serious behaviors. Providing safe spaces for all children to express their emotions through music can help break down barriers to emotional expression.

Role Models: Introducing and using diverse (male and female) music makers, performers, and educators as role models can encourage both boys and girls to learn to express their feelings more freely, and show them that emotional expression through music is possible for everyone.

4. Building Empathy and Acceptance

Understanding Differences: Music can serve as a tool to help children understand and appreciate differences between genders. Activities that involve making music together can foster respect and empathy for each other and the opposite sex.

Listening to and discussing music can help children become aware of their own and others' feelings, leading to greater empathy and improved relationships. For example, songs about friendship can spark discussions about caring for friends and being sensitive to the feelings of others.

4- Sample Participatory Music Making Activity for Young Children

An example of an activity that involves participatory music making for young children is "Music Story Circle." This group work activity encourages creativity and emotional expression while allowing children to engage with music in a fun and interactive way.

Purpose of the Music Story Circle Activity

To promote collaboration, communication skills, and emotional expression through music and storytelling.

Materials Needed

- Simple musical instruments such as percussion instruments (e.g., drums, bells, cymbals).

- Or simple, accessible materials such as pots, pans, and wooden spoons for drumming that can spark creativity in making music.

- A storybook with a clear narrative (preferably with pictures of different emotions).

- A space for children to sit in a circle.

Activity Steps

Gather the Children Together: Have the children sit in a circle, making sure everyone can see each other and feel included.

Story Introduction: Read a short, engaging storybook aloud to the children. Pause at key moments to talk about the characters' feelings and actions (e.g., happy, sad, excited).

Divide the Instruments: Give each child different musical instruments. Make sure they are familiar with how to play them. For example, the sound of beats on drums can represent a heartbeat, and the sound of bells can represent excitement.

Make Music Together

After reading the story, invite the children to make music that reflects the mood of the different sections. For example, children could play happy rhythms or melodies while reading a section that describes a character feeling happy.

When the story reaches a more challenging moment (for example, a character feeling sad), encourage slower, quieter sounds of instruments.

Let children take turns leading the music for different parts of the story, this practice encourages them to share their ideas and listen to each other more easily.

Reflect and Discuss: After finishing the storytelling with music, talk to the children about how they felt during specific parts of the story and the music they made. Questions such as:

"How did the happy music make you feel?"
"What sound did you choose for the sad part and why?"

Repetition and Development: Depending on the children's interests, you can repeat the activity with different stories and encourage them to choose the instruments and sounds that they feel best represent each part of the story.

Benefits of the Musical Story Circle Activity
Collaboration: Children need to listen to each other and work together to create a coherent musical experience.

Emotional Development: This activity provides opportunities for emotional exploration and helps children identify, express, and understand their feelings.

Creativity: Children can express their feelings artistically and practice, experiment, and experiment with sounds, fostering creativity in a supportive environment together.

This "Music Story Circle" not only engages children in collaborative music making, but also integrates storytelling with music to enhance their social and emotional learning experiences.

Diverse Perspectives: Combining music from different cultures and perspectives can help all children recognize the value of different and diverse expressions and experiences.

5. Promoting Leadership Skills
Encourage All Children: Providing opportunities for boys and girls to take turns leading musical activities can help develop leadership skills and increase confidence in all students.

Challenging Stereotypes: Allowing boys and girls to participate in a wide range of musical activities (e.g., playing an instrument, singing, dancing) helps challenge gender stereotypes and promotes equality in participation.

6. Diverse Learning Styles
Diverse Learning Preferences: Recognizing that boys and girls may have different learning styles can help educators design music-based activities to

meet diverse needs. For example, some children may prefer more active and kinetic interactions (such as boys or hyperactive children), while others may thrive in quieter environments.

Strategies for Inclusive Music Activities

Variety of Options: Offer a wide range of musical activities (singing, playing instruments, moving) to suit different interests.

Encourage Collaboration between Boys and Girls: Design activities that require boys and girls to work together and that foster teamwork and cooperation.

Celebrate All Contributions: Acknowledge, encourage, and reinforce the contributions of all children, regardless of gender, because the opinions of all boys and girls are important, respected, and valued.

By considering gender considerations for girls and boys in music learning and creating an inclusive environment, educators can increase the effectiveness of music as a tool for teaching social and emotional learning to all children and ensure that all children (regardless of gender) feel valued, included, and empowered in their social and emotional development.

Practical Strategies for Implementation

Incorporate Movement into Your Workouts: Use songs that encourage dancing or movement, which can help channel energy constructively, especially for children with ADHD.

Use Interactive Songs: Choose songs that require participation and encourage social interaction.

Create Playlists of Emotion-Focused Songs: Choose songs that resonate with different emotions and allow children to explore and identify different emotions.

Encourage Playing an Instrument: Introduce simple instruments that children ages 2 to 6 can play. Music lessons can help improve cognitive abilities such as memory, language, and spatial reasoning. By learning to play an instrument, children use both sides of the brain, which can help improve their brain function in learning.

Young children with ADHD often grow up with difficulty learning, focusing, and sticking to difficult tasks. This often leads to low self-esteem. Studies show that when hyperactive children learn a musical instrument, attention, concentration, impulse control, social functioning, self-esteem, self-expression, motivation, and memory improve. For hyperactive children who prefer not to sit still, instruments that allow them to stand and move while playing (such as guitar, drums, percussion instruments) are more suitable.

5- Challenges of Attending Music Classes for Normal and ADHD Children Aged 2 to 6 Years

Encouraging children aged 2 to 6, especially those with ADHD, to participate in music or instrumental lessons can present several challenges for parents and teachers. Here are some of the main issues:

- Attention Span: Normal children generally have a more sustained attention span, allowing them to participate in music lessons, follow instructions, and practice consistently. ADHD children often experience challenges with sustained attention, which can make it difficult to focus on lessons or practice. This can lead to shorter periods of successful engagement during music activities. This problem is challenging and can be frustrating for both the child and the teacher if left untreated.

- Impulsivity: Normal children are more likely to wait their turn and follow the group's lead during music lessons. Hyperactive children may struggle with impulsive actions, which can lead to interruptions or difficulty waiting their turn to play an instrument or responding in group settings (such as interrupting, playing an instrument inappropriately). This can be disruptive in a group setting and make it more difficult for them to enjoy the class.

- Difficulty Following Directions: In music classes, where directions may be crucial for learning new concepts or pieces, following directions can be a challenge for children aged 2 to 6, which can hinder their progress and confidence. Following directions is more challenging and difficult for hyperactive children aged 2 to 6. Hyperactivity can affect a child's ability to listen and follow multi-step instructions.

- Social Interactions: Participation in group music classes often requires social skills such as sharing attention, waiting for turns, and peer collaboration is needed. ADHD children may have more difficulty in these areas, which can affect their enjoyment and willingness to participate.

- Frustration and Anxiety: If children find music lessons challenging, they may become frustrated or anxious. The pressure to perform or learn can be overwhelming, especially for ADHD children who are often struggling to keep up with their peers.

- Consistency and Routine: If music classes do not provide consistent routines or clear expectations, children may have more difficulty adjusting and participating effectively. This is especially true for ADHD children who often need to thrive in structured environments.

- Parental and Teacher Support: Parents and teachers may need to invest additional time and energy in creating supportive environments for their young children, especially for ADHD children who have unique needs. This can require additional training, support resources, and patience, which can be challenging in busy or less supportive environments.

- Balancing Interests: Children aged 2 to 6, especially those with ADHD, may have a variety of interests that change frequently. They may quickly switch to other interests, which can lead to inconsistencies in their learning. Without balancing interests, it can be very challenging and often difficult for them to sustain sustained engagement in an activity (such as music).

Despite these challenges, with the right strategies, understanding, and support, many children, including those with ADHD, can enjoy and benefit from music education. Recognizing these challenges can help parents and teachers adjust their approaches to fostering positive music learning experiences and ways to encourage children to learn and play an instrument.

6- Ways to Encourage Children to Learn and Play an Instrument in 2 to 6 Years Old Children

Encouraging children aged 2 to 6, especially those with ADHD, to take music lessons or play an instrument can be challenging. Here are some strategies parents and teachers can use to create a positive music experience:

1. Create a Positive Environment
Comfortable Environment: Make sure the environment is quiet and free of distractions. A clean and organized space can help children focus better.

Positive Reinforcement: Celebrate and praise their small musical achievements, whether it's playing a note or participating in a class. Use praise to boost their confidence.

2. Choose the Right Instrument
Age-Appropriate Options: Choose instruments that are appropriate for young children; instruments that are easy to handle can increase engagement.

Hands-on Experience: Let children try out different instruments to find the one they really enjoy. They are more likely to engage and learn better with something they love.

3. Incorporate Movement into Your Music Activities

Interactive Activities: Incorporate movement and dancing into music activities. This can help hyperactive children release and channel their energy in an appropriate way while enjoying learning music.

Musical Games: Use games that involve rhythm or movement to music. Activities such as "freeze dancing" (children move with the music and stop when the music stops) can be fun and help children self-regulate.

4. Keep Learning Sessions Short and Engaging

Short-Term Lessons: Keep music sessions engaging and short. To maintain focus, keep music sessions short and dynamic, about 10 to 15 minutes. Gradually increase the duration as attention spans improve.

Variety: Introduce a variety of musical styles and activities in each session to keep them interested.

5. Set Up Learning with Routine and Structure

Regular Schedule: Having a regular schedule can help children know what to expect, which can reduce anxiety and improve concentration during music lessons.

Clear Instructions: Use clear, simple instructions and visual aids to help convey what they are expected to do during a music session.

6. Focus on Enjoyment, Not Set the Tone for Perfection

Focus on Fun, Not Formal Classes: Emphasize the joy of learning music rather than achieving perfection. This practice reduces the pressure and stress of formal classes for children and allows for more creative expression and joy.

Encourage Expression: Support children to express their thoughts and feelings through music in their own unique way without fear of making mistakes.

7. Involve Parents in the Music Learning Process

Practice at Home: Encourage parents to practice music at home with children aged 2 to 6. Simple activities, such as singing nursery rhymes or playing simple instruments, can foster children's interest in learning music.

Support Network: Create a channel of communication between parents and teachers to discuss their progress and challenges in learning music and ensure a unified approach to helping them learn.

8. Teach Self-Regulation Skills

Young children, especially those with ADHD, may exhibit greater difficulties in emotional self-regulation, leading to outbursts or challenges when required to adhere to classroom rules, which can negatively impact their learning environment and that of others. Normal young children often demonstrate a stable level of self-control that allows them to more easily follow classroom norms and expectations.

Mindfulness and Breathing: Introduce simple mindfulness or breathing exercises to help children learn to calm themselves before or during music class.

Emotional Exploration: Encourage children to express their feelings about music activities and teach them to recognize and say when they are feeling tired.

9. Use Educational Technology

Music Apps: Combine music apps and digital tools to enhance learning. Many children respond well to technology-based activities (e.g., tablets, computers).

Visual Supports: Use diagrams or visual programs to help children understand the flow of music class, including transitions between activities.

10. Create Collaborative Learning

Interaction with Peers: Create opportunities for group music activities, allowing children to learn from each other while developing social skills.

Paired Learning: Pair 2- to 6-year-olds with ADHD with peers who can model appropriate behavior and focus in the classroom.

By focusing on these strategies, parents and teachers can help both normal and hyperactive 2- to 6-year-olds engage with music in an enjoyable and productive way, fostering their love of music and enhancing their overall growth in learning, academic achievement, and life skill competence.

In short, while both normal and ADHD children can learn music, and teaching approaches may vary significantly based on their level of attention, impulsivity, and social interaction. ADHD children may also have unique strengths or talents. Particularly in creativity, emotional expression, and potentially other areas related to music, children with ADHD may have greater emotional responsiveness, which can lead to more passionate and expressive musical performances. This talent allows them to express emotions through music in ways that resonate deeply with others and to better connect with others. While most children diagnosed with ADHD have difficulty paying attention, some ADHD children may experience periods of hyper-focus or "immersion." If they find an instrument or activity that captures their interest, they may become intensely focused on a particular activity for long periods of time.

This distinction can lead to the development of significant skills in their musical learning. Successful music education for children with ADHD often involves tailored strategies (such as providing engaging and varied lessons, incorporating movement, and fostering a flexible learning environment) that utilize their strengths as well as their challenges.

By weaving music into the fabric of social-emotional learning instruction, appropriate educational programs for children aged 2 to 6 can often create rich, engaging, and unique experiences for them that enhance emotional and social development for all children, regardless of their individual challenges, throughout their lives from childhood to adulthood.

CHAPTER 11: THE ROLE OF TIME MANAGEMENT IN SOCIAL-EMOTIONAL LEARNING

1- THE RELATIONSHIP OF TIME MANAGEMENT TO CHILDREN'S SOCIAL-EMOTIONAL LEARNING

2- TEACHING TIME MANAGEMENT STRATEGIES TO NORMAL YOUNG CHILDREN

3- ADAPTING TIME MANAGEMENT TEACHING STRATEGIES FOR CHILDREN AGED 2 TO 6 YEARS WITH ADHD

Time management refers to the ability to plan and control how you spend your time each day to achieve your goals. This includes organizing tasks, setting priorities, and allocating the right amount of time to achieve desired outcomes. For children aged 2 to 6, time management involves learning how to transition between activities, understanding the concept of time, and developing routines that help them manage their daily responsibilities and activities. Children usually begin to understand the concept of time around age 4 or 5, although some may develop this understanding earlier or later. At this age, they can understand the difference between short and long periods of time and can match time words like "morning," "afternoon," and "evening" to the appropriate parts of the day. They can also understand the concept of time in relation to daily routines, such as knowing when it is time for breakfast or bedtime. Use games and songs to make learning about time more engaging. For example, you can sing songs that include lyrics about time.

1- The Relationship of Time Management to Social and Emotional Learning in Children 2 to 6 Years Old

Time management is closely related to several components of social and emotional learning in children 2 to 6 years old, in particular:

- Self-Management: Self-management is perhaps the most direct link, involving the ability to regulate emotions, thoughts, and behaviors in different situations. Effective time recognition and management requires skills such as setting goals, planning ahead, prioritizing tasks, and managing stress. Children 2 to 6 years old learn to allocate their time effectively to achieve their goals, whether in the academic field, in extracurricular activities, or in personal responsibilities.

- Social Skills: Knowing how to recognize and manage time allows children 2 to 6 years old to participate in group activities such as sports and games, where time management is important, leading to strengthening their social skills.

- Independence: Time management encourages independence. As children aged 2 to 6 learn to tell the time, they become more independent and can manage their own time.

- Goal Setting: Time management is an essential aspect of setting and achieving personal goals. Children who practice effective time management are able to break down larger tasks into manageable chunks, prioritize, categorize important tasks, and track their progress toward achieving those goals.

- Decision Making: Time management also plays a role in the decision-making process. Children need to evaluate how they use their time to balance different activities and responsibilities, which can include school, friendships, and leisure time. This involves weighing the pros and cons of dedicating their time to different activities and consciously choosing each activity accordingly.

- Stress Management: Effective time management can reduce stress and anxiety. Children who struggle with managing their time may have difficulty managing the start and end of tasks, while those who employ good time management strategies can manage their workload more effectively, leading to a sense of calm and control over their lives.

- Responsibility: Understanding time is an important aspect of personal responsibility. As children learn to tell time, they learn to take greater responsibility for their actions and how they use their time. Developing time management skills fosters a sense of responsibility in children. When they learn to manage their time, they also learn to take responsibility for their commitments and understand the impact of their choices on their own and others' success.

- Punctuality: Understanding time management helps children develop a sense of responsibility and punctuality. They will learn to be on time for school, appointments, and other activities.

- Cognitive Development: Recognizing and managing time fosters children's cognitive development. The ability to understand and manage time is a cognitive skill and helps children understand the concept of the past, present, and future. It is used for planning and other basic life skills in social-emotional learning.

- Planning and Organizing: Teaching time management helps children understand how to plan and organize their day. They will learn to manage their time more effectively and be able to prioritize tasks.

- Academic Progress: Recognizing and managing time supports academic progress. Understanding, telling, and managing time is a fundamental math skill. Timing is important for understanding more complex learning concepts such as measuring and timing.

2- Teaching Time Management Strategies to Normal Children 2 to 6 Years Old

Strategies for Parents at Home
Create a Routine

Create a consistent daily schedule for activities such as mealtimes, playtime, and bedtime. Visual schedules with pictures can be especially helpful for children aged 2 to 6 to help them understand what comes next.

Use Visual Timers

Use visual timers (such as an hourglass or digital timer) to give children a tangible sense of how much time is left for an activity (such as bedtime). This helps them understand the concept of time passing.

Break Tasks into Smaller Steps

For larger tasks (such as cleaning up toys), break them down into smaller, more manageable steps. This makes it easier for children to engage without feeling overwhelmed.

Use Timed Activities

Introduce games or activities that require them to complete tasks within a set amount of time (for example, "Let's see how many blocks you can stack in 2 minutes"). This helps them get things done within a "time frame."

Model Time Management

Demonstrate time management behaviors in your daily activities, such as setting specific times for different tasks and explaining your thought process. (Such as, since my free time is every afternoon and evening, I can schedule cooking and shopping. Cooking time afternoons and shopping time evenings.)

Positive Reinforcement

Praise and reward children when they follow a routine or manage their time well. This encourages them to repeat positive behaviors.

Incorporate Transition Time

Provide cues, clues, or warnings before moving from one activity to another to help children adjust. For example, give a 5-minute warning before lunchtime.

Five minutes before the end of playtime and the start of lunchtime, ring a bell or music to signal the children that it is time to switch activities from play to lunch so that they are ready to move to the lunch table.

Time Management Training Strategies for Teachers at School (Kindergarten, Preschool)

Classroom Routines
Create clear, consistent routines for daily classroom activities. Use visual aids such as charts to help children understand the sequence of events throughout the day.

Structured Activity Time
Implement structured time for activities with clear start and end signals (such as a bell or music). This helps children learn to focus and complete the task within a specific time frame. The sound of the bell means that the time for the assigned task is over. For example, you can tell them that whenever you hear the "bell ring," it means "five minutes" are up.

Attractive Visual Timers
Use attractive, colorful visual timers or countdown clocks during activities. This will keep children's attention and at the same time, there should be a clear indication of the time remaining.

Transitional Activities
Incorporate short-term transitional activities (such as songs or movements) with each activity to signal the end of one activity and the beginning of another, helping children adapt to the changes. For example, children should hear a "bell" to signal the end of one activity or game, such as play dough, and the start and transition to the next activity or game, such as painting.

Or, for example, give a 5-minute warning before the painting bell starts.
Five minutes before the end of recess and the start of the drawing bell, announce to the children that it is time to switch activities from recess to drawing with a bell or red light so that the child is ready to move on to the next class.

Goal-Setting Activities
Teach children to set simple and achievable goals for tasks such as completing a puzzle or drawing a picture. Talk and discuss with the children about the actions they can take to achieve that goal within a specific time frame.

For example, to teach them how to choose the right puzzle, you can tell them that completing a "small puzzle" like eating a "small cake" is finished faster, meaning it takes "less time", so a "large puzzle" is not suitable.

Games that Promote Time Management

Include fun games that involve time challenges, such as "coloring contest" activities. This can help children learn time awareness better in a fun context.

Modeling and Role-Playing

Draw different scenarios that develop time management skills model through play and role-playing (such as when to start getting ready for home or how to plan a short activity).

3- Adapting Time Management Teaching Strategies for Children Aged 2 to 6 Years with an ADHD Diagnosis

When teaching time management to children aged 2 to 6 with ADHD, pay attention to their learning weaknesses and challenges. Adapt time management strategies for normal children to meet their unique needs.

For example, provide opportunities for movement or rest to help them maintain focus.

ADHD children often experience a unique perception of time, which can lead to challenges with time management and emotion regulation. Their difficulties with time perception can be attributed to several factors:

Present-Moment Focus

Children with HD may focus primarily on the present moment, and this preoccupation with the present can often make it difficult for them to anticipate the importance of future tasks. This problem can lead to a misperception of how much time they actually have for a given task.

Working Memory Challenges

ADHD can affect working memory, which is the ability to hold and manipulate information for short periods of time. This effect can lead to problems remembering tasks or time frames.

Problem with Delay Sensitivity

Many children with ADHD have difficulty with waiting and can feel that time is getting longer when they are anticipating something (such as waiting for a favorite activity). This problem can cause them to often feel restless, anxious, or angry.

Task Switching

When children with ADHD are asked to change tasks or complete activities within a given time frame, they may feel overwhelmed, leading to a very short perception of time. The pressure to quickly change focus can lead to increased anger or anxiety and frustration.

Impulsive Emotional Responses

Emotion regulation disorders are common in children with ADHD. When faced with time constraints or expectations, they may display impulsive emotional responses, in part because of their strong feelings about time and urgency, with anger or fatigue.

Common Strategies for Parents and Teachers
Use Visual Timers

Visual timers can provide a clear sense of how much time is left for a task. This visual cue can help children with ADHD become aware of time without feeling overwhelmed.

Create Routines

Establish regular routines at home and in the classroom. Predictability can help children with ADHD know what to expect and make it easier for them to plan and manage their time.

Break Tasks into Smaller Steps

If a task seems too overwhelming, break it down into smaller, more manageable chunks. This can reduce feelings of urgency or pressure. and helps children focus on completing one step at a time.

Set Clear Expectations and Reminders

Plan clearly what is expected in the lesson and provide gentle reminders about tasks or assignments. Giving advance notice can reduce anxiety related to time constraints in children.

Include Transition Time

Include adequate transition time between activities in the lesson. For example, give a warning a few minutes before moving on to a new task to prepare them mentally.

Include Engaging Activities

Use engaging, hands-on activities in the lesson that keep children interested and focused. These can provide positive experiences over time and help them feel more in control.

Teach Coping Strategies

Teach children strategies to cope with feelings of boredom or frustration when waiting. Deep breathing, counting down, etc. can often help.

Time Management Praise and Reward

Provide positive verbal or nonverbal reinforcement when children successfully complete tasks on time. Recognizing their efforts and achievements can help reinforce their learning of time management skills.

Be Patient and Understanding

Understand that time management issues are part of the challenges of both normal and hyperactive young children. Being empathetic and patient can help children feel supported rather than criticized as they struggle to manage their time effectively.

Conclusion

Children with ADHD may experience unique challenges with time management and perception. By implementing supportive strategies at home and in the classroom, parents and teachers can help these children better understand and manage their sense of time and reduce frustration, impatience, and impulsive emotional responses. Consistency, visual aids, and patience are key elements in supporting children's progress in learning time management.

Teaching time management to children aged 2 to 6 involves creating supportive environments that reinforce the understanding of routine, time concepts, and task organization. By providing clear structures at home and in the classroom, and using interactive methods, parents and teachers can strengthen children's time management skills that will be useful in their social-emotional learning and throughout their lives.

CHAPTER 12: ACCURATELY ASSESSING THE LEVEL OF PROGRESS IN NURTURING AND EMPOWERING SOCIALLY AND EMOTIONALLY OF 2 TO 6 YEARS OLD CHILDREN

1- REVIEWING PROGRESS AND PROVIDING APPROPRIATE FEEDBACK

2- ENCOURAGING CONTINUOUS REFLECTION AND ADAPTATION

3- LOOKING TO THE FUTURE

4- PREPARING FOR THE TRANSITION TO KINDERGARTEN AND BEYOND

1- Accurately Assessing and Evaluating the Progress of Children Aged 2 to 6 Years

Progress monitoring means spending time observing, documenting, and evaluating the growth and development of basic life skills in children aged 2 to 6 over a period of time. This monitoring includes:

- Observation: Regularly watching how children participate in activities, interact with others, and manage their emotions and behaviors.

- Documentation: Keeping records of observations by parents, caregivers, and teachers, such as notes, checklists, and work samples, to track changes and improvements.

- Evaluation: Analyzing documented information to assess a child's progress in various areas of skill development.

- Appropriate Feedback: Sharing this assessment with parents, caregivers, and teachers to provide constructive feedback and set goals for skill development. Constructive and appropriate feedback from parents, caregivers, and teachers means encouraging children's strengths and progress and supporting the child to address weaknesses and make appropriate efforts to achieve the educational goal.

Therefore, examining the development progress of basic life skills in normal and hyperactive children aged 2 to 6 helps educators and parents understand the strengths and weaknesses of the child's social-emotional learning and provide the basis for addressing the problems and weaknesses of children's learning and development. Identify the strengths of development and celebrate their achievements and ultimately guide the child on the path of progress and success.

Accurately Assessing the Level of Progress in Nurturing and Empowering the Social-Emotional Learning of Normal Young Children

- Observation and Documentation: Regularly observe the activities of children aged 2 to 6 in different settings and record their interactions, behaviors, and feelings for documentation. Look for signs of progress in social skills, emotion regulation, for example, in children's cooperative play.

- Anecdotal Records: Written records of teacher observations of children aged 2 to 6. Collect specific instances when children demonstrate progress in social and emotional learning to assess children's progress. (For example, note moments when children successfully resolve a conflict or show empathy for their peers.)

- Assessment Tools: Use age-appropriate assessment tools and checklists to assess the social-emotional learning skills of children aged 2 to 6. These tools can help identify strengths and areas that need additional support. (Such as, the Social-Emotional Questionnaire, 2nd Edition (ASQ:SE-2). This questionnaire can help identify your child's strengths and weaknesses in social-emotional learning.)

- Portfolio: Create a folder of homework and work completed by children aged 2 to 6, photos, and records of their participation in activities.

- Feedback and Reflection: Based on the results of the assessment and evaluation, provide regular feedback to children aged 2 to 6, celebrate their achievements, and gently guide them towards areas of improvement if they are weak in some areas.

Accurately Assessing and Evaluating the Level of Progress in Nurturing and Empowering the Social-Emotional Learning of Children with ADHD

- Attention and Focus: Regularly observe children 2 to 6 years old with a diagnosis of ADHD in a variety of settings. Track progress in maintaining attention throughout activities, following instructions, and completing tasks without long breaks or frequent redirection.

- Impulse Control: Observe progress in controlling impulsive behaviors (such as waiting for turns, following rules, and responding appropriately to cues).

- Emotion Regulation: Monitor improvement in skills in managing emotions, such as reducing outbursts and using calming strategies effectively.

- Social Interactions: Observe and monitor progress in the ability to interact positively with peers, engage in cooperative play, and resolve conflicts with guidance.

- Time Management: Observe and monitor improvement in time management. Assess the extent to which children aged 2 to 6 can follow regular routines, use visual schedules, and complete tasks within manageable time frames.

Methods to Accurately Examine and Evaluate the Level of Progress in Fostering and Empowering Social-Emotional Learning of Children with ADHD

- Observation and Anecdotal Records: Regularly record the behaviors and interactions of children aged 2 to 6 years. Observe and record your 6-year-old in different settings and note specific examples of progress.

- Checklists and Rating Scales: Use checklists and rating scales to assess specific skills and behaviors of children aged 2 to 6, providing a clear picture of development over time.

- Portfolios: Collect examples of your 2- to 6-year-old's work, including art projects, writing samples, and photos of activities, in a designated folder.

- Home-School Parent-Teacher Meetings: In regular parent-teacher meetings (classroom and nursery), discuss and discuss observations of the social-emotional learning progress of children aged 2 to 6, share insights, and set goals for further development.

Using these methods, teachers, educators, and parents can effectively reflect on the progress of normal and hyperactive 2- to 6-year-olds, and adequately support them by comprehensively reviewing and assessing the level of progress in learning and developing social-emotional skills of each child, and ensure that they receive the necessary guidance and encouragement they need to progress.

Carefully reviewing and assessing the level of progress of children aged 2 to 6 (reflecting on progress) by celebrating, appreciating, and celebrating each child's achievements, efforts, and growth (however small), often leads to the following results:

- Increased Self-Esteem: Increase the self-esteem and self-confidence of children aged 2 to 6 and encourage them to better tolerate new challenges.

- Motivates Learning: Recognizing progress, motivates children aged 2 to 6 to continue learning and strive for improvement.

- Develops Self-Awareness: Helps children aged 2 to 6 develop a sense of self-awareness, understanding their strengths, weaknesses, and areas for improvement.

- Strengthens Emotional Intelligence: Promotes emotional intelligence by validating children aged 2 to 6's feelings (such as excitement, pride, or disappointment).

- Builds Relationships: Strengthens relationships between parents, caregivers, and teachers with children aged 2 to 6 because it shows that the child's efforts are valued and appreciated.

General Tips for Accurately Assessing the Level of Progress of Children Aged 2 to 6 Years

- Verbal Praise: Acknowledge specific successes and efforts with verbal praise, such as "I'm proud of you for using your words to solve a problem!"

- Visual Reminders: Provide visual reminders, such as charts or pictures, to track progress and celebrate milestones.

- Celebrations: Provide special celebrations or events for children to encourage and praise their achievements or important milestones of progress. (such as a "talent show" or "progress celebration party").

- Open-Ended Conversations: Talk to children about their progress and ask open-ended questions such as "What did you do well today?" or "How do you feel about your success?"

- Progress Notebook: Provide a notebook or folder to document and display children's progress over time and highlight their growth and development.

- Incorporating Technology: Use tools or programs specifically designed to assess children's homework to track progress and create interactive displays of achievements.

- Involve Children in Thinking: Encourage children to reflect on their progress and ask them to identify what they did well and what they could improve.

Remember to assess progress in a way that is valid and meaningful for children aged 2 to 6, and that considers their individual needs, interests, and personality.

Some Tips for Parents and Teachers to Accurately Assess and Evaluate the Level of Progress of Children in Social-Emotional Learning

Parents
- Schedule Regular Discussion Sessions: Set aside time to talk with your child about their feelings, strengths, and challenges.

- Use a Growth Mindset: Focus on children's growth, not just their perfection and success, to assess progress. Appreciate every good effort, no matter how big or insignificant, and celebrate small victories. (Growth Mindset: The belief that a person's abilities are not innate, but can be improved through effort, learning, and perseverance.)

- Think about Children's Feelings: Ask open-ended questions to assess children's progress, such as "How did you feel today?" or "What made you feel upset/sad/happy?"

- Identify Strengths and Weaknesses: Identify your child's strengths and areas for improvement in social-emotional learning skills such as self-awareness, self-regulation, and empathy.

- With Teachers Communicate: Share your observations and concerns with teachers to ensure a cohesive approach to supporting your child's social-emotional learning development.

Teachers
- Use Data-Driven Reflections: Analyze and use data from assessments, tests, and classroom discussions to identify children's strengths and weaknesses in social-emotional learning skills.

- Classroom Observations: Observe students during their activities and interactions with each other to gain insight into their social-emotional behaviors.

- Student Self-Assessments: In simple, understandable language for any 2- to 6-year-old child, encourage students to think about their social-emotional learning skills and set simple, age-appropriate goals to improve their social-emotional learning.

- Home-School Parent-Teacher Meetings: Use home-school meetings as an opportunity to share observations and insights into children's social-emotional learning with parents and set shared goals to support children's social-emotional learning development.

- Interventions and Accommodations: Provide targeted interventions or accommodations to support students who are struggling with specific social-emotional learning skills (such as children diagnosed with ADHD).

By checking and evaluating the level of progress of 2- to 6-year-old children in social-emotional learning, (reflecting on progress), parents and teachers can:

- Identify children's strengths and weaknesses in social-emotional learning skills.

- Develop targeted strategies to improve children's social-emotional learning skills.

- Enhance children's growth mindset and focus on progress.

- Enhance children's communication and collaboration.

- Celebrate children's success and progress.

Remember, assessing children's (2- to 6-year-olds) progress in social-emotional learning is an ongoing process that requires regular communication, data analysis, and collaborative effort between parents, teachers, and children.

2- Encouraging to Check and Evaluate the Progress Level of 2 to 6 Years Old Children and Continuous Adaptation

What does it mean to encourage close monitoring and continuous adaptation in assessing the progress of children aged 2 to 6 in social-emotional learning? In what ways can this be made possible at home and at school?

Encouraging continuous monitoring and continuous adaptation in assessing the progress of children aged 2 to 6 in social-emotional learning means regularly reviewing and adjusting educational strategies, activities, and goals based on development and in line with the needs of the children. This ongoing process often results in effective and responsive support to the appropriate developmental needs of each child aged 2 to 6.

At School (Kindergarten, Preschool)
- Regular Observations: Teachers can routinely observe children regularly during various activities and record their social-emotional behaviors and interactions.

- Flexible Planning: Based on observations, educators can adapt lesson plans and activities to better support each child's development.

- Feedback Sessions: Hold regular meetings with children to discuss their progress, celebrate achievements, and set new goals.

- Professional Collaboration: Teachers can collaborate with colleagues and child specialists to share insights and strategies to support children's social-emotional learning.

- Use Assessment Tools: Implement tools such as the ASQ:SE-2 assessment questionnaire to systematically track the progress of social-emotional behaviors and interactions and identify areas that need attention.

At Home
- Routine Conversations: Parents can talk to their children about feelings, experiences, and daily interactions in a consistent and regular routine.

- Observation and Documentation: Parents can observe and document their children's behavior in different settings and keep a journal to track changes and progress in social-emotional skills.

- Adapt Activities: Based on observations, parents can introduce new activities or modify existing ones to better support their child's social-emotional learning.

- Family Meetings: Regular family discussions can provide a platform for children to express their thoughts and feelings, review and evaluate their behavior, and set goals for improvement.

- Collaborate with Educators: Parents can connect with teachers to better share their insights and work on strategies that support their child's development at home and at school.

By fostering careful monitoring and evaluation of children's progress (reflection on progress) and ongoing adaptation, both at home and at school, young children receive consistent and appropriate support that effectively promotes their social-emotional development.

3- Looking to the Future

Here are some tips for parents and teachers to help children aged 2 to 6 with ADHD be forward-thinking and prepare for future challenges in social-emotional learning:

Parents

- Teach Problem-Solving Skills: Encourage your child to think critically and find solutions to problems they may face in the future.

- Role-Playing Scenarios: Play out different scenarios with your child, such as managing peer pressure or dealing with frustration, to help them prepare for potential future challenges.

- Encourage Goal-Setting: Use simple, understandable language to help your child set realistic goals for their future and develop a plan to achieve them, teaching them to focus on progress rather than perfection.

- Talk about Anxiety and Worries: Talk to your child about their worries and help them learn simple coping strategies, such as slow, deep breathing, to manage their anxiety with practice.

- Foster Resilience: Teach your child that it's okay to make mistakes and that they can always learn from failures.

Teachers

- Teach Time Management Skills: Help students learn to prioritize tasks and manage their time effectively to reduce stress and anxiety.

- Encourage "Self-Advocacy": Teach students to advocate for themselves and clearly communicate their needs in and out of the classroom.

- Develop Emotion Regulation Strategies: Teach students various emotion regulation strategies (such as deep breathing or physical activity) to help them manage stress and control and regulate emotions.

- Focus on Effort, Not Just Grades: Emphasize the importance of effort and perseverance rather than just grades, and help students develop a growth mindset.

- Prepare for Transition: Prepare students for transitions, such as moving to a new class or changing classes, by teaching coping strategies such as self-soothing and encouraging them to ask for help (if needed).

Tips for Parents and Teachers

- Stay Positive and Supportive: Have a positive and supportive attitude toward the child and focus on their strengths and abilities rather than their weaknesses.

- Encourage Independence: Encourage the child to take responsibility for their own learning and decision-making processes, and gradually increase their independence as they grow.

- Enhance a Growth Mindset: Teach the child that intelligence, abilities, and talents can be cultivated through hard work, dedication, and perseverance.

- Practice Mindfulness: Practice mindfulness together as a family or class, teaching children to always be present in the moment and focus on their thoughts, feelings, and physical senses.

- Stay Connected with Teachers: Stay in touch with your child's teacher or school counselor to stay informed about their progress and get support if needed.

By looking ahead and preparing normal 2- to 6-year-olds and hyperactive children for future challenges in social-emotional learning, parents and teachers can help them develop essential skills for success in academics, social situations, and life beyond school.

4- Preparing Children for the Transition to Kindergarten, Preschool, and Beyond

Why is it important to prepare children aged 2 to 6 for the transition to kindergarten, preschool, and beyond? What are the differences between normal and hyperactive children in this regard?

Preparing children aged 2 to 6 for the transition to kindergarten, preschool, and beyond is crucial for several reasons:

Emotional Readiness: The transition to a new environment can be emotionally challenging for young children. Emotional readiness helps children feel more secure, less likely to experience separation anxiety, and more positive attitudes toward change.

Social Skills: Early preparation allows children to learn and develop essential social skills, such as sharing, cooperation, and communicating with peers and teachers, to some extent before the transition.

Academic Readiness: Exposure to preschool concepts and programs helps children adjust to the structured environment of kindergarten and preschool and build a strong foundation for future learning.

Emotional Self-Regulation: Teaching children to manage, moderate, and regulate their emotions and behaviors prepares them to handle expected demands in an environment outside their home (such as daycare, preschool), such as following instructions and adapting to structured routines.

Building Self-Confidence: Familiarity with new environments, routines, and expectations increases children's self-confidence and makes them feel capable and ready to tackle new challenges.

Differences between Normal 2 to 6 Years Old Children and Children Diagnosed with ADHD
Normal Children
Adaptability: They usually adapt to new environments and routines more quickly with minimal support.

Attention and Concentration: They generally have fewer problems with attention and can stay focused on tasks for longer periods of time.

Impulse Control: They have a better ability to control impulsive behavior and follow instructions.

Social Interactions: They are more likely to pick up social cues (such as tone of voice) They understand and respond to sounds, body language, and more easily form appropriate relationships with peers.

Children Diagnosed with ADHD
Adjustability: May have more difficulty with changes in routines and environments and may need more support to adjust.

Attention and Focus: Often have challenges maintaining attention and focusing on tasks, which can affect their learning and participation.

Impulse Control: Have more difficulty controlling impulsive behavior and following instructions.

Returning to frequent interruptions and challenges in the following instructions:

Social Interactions: May have difficulty understanding social cues and establishing relationships, leading to social isolation or potential conflicts with others due to misunderstandings.

Transition Support Strategies

For Normal Children
Regular Introductions: Introduce children to school routines through conversation and practice at home.

Visits and Tours: Arrange visits to the new school to familiarize children with the environment, classrooms, and teachers.

Social Play: Encourage playdates with prospective classmates so they can make social connections before school starts.

Storytelling: Use books and stories about starting school to discuss expectations and address concerns.

For Children with ADHD
Structured Routines: Create and practice a structured routine at home that mimics the school schedule. to help children adjust.

Visual Programs: Use visual aids and programs to provide clear, consistent information about daily activities and transitions.

Individualized Support: Work with teachers to develop personalized strategies and support programs to address each child's specific needs and challenges.

Social Skills Training: Provide more opportunities for social skills training and practice to help children better understand and navigate social interactions.

Positive Reinforcement: Use positive reinforcement to encourage desirable behaviors and build children's self-confidence.

By preparing children aged 2 to 6 for the transition to kindergarten, preschool, and beyond, educators and parents can create a supportive and empowering environment that promotes successful social-emotional and academic development.

Here are some tips for parents and teachers to help prepare normal and hyperactive children aged 2 to 6 for the transition to kindergarten and beyond:

Parents

- Create Routines: Establish consistent routines and changes at home, such as bedtime and wake-up times, to help your child adjust to the structure of school.

- Practice Independence: Encourage your child to dress themselves, use the bathroom, and do simple tasks on their own to gradually gain independence.

- Labeling and Organizing: Teach your child to label and sort their belongings, such as toys and clothes, to help them develop responsibility.

- Practice Social Skills: Practice social skills, such as sharing, taking turns, and using appropriate, prosocial behaviors with your child through fun games and role-plays to prepare them for interactions with peers.

- Encourage Curiosity: Encourage your child's natural curiosity by providing a variety of simple play materials available and asking open-ended questions.

Teachers

- Create a Smooth Transition: Create a smooth transition, for example from kindergarten to preschool, by establishing a consistent routine, providing familiar materials, and gradually introducing new activities.

- Differentiated Instruction: Provide differentiated instruction to meet the unique needs of each child, including children with ADHD.

- Provide Visual Aids: Use visual aids such as pictures or charts to help children with ADHD follow directions and stay focused.

- Build Relationships: Build positive relationships with each child, including children with ADHD, by being patient, understanding, and supportive.

- Offered Choices: Offer choices throughout the day to give children a sense of control and autonomy, which can be especially helpful for children with ADHD.

Tips for Parents and Teachers

- Communicate Regularly: Teachers should communicate with parents regularly about their child's progress, strengths, and challenges to ensure a collaborative approach to helping children thrive.

- Provide Additional Support: Provide appropriate and adequate support for children with ADHD by providing additional resources, such as speech therapy or occupational therapy, as needed.

- Strengthen Your Advocacy: Strengthen children's self-love or "self-advocacy" skills by encouraging children to express their needs and wants clearly and respectfully.

- Stay Flexible: Be flexible and adapt your intended educational program as needed to meet each child's unique needs.

- Celebrate Your Child's Small Successes: Celebrate your child's small successes and progress toward a goal to build confidence and motivation.

Special Tips for Children 2 to 6 Years Old with ADHD

- Use Visual Reminders: Use visual reminders such as charts or pictures to help hyperactive children remember routines, tasks, and expectations. (To help with remembering routines and tasks.)

- Allow Extra Time: Allow extra time for children with ADHD to complete tasks or transition between activities, if needed.

- Suggest Movement Breaks: Provide movement breaks throughout the day to help children with ADHD release excess energy and focus better.

- Use Educational Technology: Use educational technology to engage children with ADHD in learning activities or provide additional support when needed. (To engage in learning activities.)

- Create a Behavior Plan: Develop a behavior plan with parents and teachers that outlines strategies for managing challenging behaviors and promoting positive behaviors. (To manage challenging behaviors.)

In short, to help both normal and ADHD children transition to kindergarten and beyond, parents and teachers can follow these tips:

Parents

- Establish routines and changes at home.

- Encourage children's independence and responsibility.

- Practice children's social and curiosity skills.

Teachers

- Gradually change the curriculum by creating a familiar routine for children.

- Differentiate instruction to meet each child's individual needs.

- Provide visual aids to help hyperactive children.

Both Parents and Teachers

- Communicate regularly with parents and teachers.

- Provide additional support when needed.

- Strengthen self-advocacy skills.

- Be flexible and praise small successes.

By following these tips, parents and teachers can help normal and hyperactive young children prepare for the transition to kindergarten and beyond, setting them up for success in their studies, social situations, and life beyond school.

CHAPTER 13: SUMMARY AND CONCLUSIONS

1- Summary

One of the basic life skills of children is the teaching of social-emotional learning, and teaching this skill to children aged 2 to 6 is very important for creating the foundation for children's overall social and emotional health throughout their lives. Key components of social-emotional learning include specific skills such as self-awareness, self-management, social awareness, communication skills, and responsible decision-making. Fundamental teaching of these skills helps children to be able to establish positive relationships with peers and adults when entering the community and school environment. For optimal teaching of social-emotional learning in children aged 2 to 6, play-based activities and discussions that promote social-emotional learning are often used. In advanced and professional educational environments, the educational and developmental needs of individual children, especially children with special needs such as children diagnosed with hyperactivity, are given significant specialized attention. In order to promote children's behavioral and academic progress, by examining their cognitive and emotional strengths or weaknesses, they are provided with professional and appropriate support by developing appropriate educational programs. Children with ADHD benefit from social-emotional learning education, along with normal children, because it helps them develop skills to manage their emotions, behaviors, and relationships, and by strengthening behavioral, cognitive, social, and emotional weaknesses, they progress at different stages of education and life. Incorporating social-emotional learning into the curriculum for children aged 2 to 6 not only strengthens their individual emotional health, but also fosters an inclusive, supportive classroom environment. When children learn to identify their own emotions and understand the emotions of others, they are better equipped to communicate effectively and resolve conflicts peacefully. This is especially helpful in diverse classrooms where children may have different emotional backgrounds and experiences. A strong foundation in social-emotional skills can reduce misunderstandings, foster inclusion, and make the classroom a safe space for all children, including those with ADHD, to understand and empathize with each other, to tolerate each other's differences and problems with greater flexibility and resilience, to express their diverse feelings more easily with others, to adapt to them, and to cooperate when necessary.

In addition, social-emotional learning can have long-term benefits that extend beyond infancy and early childhood. Research shows that children who master social-emotional skills perform better academically at different levels of school, have better mental health, and are more resilient in the face of challenges throughout life. Prioritizing these skills in early childhood education can help all children, especially children with special needs such as ADHD, who often face various cognitive, behavioral, and emotional difficulties.

Early intervention through social-emotional learning can lead to more positive outcomes in most of them, such as:

Enhancing Emotion Regulation

Importance: Hyperactive children aged 2 to 6 often have difficulty regulating emotions, experiencing intense emotions and finding them difficult to manage.

Benefits of Social-Emotional Learning Education

Social-emotional learning education teaches children aged 2 to 6 to identify their emotions, understand triggers, and use strategies such as deep breathing to manage their emotions.

Case Study: Teaching hyperactive children aged 2 to 6 to recognize signs of frustration and using a "calm corner" can prevent the child's emotional outbursts and strengthen self-control.

Improving Social Skills

Importance: ADHD children may have difficulty interacting socially, understanding social cues, and forming positive relationships.

Benefit of Social-Emotional Learning Education

Social-emotional learning education helps children empathize, learn to read social cues such as tone of voice, body language, and engage in positive social behaviors.

Case Study: Role-playing various social scenarios can help an ADHD child to practice appropriate responses and build better relationships with peers.

Promote Responsible Decision-Making

Importance: Impulsivity is a common challenge for hyperactive children, affecting their ability to make thoughtful decisions.

Benefit of Social-Emotional Learning Education

Social-emotional learning education guides children to think about the consequences of their actions before taking an action and making decisions.

Case Study Example: Using decision-making games, such as choosing the best way to share toys, teaches children to pause and consider the consequences of their choices.

Support Academic Success

Importance: Hyperactivity can affect attention and concentration, making academic tasks more challenging.

Benefit of Social-Emotional Learning Education

Social-emotional learning education encourages goal-setting and perseverance, helping children stay focused and motivated.

Case Study Example: Setting small, achievable academic goals. Praising and celebrating progress can improve a child's focus and academic performance.

Build Self-Confidence and Resilience

Importance: Hyperactive children may struggle with challenges Face repeated setbacks and failures that affect their self-confidence.

Benefit of Social-Emotional Learning Education

Social-emotional learning education activities that celebrate even small successes build a child's self-confidence and resilience.

Case Study: Praising a child for successfully completing a task or effectively managing their emotions boosts their self-confidence and encourages perseverance.

By integrating social-emotional learning education into the education of children with ADHD, educators and parents can provide them with the skills and strategies they need to thrive academically and socially, leading to more balanced and fulfilling lives.

Many inspiring success stories show how effectively managing ADHD and social-emotional learning and paying attention to their specific interests can lead to significant improvements in children's lives. Incorporating interests helps children stay focused on their goals and feel accomplished. Parents can talk to their child about what they liked about a particular task, which helps both the child and the parent understand what motivates them and what challenges them. Each particular interest path may seem more challenging for children with ADHD. Social emotional learning teaches children these skills to feel confident in their ability to create their own passion path by recognizing their strengths or superpowers. An ADHD child's impulsiveness may drive them to move forward at full speed in a particular direction, but by understanding their strengths and weaknesses, children aged 2 to 6 can make sure that each step is based on a responsible decision. By controlling their automatic impulsive emotional response on the path to achieving a goal, they can slow down their pace. When a child is not connected to a goal or task, such as homework, they feel more lost and distracted. Connecting goals to interests not only helps 2- to 6-year-olds identify their interests, but they can also connect these interests to feelings, passions, or experiences that make them happy, as opposed to other experiences that may be a source of stress for them. Social-emotional learning provides 2- to 6-year-olds with ADHD with the tools they need to create a path to success, face difficult challenges, manage anxiety and anger, and maintain positive relationships.

One notable example is the story of a preschooler (a 5-year-old boy) who struggled with hyperactivity and difficulty concentrating. At first, teachers saw him as a disruptive presence in various educational classes, but after the participation of his parents and a pediatrician and a specialized educational psychology consultant, they began to develop and implement a comprehensive educational program for him, starting with social-emotional learning. With the support of his family and school, he gradually learned to direct his energy towards positive activities that he liked, such as sports and art. Over time, in later grades, he became a star on his school's soccer team in sports and found a passion for painting in art, demonstrating his creativity and focus. He was able to participate in painting exhibitions with considerable success by creating beautiful paintings of his surroundings with the help of his parents and teachers. These successes not only improved his academic performance, but also increased his self-esteem and social interactions. This experience is an example of how social-emotional learning can affect the academic, artistic, and behavioral success of hyperactive children. It shows how social-emotional learning can pave the way for the success of difficult students, such as hyperactive children, with timely and appropriate specialized interventions.

Another inspiring success story is that of a girl who faced challenges with emotion regulation and attention in her early school years, such as kindergarten and preschool. For example, whenever other children wouldn't let her in their playgroup, she would start screaming and crying or try to disrupt their play. Realizing the importance of social-emotional learning, her parents enrolled her in a program that included mindfulness exercises, emotion regulation, and appropriate and positive interactions with her peers. Through these interventions, he was able to learn how to identify and control his emotions, use positive self-talk, and communicate better with his classmates through coping strategies such as calming down and controlling his impulsive behavior. By practicing mindfulness, he learned techniques to calm himself down in stressful situations, which significantly improved his ability to focus and participate in class. Years later, when he entered middle school, he faced teasing and bullying from children who were taller and larger than him. In those challenging and difficult situations, he began to learn appropriate ways to defend himself by paying attention and using the social-emotional skills he had learned earlier, controlling his emotions and staying calm. When necessary, he sought advice and help from his parents, teachers, or school counselors until he was finally able to solve his problem with the help of counselors. He also helped other students who were facing similar challenges. His story serves as a testament to the transformative power of early intervention. And it is appropriate. Empowering hyperactive children for their academic and social development throughout life is very necessary and important. Many famous historical figures, while perfecting their work skills, artistic works, or important scientific hypotheses, lived for many years in challenging and difficult conditions with hyperactive symptoms and achieved important successes, such as:

-Alexander Graham Bell - Inventor

-Agatha Christie - Mystery Writer

-Leonardo da Vinci - Painter, Scientist

-Thomas Edison - Inventor

--Albert Einstein - Physicist

-Harvey Cushing - Father of Neurosurgery

-Nikola Tesla - A Man Ahead of His Time, Inventor and Engineer

-Bill Gates - Co-Founder of Microsoft Software

2- Conclusions

Conclusions for Parents

As a parent, you play a crucial role in your child's social-emotional development. By supporting your child's social-emotional learning from ages 2 to 6, you can help them develop the skills they need to thrive in school and beyond throughout life, in both challenging and easy situations. To help empower your child, you can look for programs specifically for young children that prioritize social-emotional learning and incorporate activities that promote social-emotional learning in simple, hands-on ways into their daily routines.

Encourage your child to express their feelings and emotions more easily with a positive, empowering parenting style, and try to model emotion regulation, positive, helpful social interactions, and a healthy lifestyle for them to observe and learn better. By working with your child's teachers and supporting your child's social-emotional learning, you can help them build a strong foundation for lifelong social-emotional well-being.

Parents of Children 2 to 6 Years Old with ADHD

When parents first learn that their 2-to 6-year-old child has ADHD, it is essential that they take the diagnosis seriously, take steps to manage their own emotions, and then help their child. Here is an example of a step-by-step guide for parents to help them calm down and then support their child:

Step 1: Calming Down and Processing the Diagnosis
-Take a Moment to Process the News: Find a quiet, comfortable space to sit and consider the diagnosis. Take a few deep breaths and notice your initial reaction.

-Let Your Emotions Flow: It is normal to feel overwhelmed, anxious, or even confused. Accept your emotions and allow yourself to identify and release them.

-Seek Support: Reach out to a trusted friend, family member, or mental health professional for emotional support. Sharing your feelings with someone who understands you can help you process your emotions.

-Educate Yourself: Learn about ADHD, its symptoms, and possible treatment options. Understanding this condition will help you better support your child.

-Write Down Questions and Concerns: Make a list of questions and concerns you have about ADHD, ways to manage and treat it, and how it affects your child's daily life.

Step 2: Helping Your Child with ADHD
-Maintain a Calm Demeanor: Children with ADHD are highly attuned to the emotions of their caregivers. Try to be calm, patient, and understanding when interacting with your child.

-Establish Daily Routines and Structures: A daily schedule that includes regular times for meals, sleep, and activities can help your child feel more secure and control hyperactivity.

-Break Down Tasks into Smaller Steps: Big tasks can be overwhelming for these children. Break down tasks into smaller, more manageable steps to help them stay focused on completing the task.

-Use Positive Reinforcement: Praise your child for their efforts and successes, no matter how small. Positive reinforcement can help boost their confidence and motivation.

-Use Positive Language: Use positive language when giving instructions or correcting behavior. Instead of focusing on inappropriate behavior, try to focus more on your child's appropriate behavior. Instead of saying "don't do it," say "do it." Instead of repeating "don't do it," say "do it."

-Provide Choices: Offer your child choices throughout the day, such as "Do you want to do your homework now or after dinner?" These choices can help them feel more empowered and in control and reduce resistance.

-Encourage Physical Activity: Regular physical activity can help these children release excess energy and improve their focus and attention.

-Teach Organization Skills: Teach your child how to organize their toys, clothes, and belongings. This can help them develop important life skills more calmly.

-Collaborate with Teachers: Communicate regularly with your child's teachers to ensure that they have appropriate and consistent support and strategies in school to teach and develop basic life skills, including social and emotional skills.

-Be Patient and Consistent: Raising a 2- to 6-year-old child with a diagnosis of ADHD is often not easy for parents and in some cases can be extremely difficult and overwhelming. Raising and teaching them basic life skills requires a lot of patience and consistency. Encourage and reinforce social-emotional learning in them through various ways, such as play and entertainment. Set clear boundaries and consequences for their various behaviors (both positive and negative) in simple, understandable language, while modeling empathy and understanding for them yourself to help them learn better. Remember that every child with ADHD is unique, so it's best to work closely with your child's caregivers, teachers, and healthcare providers to create a personalized support and education plan that's tailored to your child's needs.

Working Together as Parents

Here are some tips for parents to work together effectively when their young child is diagnosed with ADHD:

Communicate Effectively

-Regular Meetings: Set up regular meeting times to talk about your child's progress, challenges, and concerns.

-Use a Shared Schedule: Keep track of your child's educational planning, appointments, and reminders on a shared schedule to stay organized and coordinated.

-Use Clear, Positive Language: Avoid jargon or technical jargon that may confuse each other. Use simple, clear language to explain your concerns and ideas.

-Provide a Consistent Message: Make sure you are sending consistent messages about expectations, boundaries, and consequences to your child.

-Set a Unified Tone: Maintain a unified tone and approach when interacting with your child to avoid confusing or contradictory messages.

-Support Each other's Strengths: Be organized and consistent in managing your child's ADHD. Recognize and appreciate each other's strengths.

-Create a Daily Routine: Create a coordinated daily schedule that includes set times for meals, activities, and chores to help your child feel a sense of predictability and security at home.

-Assign Responsibilities: Assign specific tasks and responsibilities to each parent or caregiver to avoid duplication of effort and ensure consistency and coordination of parenting.

-Use Visual Reminders: Use visual reminders such as charts, schedules, or daily routine boards to help your child remember their responsibilities and tasks.

-Understand Each other's Feelings: Understand and validate each other's feelings when dealing with stress, frustration, or anxiety related to your child's ADHD.

-Provide Emotional Support: Be available to each other to offer emotional support and encouragement as you face the challenges of parenting a child with ADHD.

-Develop an Appropriate Parenting Style: You should work together to create a strong parenting style that focuses on positive reinforcement and gentle discipline. By setting clear boundaries and responding to your child's needs, you can help your child develop self-regulation skills and build a strong, loving relationship. Use a parenting style that acknowledges your child's ADHD and is consistent with managing their specific problems appropriately.

Decades of research by ADHD scientists and experts show that authoritative parenting is the most effective style for raising productive, well-adjusted, and functioning children with ADHD. Your child likely doesn't understand the stress his condition can cause. It's important to remain positive and encouraging. Praise your child for good behavior so that he or she knows when something is done right. An authoritative parenting style that combines high control with high warmth and support can be helpful and productive for your child.

-Practice Self-Care: Make self-care a priority and make time for rest and stress-reducing activities to maintain emotional well-being.

-Seek Professional Help if Needed: Work with qualified doctors and psychologists, healthcare providers, therapists, or other professionals who can provide guidance and support in managing your child's ADHD.

-Attend Educational Sessions Together: Attend educational sessions together as a family to address challenges and develop strategies for managing your child's ADHD.

Join Support Groups: Join online or in-person support groups for parents of children with ADHD to connect with others who understand the same difficult and sometimes overwhelming challenges you face.

By following these tips, you can effectively empathize and collaborate with each other as parents to support and provide better educational conditions, nurture your children's special needs, and create a stable and loving environment that promotes their social-emotional empowerment and optimal growth and development.

Conclusions for Teachers

As a teacher, you have the power to promote the social-emotional development of your students from ages 2 to 6 by working with parents, professionals, and counselors. Make social-emotional learning a priority for all students, including those with ADHD who need additional special educational supports. Use well-designed, specific activities, programs, and games to teach social-emotional learning skills, and be sure to involve parents in the process. By doing so, you can create a positive environment that effectively supports the social-emotional development of all students with different needs.

In short, it is important to incorporate social-emotional learning into the daily lives of children aged 2 to 6, including those diagnosed with ADHD. Social-emotional learning helps children develop essential life skills such as self-awareness, self-regulation, and social awareness, which are essential for building strong relationships, achieving academic success, and navigating the complexities of life. In addition, social-emotional learning promotes positive relationships with others, reduces stress and anxiety, and strengthens a sense of belonging. In a diverse society, social-emotional learning is especially important for preschoolers from different cultural backgrounds, as it helps them develop an understanding of different perspectives, empathy, and cultural competence.

For children aged 2 to 6 with ADHD, social-emotional learning is even more critical because they struggle with cognitive (such as lack of attention and concentration) and emotional (such as impulsive emotional behavior) challenges and difficulty in social interactions. Incorporating social-emotional learning into their daily routines can help them develop these skills. In today's multicultural societies, social-emotional learning provides an opportunity to promote awareness of cultural diversity and acceptance of differences. By incorporating social-emotional learning into the daily lives of all children, including children with ADHD, we can create a supportive and inclusive environment that promotes social-emotional development and the empowerment of essential life skills for all children in different societies from childhood to adulthood, and pave the way for the development of a safe, happy, peaceful, and healthy society by teaching, strengthening, and promoting understanding, empathy, cooperation, and positive and constructive relationships for all people around the world.

CHAPTER 14: SCIENTIFIC AND PRACTICAL TIPS AND RESOURCES

1- INTEGRATING SOCIAL-EMOTIONAL LEARNING INTO DAILY ACTIVITIES

2- CREATE A BALANCED SCHEDULE WITH PLAYTIME, LEARNING, AND RELAXATION

3- LIST OF BOOKS, GAMES, AND SOCIAL-EMOTIONAL LEARNING PROGRAMS

4- CONNECT WITH OTHER PARENTS AND SUPPORT GROUPS

5- FIND LOCAL RESOURCES AND COMMUNITY PROGRAMS

1- Integrate Social-Emotional Learning into Everyday Activities

Tips for Parents, Educators, and Teachers

Integrating social-emotional learning into daily activities is beneficial for both normal and hyperactive children aged 2 to 6, helping them develop essential skills for managing emotions, building relationships, and making responsible decisions. Here are some tips and various scientific and practical resources to guide parents and teachers in integrating social-emotional learning into children's daily routines:

For Parents

Books and Reading Materials

Recommendations: Look for storybooks that explore children's emotions, empathy, and social interactions, and can be good conversation starters. A variety of educational books in this area are written in different languages, in the form of poems, songs, or children's stories, with the aim of teaching different emotions appropriate to the developmental age and grade level of children. You can obtain them online or from a bookstore, depending on the level and field of interest of each child.

Books Like:

1. "The Color Monster" by Anna Lenas teaches children about different emotions through the use of different colors in a children's story. This book encourages children to identify and talk about their emotions in simple language - "As parents, we teach toddlers to identify colors, numbers, shapes, and letters - but what about their feelings? "

2. "I Feel Silly Today! and other Moods that Make My Day" by Jamie Lee Curtis.

Silly, grumpy, excited, or sad - everyone has feelings that can change from day to day. And that's okay! This fun book teaches children about different emotions in simple, understandable language. A book with whimsical illustrations that helps children identify and even enjoy their ever-changing moods.

1. "The Color Monster" by Anna Lenas.

2. "I Feel Silly Today! and Other Moods That Make My Day" by Jamie Lee Curtis.

Family Discussions

- Conversation Starters: Use mealtime or bedtime routines to talk about feelings, problem-solving strategies, and ways to show kindness. Open-ended questions like "How did you feel when…?" or "What would you do if…?"

- Daily Reflection Journal: Encourage children to keep a journal where they can think, draw, or write about their daily adventures, including how they felt, what made them happy or sad, and how they dealt with challenges.

Feeling-Focused Activities

- Arts and Crafts: Engage in creative activities where children can express their feelings through drawing, painting, or crafting.

Mindfulness and Relaxation Techniques

- Guided Imagery: Do simple guided imagery or relaxation exercises before bed to help children release their feelings. "For example, imagine yourself lying on the grass in a beautiful park under a tree with your eyes closed listening to the song of a bird high in the tree! Breathe slowly and deeply! Visualize how relaxing it is!"

For Teachers and Educators (Kindergarten, Preschool)

Curriculum and Lesson Plans

- Social-Emotional Learning Programs: Use structured social-emotional learning programs that offer comprehensive lesson plans and activities tailored to different age groups and needs.

Classroom Discussions and Activities

- Morning Meetings: Start each day with an emotion check-in where students share their feelings and discuss strategies for managing emotions.

- Group Projects: Prepare collaborative projects that require teamwork, communication, and problem-solving skills.

Social-Emotional Learning Games and Exercises

- Role-Playing: Use role-playing activities to simulate social situations and practice conflict resolution skills.

- Games: Use interactive board games or online games that promote empathy, decision-making, and collaboration.

Parents Involvement

Workshops: Host workshops for parents on integrating social-emotional learning at home. Recommend or share strategies, books, and activities that parents can do with their children.

Social-Emotional Learning Assessment and Evaluation

Assessment Tools: Use social-emotional learning assessment and evaluation tools to monitor student progress and identify areas for growth. Provide feedback that emphasizes effort, improvement, and social-emotional development.

Additional Resources

1. CASEL: (Collaborative for Academic, Social, and Emotional Learning): CASEL stands for Collaborative for Academic, Social, and Emotional Learning. It is a trusted center of expertise dedicated to advancing the practice of promoting integrated academic, social, and emotional learning for all students. CASEL provides research, resources, and guidance for educators, policymakers, and parents interested in implementing effective social-emotional learning programs and practices. It provides resources, guidelines, and research-based curriculum recommendations for integrating social-emotional learning in schools and homes.

2. Edutopia: Provides articles, videos, and classroom strategies for effectively implementing social-emotional learning practices.

3. Mindful Schools: Provides online courses and resources for teachers and educators on integrating mindfulness and social-emotional learning into classrooms.

By incorporating these practical resources and strategies into daily activities, parents and teachers can effectively support the social and emotional development of normal and hyperactive children, fostering positive relationships, resilience, and overall well-being.

1. CASEL: casel.org
2. Edutopia: www.edutopia.org
3. Mindful Schools: www.mindfulschools.org

2- Create a Balanced Schedule with Playtime, Learning, and Relaxation Time – Normal and ADHD Children

Creating a balanced schedule that includes playtime, learning, and relaxation time is essential for both normal and ADHD children. Here are a few tips for parents and teachers to consider:

Tips for Parents

Create Consistent Routines
Create a daily schedule with wake-up times, mealtimes, and bedtime routines. Predictability helps children feel secure and reduces anxiety.

Allocate Playtime and Physical Activity
Make sure children have ample opportunities for free, unstructured play and physical exercise. Outdoor play is especially helpful for releasing excess energy in ADHD children.

Break Tasks into Manageable Chunks
Break learning activities into smaller tasks. Use timers or visual schedules to help ADHD children stay focused and manage time effectively.

Teach Mindfulness and Relaxation Exercises
Teach simple mindfulness exercises or relaxation techniques, such as deep breathing or muscle relaxation, to help children release stress.

Limit Screen Time
Set firm and consistent limits on screen time, such as TV, tablets, and phones, and instead encourage activities that promote creativity and social interaction.

Encourage Self-Expression
Provide opportunities for children to express their thoughts and feelings through art, music, or journaling. This will foster their creativity and emotional expression.

Tips for Teachers

Use Visual Schedules and Timers
Use timers and digital instructional technology or charts and visual schedules in the classroom to help students understand time constraints and to help them complete assignments and tasks and transition from one task to another.

Create Structured Learning Activities
Plan structured activities that include movement breaks and hands-on learning experiences. These activities help maintain interaction between students and support different learning styles.

Promote Group Play
Facilitate activities that encourage teamwork and collaboration among students. This strengthens social skills and empathy.

Provide Flexible Seating and Standing Desk Options
Provide flexible seating (such as bean bags) and standing desks to meet children's need for movement and activity.

Provide Positive Reinforcement
Recognize and reward children for following the schedule, completing tasks, and showing effort. Positive reinforcement increases their motivation and self-esteem.

Collaborate with Parents
Communicate regularly with parents to ensure that necessary and appropriate programs and strategies are implemented to support children's learning and development at home and at school.

General Tips for Both
- Monitor and Adjust: Regularly evaluate the effectiveness of the developed educational programs and make adjustment and modifications as needed based on the child's progress and feedback.

- Be Flexible: While consistent routines are important, be flexible and allow for each child's individual needs to be met when unexpected changes occur or in special and necessary situations.

- Model Healthy Habits: Healthy habits such as model and demonstrate time management, stress management, and self-care so that children can imitate and learn more easily.

By implementing these tips, parents and teachers can create a balanced curriculum that supports the social, emotional, and academic development of both normal and hyperactive children, creating a positive and nurturing environment for them to learn and thrive.

Resources
Creating a balanced schedule that includes playtime, learning, and relaxation is important for both normal and hyperactive children. Here are some examples of resources that provide guidance on how to structure such schedules:

American Academy of Pediatrics (AAP): www.aap.org

The AAP emphasizes the importance of balanced routines for children's development, including adequate time for play, learning, and relaxation.

Childmind Institute: childmind.org

Provides articles and resources on managing hyperactivity and creating routines that support children's social, emotional, and educational needs.

National Institute of Mental Health (NIMH): www.nimh.nih.gov

Provides information on strategies for managing hyperactivity, including tips for creating structured routines that balance academic tasks with play and relaxation.

ADDitude Magazine and Website: www.additudemag.com

Provides articles, guides, and expert advice on managing ADHD in children, including tips for creating effective programs that meet their unique needs.

Understood.org: www.understood.org

Provides resources and tools for parents and educators on supporting ADHD children, including strategies for structuring daily routines that promote each child's learning and overall well-being.

Most of these resources provide evidence-based guidance and expert scientific and practical tips for creating programs that significantly meet the needs of both normal and hyperactive children, including important educational tips for playing, learning, and calming children throughout the day.

3- List of Books, Games, and Social-Emotional Learning Programs that Support Normal and Hyperactive Children

Books

"The Social Skills Picture Dictionary" by Joseph P. Kelly - A visual dictionary to help students understand social skills and behaviors.

"The Feelings Book" by Todd Parr - A colorful and engaging book to help students identify and express their emotions.

"The Zones of Regulation" by Leah Kuypers - A book to help students understand and manage their emotions and behaviors.

"Have You Filled a Bucket Today?" by Carol McCloud - A story about the importance of kindness and positive interactions.

"The Berenstain Bears' Trouble with Friends" by Stan and Jan Berenstain - A story about dealing with friendship issues.

Games
"Feelings Charades" - A charades game that helps students express and identify different emotions.

"Social Skills Bingo" - A bingo game that promotes social skills and interaction.

"Emotion Charades" - A charades game that focuses on emotional intelligence.

"Kindness Cards" - A deck of cards that encourages students to practice kindness and empathy.

"Feelings Match" - A matching game that helps students identify and express different emotions.

List of Social-Emotional Learning Programs for Children Aged 2 to 6 Years
Programs
MindUP: A comprehensive SEL program that focuses on social-emotional learning, self-awareness, and resilience.

Mindfulness-Based Stress Reduction (MBSR): A program that teaches mindfulness techniques to reduce stress and improve emotion regulation.

Second Step: A program that teaches social-emotional skills, problem-solving, and self-regulation strategies.

Calm Classroom: A program that promotes mindfulness, self-regulation, and emotional intelligence in the classroom.

Gumdrop: A program that uses gamification to teach social-emotional skills, such as empathy, self-awareness, and self-regulation.

Apps
Moodfit: An app that helps students track their emotions and develop emotion regulation strategies.

Happify: An app that offers interactive activities to help students manage stress, anxiety, and negative thoughts.

Breathe, Think, Do: An app that teaches mindfulness techniques to reduce stress and improve focus.

Pebble Pad: An app that helps students develop emotional intelligence, self-awareness, and self-regulation skills.

Class Craft: An app that promotes social-emotional learning, teamwork, and classroom management.

Online Resources

SEL4Kids: A website offering SEL resources, lessons, and activities for teachers and parents.

Edutopia: A website offering articles, lesson plans, and resources on SEL and character education.

PBS Parents: A website offering articles, games, and resources on social-emotional learning for parents and educators.

Please note that while these resources can be beneficial for both regular and ADHD students, it's essential to consider individual student needs and adapt the materials accordingly.

4- Connect with other Parents and Support Groups - Normal and ADHD Children

Here are some tips for parents, teachers, and caregivers to connect with other parents and support groups to teach social-emotional learning to normal and ADHD children:

Parents

- Join Online Forums: Look for online forums, social media groups, and online communities dedicated to social-emotional learning, parenting, and ADHD.

- Local Support Groups: Look for local support groups in your area that focus on social-emotional learning, ADHD children. Attend local support group meetings, discussions, Parenting Reddit to connect with people who have similar experiences and concerns.

- Parent-Teacher Conferences: Use parent-teacher conferences as an opportunity to talk and discuss your child's social-emotional learning needs and get guidance on how to support their development.

- Collaborate with other Parents: Connect with other parents of children with similar needs and challenges to your child. Share strategies, resources, and experiences to learn from each other.

- Professional Development: Attend workshops, webinars, and conferences on social-emotional learning for normal and hyperactive children to learn about current best practices and strategies.

Teachers

- Collaboration with Colleagues: Work with colleagues who share and teach strategies, resources, and ideas to students with similar needs.

- Parent-Teacher Conferences: Use parent-teacher conferences as an opportunity to discuss students' social-emotional learning needs and create individualized plans to support each student.

- Classroom Discussions: Encourage open-ended discussions in the classroom about social-emotional learning topics such as empathy, kindness, and self-awareness.

- Lesson Planning: Incorporate social-emotional learning lessons into your curriculum using programs or activities that align with your teaching style.

- Consult with Experts: Consult with school psychologists, counselors, or special education teachers for guidance on supporting students with special needs, such as ADHD, and developing social-emotional learning education programs.

Support Groups

- National Associations: Join national organizations like the National Association of School Psychologists (NASP), the American Academy of Pediatrics (AAP), or the Attention Deficit Hyperactivity Disorder Association (ADDA) for resources and support.

- Social Media Groups: Join social media groups focused on social-emotional learning, ADHD, or parenting to connect with people who share similar interests and concerns.

- Workshops and Conferences: Attend workshops and conferences related to social-emotional learning, ADHD, to learn from experts and connect with people with similar goals.

5- Finding Local Resources and Community Programs - Normal and Hyperactive Young Children

Here are some ways to find local resources and community programs for normal and hyperactive young children:

Search Online
- Google Search: Enter keywords like "social-emotional learning programs near me" or "support groups for hyperactive children near me" to find local resources.

- Online Community Websites: Use the websites of online communities like the National Association of Social Workers (NASW) or the Attention Deficit Hyperactivity Disorder Association (ADDA) to find local resources.

Community Centers
-"Extracurricular" Educational Centers: "Extracurricular" educational centers offer after-school programs that promote character development, education, and healthy lifestyles.

- Community Centers: Local community centers often offer classes, workshops, and programs focused on social-emotional learning, parenting, and supporting hyperactive children.

- School Resources (Kindergarten, Preschool)

- School Counselor or Psychologist: Contact your child's school counselor or psychologist for guidance on local resources and programs. Special Education Department: If possible, contact your school district's special education department for information about services and programs for students with ADHD.

School Educational Forums
Parent-Teacher Associations: Offer many events, workshops, and programs focused on parenting, education, and community building.

Community Forums: Look for community educational forums that focus on the social issues of ADHD, mental health, or child development.

Networking
Ask Around: Ask friends, family members, or colleagues for recommendations on relevant educational resources and programs if they know of any.

Social Networks: Join educational social networks that focus on parenting, education, or ADHD to connect with people who may have similar experiences.

Attend Social Events: Attend parenting conferences or workshops to learn about available resources and connect with experts in the field.

Additional Tips
- Be Aware and Specific: Be aware and specific about your needs and what you are looking for in a resource or program. Be clear about exactly what questions or training you are looking for answers to in relation to your child's specific needs and challenges.

- Be Patient: Finding the right resource or program can take time, so be patient and persistent in your search.

- Check Credibility: Be sure to check the credentials and qualifications of the program providers or professionals providing the services.

- Start Small: Start by participating in small programs or resources and gradually increase your involvement as needed.

- By using these strategies, you can find local resources and community programs that support the social-emotional development of both normal and ADHD children.

The main goal of this book is to help educate and strengthen the development of social and emotional skills of 'Early Childhood', 2 to 6 years old, especially children diagnosed with ADHD, which is provided in order to empower their basic life skills. The writing of this book is based on a summary of the study of the latest research articles and published books in the field of basic social and emotional life skills for children 2 to 6 years old, so that it can be useful for all of you: parents, counselors, teachers, children, and students. It is hoped that the important educational and training key tips and advice in this book will be fruitful for you.

ADDENDUM
ADDITIONAL NOTES

1- A General Comparison of the Process of Social and Emotional Development in Children Aged 2 to 6 Years Diagnosed with ADHD, Compared to Normal Children

Here is a summary of key points about social and emotional development in children aged 2 to 6 years with a diagnosis of ADHD compared to normal children:

Children with a diagnosis of ADHD often have delays in their social and emotional development and maturation compared to normal children, leading to hasty, impulsive behaviors, emotional outbursts, and problems with stress-coping behaviors, but with special help and support, they can develop these social and emotional skills.

- They have specific challenges in social and emotional development due to their condition, more so than their normal peers without ADHD. They often have difficulty with their social-emotional learning (such as poor understanding of social cues, regulating their own emotions, and understanding the empathy or feelings of others). These challenges can lead to problems relating to others and forming and maintaining friendships.

- They become easily bored, distracted, or withdrawn in social situations compared to normal children.

- ADHD is associated with higher rates of emotional disorders, such as problems controlling impulses, impulsivity, and managing emotions, which can lead to problems such as sensitivity to rejection by others, social anxiety, and poor self-awareness.

- They may have difficulty with planning, organizing, self-regulation, bullying, sharing, taking turns, listening, and taking social cues, waiting for what they need, following or changing daily routines, and other social and emotional skills.

However, it is important to note that with the right guidance, support, and strategies, children diagnosed with ADHD can still develop their social and emotional skills. Parents, caregivers, and teachers can play a vital role in helping children with ADHD develop these skills.

By understanding the challenges that children with ADHD face in social and emotional development, and by providing targeted support and positive strategies, we can help them develop the social and emotional skills they need to thrive in life.

Creating a specific and engaging daily learning program appropriate for children aged 2 to 6, especially those with ADHD, includes simple activities that help them focus, relax, and enjoy their day in a structured way.

2- "Daily Relaxation Routine" Training Program

Creating a daily relaxation routine for children aged 2 to 6, especially those with ADHD, includes activities that help them focus, relax, and enjoy their day in a structured way.

A balanced routine, including a variety of activities that are engaging and relaxing for children aged 2 to 6, could be designed as follows:

Morning Routine
1. Calm Wake Up (7:00 A.M.)
   - Activity: Wake up gently with soft music in a quiet, comfortable environment.

   - Tip: Take your time to slowly transition your child from sleep to wakefulness, and don't rush them to wake up.

2. Morning Stretches and Deep Breathing (7:15 A.M.)
   - Activity: Do simple stretches and deep breathing exercises to start the day off on a calm note.

   - Tip: Use visual aids or game-like movements to make it engaging for your child.

3. Healthy Balanced Breakfast (7:30 A.M.)
   - Activity: Prepare a nutritious, balanced breakfast, with a variety of textures and flavors that your child will enjoy.

   - Tip: Allow for choices among healthy foods to encourage your child's independence.

Midmorning
4. Creative Activity Time (8:00 A.M.)
  - Activity: Do activities such as building with blocks, painting, or playing with sensory bins.

  - Tip: Choose activities that can be done quietly and allow for focused, calm play.

5. Outdoor Time or Nature Walk (9:00 A.M.)
  - Activity: Take a walk in the park or garden or play a simple outdoor game.

  - Tip: Keep the walk short and engaging, and create opportunities to observe nature.

6. Snack Time (10:00 A.M.)
  - Activity: Have a healthy, easy-to-eat snack.

  - Tip: Provide a quiet environment during snack time. Like a quiet corner with soft lighting.

Noon
7. Story Time or Audiobooks (10:15 A.M.)
  - Activity: Read a book together or listen to an audiobook story.

  - Tip: Choose soothing stories and create a cozy corner for story time.

8. Rest Time, Nap (11:00 A.M.)
  - Activity: A short nap or break with dim lights and soft music.

  - Tip: Establish a regular nap routine to help your child relax and unwind.

9. Lunch (12:00 P.M.)
  - Activity: A well-balanced meal that your child enjoys.

  - Tip: Make mealtime enjoyable and relaxing for your child by avoiding distractions like TV or tablets.

Afternoon
10. Quiet Play or Learning Activities (1:00 P.M.)
  - Activity: Engage in quiet play or activities like puzzles, coloring, or simple educational games.

- Tip: Focus on activities that encourage and strengthen your child's focus without being overly stimulating.

11. Creative Art or Music Time (2:00 P.M.)

- Activity: Art projects or playing music (such as using simple instruments).

- Tip: Consider free-form art activities to prevent stress.

12. Outdoor Play or Physical Activity (3:00 P.M.)

- Activity: Active playtime, such as playing in the sandbox, riding a tricycle, or gentle games.

- Tip: Make sure the activities are fun and engaging for your child, and not too competitive or complicated.

13. Snack Time (4:00 P.M.)

- Activity: A light, healthy snack.

- Tip: Provide a calming activity for your child, such as listening to soft music.

Evening
14. Calming Activities (4:30 P.M.)

- Activity: Engage in calm play, such as making shapes with soft materials or simple board games with your child.

- Tip: Make sure the activities are simple and help reduce your child's rush.

15. Dinner (5:30 P.M.)

- Activity: A balanced meal in a quiet setting with your family.

- Tip: Provide opportunities for conversation and a calm environment for your child.

16. Bedtime Routine (6:30 P.M.)

- Activity: Follow a regular, relaxing routine, including bath time, story time, and a designated time for rest.

- Tip: Use a consistent bedtime routine to signal to your child that it's time to rest and to mentally prepare for sleep.

17. Bedtime (7:00 P.M.)

- Activity: Bedtime with relaxing activities, such as soft music or lullabies.

- Tip: Keep your child's bedroom dark and quiet to help them sleep soundly.

Additional Tips

- Visual Schedules: Use visual schedules or charts to help your child better understand the flow of the day.

- Flexibility: Don't be too strict with the schedule. Be flexible if necessary to meet your child's mood and needs.

- Sensory Breaks: If needed, incorporate sensory breaks, such as using sensory boxes or fidget toys, into activities.

- Positive Reinforcement: Use positive reinforcement to encourage your child's cooperation and calm behavior.

This plan, for example, reinforces children's adherence to a schedule and structured activities and flexibility, and aims to provide a calm and engaging day to help children aged 2 to 6 with ADHD.

3- "Mindfulness" Training Program

The purpose of creating a mindfulness training program to help children aged 2 to 6, especially those with ADHD, is to provide a home environment for practicing mindfulness, including simple and engaging activities that are developmentally appropriate for children aged 2 to 6. The overall goal of the program is to introduce mindfulness concepts in simple language that is understandable, fun, and manageable for children aged 2 to 6. Here is a structured yet flexible and simple program to help integrate mindfulness into the daily routines of children aged 2 to 6, as an example:

Daily Mindfulness Practice Program

1. Explain an Introduction to Mindfulness (10-15 Minutes a Day)

- Objective: Introduce the concept of mindfulness in a simple and engaging way for the child.

- Activity: Start with a short story or video about introducing mindfulness that is designed for children. Choose stories that explain mindfulness in a simple and understandable way for them.

2. Mindful Breathing (5 Minutes a Day)

- Goal: Teach children how to focus on their breath to help them calm their minds.

- Activity: Practice "balloon breathing," where children imagine that they are slowly blowing up balloons as they breathe in. Encourage them to take a deep breath and slowly exhale as they imagine the balloon is being blown up.

- Tip: Use a visual aid like a "breathing toy" (a soft toy placed on the child's stomach that moves up and down with the inhale and exhale) to help them watch their breath and stay focused on their breathing.

3. Mental Activity (10 Minutes a Day)

- Goal: Combine physical activity with mindfulness practice.

-Activity: Engage in activities such as gentle children's yoga, stretching, or "mindful walking," where children walk slowly and pay attention to the movements of their feet as they move.

- Tip: Use simple instructions and make the exercise engaging. For example, for slow stretching, say, "Let's be a slow turtle."

4. Sensory Exploration (10 Minutes a Day)

- Goal: Help children become aware of their senses (e.g., sight, hearing, smell) and their surroundings.

- Activity: Use sensory bins filled with items such as rice grains, sand, yarn, or water. Encourage children to touch and explore these items with their hands and describe what they feel, see, and hear.

- Tip: Create a "sensory scavenger hunt" where children find objects based on different sensory experiences (e.g., "Find something that feels soft. Like yarn").

5. Mindful Eating (10 Minutes at Mealtime)

- Goal: Encourage focus and presence during meals.

- Activity: Practice mindful eating by paying attention to the colors, textures, and flavors of their food. Use a "mindful eating" routine where children take a moment to notice the taste and smell of their food before eating and express how they feel about it.

- Tip: Use a timer to practice eating slowly and savoring each bite.

6. Calm Time (10 Minutes before Bed)

- Goal: Create a relaxing transition from daily activities to rest time.

- Activity: Create a bedtime routine that includes calming activities such as listening to soft music, reading a calming story (e.g., "butterfly breathing," where children imagine their breaths closing like a butterfly's wings as they inhale and opening them as they exhale.

- Tip: Keep the repetition of this routine consistent and calming to indicate that it's time for it.

Weekly Activities

1. Mindfulness Calm Bottle Craft (1-2 Times a Week)

- Goal: Create a visual aid for mindfulness.

- Activity: Make a "calm bottle" by filling a bottle with water, glitter paper shreds, and glue. When the bottle is shaken, the glitter paper shreds scatter and swirl around, and after a while, they slowly settle, making the bottle seem calm. Watching this bottle helps your child calm down.

- Tip: Use this bottle when children need to calm down.

2. Nature Walk (1-2 Times a Week)

- Goal: Strengthen your connection to nature and mindfulness.

- Activity: Go for a nature walk and encourage your children to observe their surroundings. Ask them to notice the different colors, sounds, and textures around them.

- Tip: Ask simple questions like "What do you hear?" or "What colors do you see?" to help them focus.

3. Mindfulness Games (1-2 Times a Week)

- Goal: Make mindfulness fun and interactive.

-Activity: Play games that encourage mindfulness, such as teacher-student: "Teacher says" with mindful instructions (e.g., "Teacher says, take a deep breath") or "mind freeze dance," in which children dance freely to music and then, when the music stops, the students freeze in a funny mental state.

- Tip: Keep games short and engaging to keep children's attention.

Tips for Parents

- Consistency: Create a regular routine for children's mindfulness activities. Following a consistent schedule helps children become familiar with the practices and become more receptive to them.

- Modeling Behavior: Demonstrate mindfulness practices yourself. Children often learn best by watching their parents do things.

- Positive Reinforcement: Encourage and praise your child's efforts in practicing mindfulness. Positive reinforcement helps build interest and engagement (immediately celebrate even small successes).

- Flexibility: Adjust activities based on your child's mood and needs. Some days may require more active or less structured and relaxed activities.

- Create a Calm Environment: Make sure the space in which mindfulness activities are carried out is quiet and free from any distractions.

This program, as an example and model, integrates mindfulness activities into daily routines in a simple way that is attractive and appropriate for children aged 2 to 6 years, helping them to gradually learn these skills naturally and effectively, practice and develop them with interest.

4- Training Program to Deal with "Resistance to Doing Homework"

Dealing with homework resistance in children aged 2 to 6 can be challenging for parents, but by designing a structured program that includes positive strategies and appropriate consequences, parents can create a more conducive learning environment for their children. Below is a sample homework plan for children aged 2 to 6 that parents can use to encourage homework completion on time, especially for children with ADHD who often struggle with homework, and to constructively address their child's academic and behavioral problems. A homework completion program includes the following key points:

- Foster a positive attitude toward homework and learning.
- Encourage homework completion on time with minimal resistance.
- Define appropriate consequences for persistent refusal to do homework, promoting accountability.

Step 1: Set a Plan for Success

1. Create a Dedicated Homework Space

Designate a specific place in the home for homework and learning activities. This space should be quiet, well-lit, and free of distractions (such as a TV, tablet, or loud music).

Make sure it is equipped with the necessary supplies (crayons, paper, scissors, etc.) to make homework more enjoyable.

2. Create a Routine

Set a consistent time each day for homework. Creating a regular routine helps children understand and get used to homework as part of their daily activities.

For example, you might tell your child, "After snack time at 4 P.M., we will sit down to work on your homework together."

Step 2: Strategies to Encourage Doing Homework on Time

1. Make Homework Fun

Turn homework into a game by introducing fun activities or rewards. Use colorful materials and interactive activities to make learning and homework fun and enjoyable.

Example: Use a timer and challenge children to complete a task before the timer goes off, and reward them with immediate praise or a sticker.

2. Break Down Tasks

Break down tasks into small, manageable chunks. This makes them seem less overwhelming and helps children focus on one task at a time.

Example: If they have multiple tasks, set a timer for 5-10 minutes of focused work on each task, then take a short break to continue working on the task.

3. Positively Reinforce Efforts

Praise Small Successes. Praise your child for completing tasks or efforts, even if the work is not perfect.

Example: "I'm so proud of you for starting your homework on time! Well done! You worked really hard on that drawing!"

4. Suggested Choices

Let your child have their say about how they want to complete their homework or which tasks to do first. This gives them power and can often reduce their resistance.

Example: "Do you want to start your homework with the notebook and coloring first? Or do you want to write your homework first?"

Step 3: Deal with Resistance with Consequences

1. Discuss Expectations

Communicate clearly with children about expectations for homework in simple, clear language. Talk about the importance of completing homework on time and how it helps them learn.

Example: "We have a specific amount of time each day to do our homework, and it is important that we work hard to finish it on time."

2. Practice a Behavioral Consequence

If necessary, let children experience a natural consequence for not doing their homework. This practice helps them better understand the importance of responsibility and the consequences of their inappropriate behavior.

Example: If they refuse to do their homework, they may miss out on playtime later or have to struggle to finish it the next morning before school.

3. Use a "Homework Contract"

Create a simple homework agreement or contract. Both parent and child can sign it to accept their responsibilities. Include both positive consequences for consistently completing homework on time, such as more playtime, and negative consequences for repeatedly resisting, or being late for completing homework, such as less playtime.

4. Time and Behavior Management

If your child continues to resist doing homework, implement a discussion session where the child thinks about their choices and how they can improve their behavior toward doing homework in the future.

Example: "Let's take a break and think about why doing homework is important and how we can do our homework better tomorrow?"

Step 4: Build Support and Collaboration

1. Encourage Parental Support
Actively participate as your child's partner in doing homework. Sit with your child, ask questions, and guide them without directly doing the homework.

Example: "I'm here to help you if you have any questions. Let's read the homework instructions together."

2. Communicate with Teachers
If homework resistance is a persistent issue, reach out to teachers for additional support and strategies.

Example: Discuss your child's strengths and challenges with his or her teachers. They may offer you insight on how to increase motivation or simplify assignments.

3. Be Patient and Flexible
Homework can be more challenging on some days than others. So, it's best to be flexible in your approach and adjust your schedule and routine as needed.

Example, if your child is tired or upset one day for some reason, acknowledge their feelings and give them a short break before returning to homework.

Conclusion

By implementing this structured plan, parents can effectively manage homework resistance in children aged 2 to 6. Creating a dedicated homework environment, establishing routines, and incorporating engaging strategies can help foster a positive attitude toward learning and completing homework. Additionally, using positive and negative behavioral consequences and reinforcing collaboration with teachers can reinforce the importance of taking responsibility for the task. Through patience and consistency, parents can foster a sense of responsibility and a love of learning in their children, making homework time an enjoyable experience.

5- Training Program to Deal with Resistance to "Observing Hygiene and Personal Hygiene Tips"

Creating a successful educational program to address the resistance of children 2 to 6 years old to hygiene and personal hygiene tasks (such as showering, washing hands, brushing teeth, and keeping rooms clean) is very important and vital for normal children and especially for children with ADHD due to the importance of observing hygiene and personal hygiene in maintaining their overall health. By using positive strategies and understanding the consequences, parents can encourage and reinforce their compliance with hygiene rules while promoting habits and routines appropriate to each child's age and specific conditions. Below is a sample hygiene and personal hygiene training model for normal and ADHD children, 2 to 6 years old. This educational program includes the following important points:

- Promptly encourage the child's timely and consistent hygiene and cleanliness behaviors.
- Use positive reinforcement strategies to promote the child's cooperation.
- Create understandable and age-appropriate behavioral consequences for each child for persistent resistance to completing tasks.

Step 1: Successful Planning

1. Create a Visual Routine
Create a visual schedule that outlines each of your child's hygiene tasks with simple, clear pictures. This can be useful as a visual reminder to help your child remember what to do.

Example: Colorful, eye-catching pictures can guide your child through easy steps like showering, washing hands, brushing teeth, and cleaning their room.

2. Set a Specific Time for Health Activities
Set a consistent time each day for activities like showering and brushing your teeth that will become part of their regular daily routine.

Example: "After dinner, it's time to brush your teeth first, then we'll take a bath or shower."

3. Make the Child's Room Attractive
Make sure the bathroom and child's room are attractive and child-friendly. For example, colorful towels or fun bath toys can make showering fun and playtime.

Provide cleaning supplies in the child's room that are easy for them to reach (small brooms, laundry baskets, etc.).

Step 2: Positive Strategies to Encourage Cooperation

1. Make the Work Steps Fun

Turn hygiene tasks into games. For example, use a timer for activities and challenge your child to complete tasks happily in the allotted time.

Example: Say, "Let's see how fast you can wash your hands before this song ends!"

2. Use Positive Reinforcement

Give your child an immediate reward for completing tasks on time and without resistance. This immediate reinforcement can include a sticker, praise, or extra playtime.

Example: "Well done! You brushed your teeth so well! Here's a sticker for your reward chart!"

3. Model Appropriate Behavior

Show your child the importance of each task by actually doing it together. Children often learn best by imitating.

Example: Brush your teeth together in the mirror with your child or pretend to brush your child's doll's teeth.

4. Provide Choices

Give your child choices when doing tasks. This often empowers children and reduces their resistance.

Example: "Do you want to use the blue or green toothbrush today?" or "Which soap do you want to wash your hands with? Solid or liquid soap?"

Step 3: Implement Behavioral Consequences for Resistance

1. Behavioral Consequences

Let your child experience the consequences of inappropriate behavior (such as not doing hygiene tasks). For example, if your child doesn't brush their teeth, they may have less playtime. Or, say something like, "If we don't wash our hands before eating, we might not get our favorite food. So, let's wash our hands together so we can enjoy our favorite snack!"

2. Establish a "Hygiene Contract"

Create an easy and fun contract that outlines expectations for hygiene tasks in simple language that your child can understand. Stickers or rewards can be tied to successful completion of tasks throughout the week.

Example: "If you complete your morning and evening hygiene tasks every day this week, we'll have a family fun day!"

3. Behavioral Reflection Assessment Time

If your child continues to resist, set aside a few minutes for a behavioral reflection assessment period. Calmly discuss with your child why these tasks are important. and how the child is able to approach personal hygiene and cleanliness differently.

Example: "Let's talk a little and think about why it's important for us to be clean. How can we do difficult tasks better and more easily?"

Step 4: Addressing Specific Tasks

1. Showering, Bathing

Make bath time fun and interesting for your child with special bath toys, bubbles or songs. Set a time limit so that it feels less like a chore with more control.

Example: "Let's play your favorite song for two minutes while you wash! When the song is over, it's time to rinse and get out of the bath."

2. Washing Hands

Teach them the importance of handwashing with a fun song or dance to help them follow along.

Example: "Let's wash our hands together while singing this song you love... together! When the song is over, we've washed our hands enough and are clean."

3. Brushing

Choose a fun toothbrush and toothpaste that your child likes. Use apps or videos to make brushing fun together.

Example: Say, "Let's pretend this toothbrush is a superhero fighting the cavity monster!"

4. Keeping Rooms Clean

Break down the cleaning process into simple, fun, and manageable tasks (like picking up toys, putting away clothes) and use a "cleaning time song" to make it fun.

Example: Say, "Let's see if we can clean and tidy your room before the song ends!"

Step 5: Monitor Progress

Regularly Check In: Talk to your child about their progress with hygiene and personal hygiene tasks on a regular basis. Find out what tasks are still difficult for them to do, and provide easier ways to do them. Reward and encourage them immediately for small successes.

Tailor the Program to Your Child's Needs: Be flexible and adjust your approach as needed. Some strategies may work better for your child than others.

Conclusion

By implementing this sample program, parents can successfully manage hygiene and hygiene resistance in children ages 2 to 6. The combination of visual cues, positive reinforcement, and engaging activities strengthens children's sense of agency and makes hygiene tasks less daunting. Establishing appropriate consequences for persistent resistance encourages accountability while creating a positive environment for learning good health habits. Through patience, consistency, and creativity, parents can help reinforce the importance of self-care and responsibility in children aged 2 to 6 years.

6- A Training Program for Appropriately Dealing with Inappropriate Behaviors During "Mealtime" at Home, at Restaurants, or at Various Events

- A training program for dealing with inappropriate behavior at home, in restaurants, or at various events.

Creating a supportive and structured program and environment for children aged 2 to 6 years, especially when inappropriate behaviors such as bullying and stubbornness are present, is key to fostering positive behavior. Below is a sample model of appropriate handling of inappropriate behavior and management at home, in restaurants, or at various events for children aged 2 to 6 years with ADHD. This training program includes the following important points:

- Encourage positive behavior at mealtimes and prevent the development of issues related to bullying and stubbornness.

- Provide an environment in which the child feels valued, understood, and supported.

Step 1: Setting Up for Success

1. Establish Regular Routines
Create a predictable daily schedule that includes set times for different meals. Consistency helps children aged 2 to 6 years feel secure and understand parental expectations.

For example, say, "We eat breakfast at 8 A.M. every day, lunch at 12 P.M., and dinner at 6 P.M."

2. Create a Positive Environment
Set the table together and involve your child in meal preparation if necessary. These can foster a sense of participation and excitement about eating. Maintain a calm, positive atmosphere during mealtimes; avoid distractions from screens (tablets, phones, TVs) or loud noises.

Step 2: Strategies for Dealing with Stubbornness

1. Suggested Choices
Instead of insisting on what your child should eat, offer simple choices to avoid a power struggle between you and your child.

Example: "Would you rather have salad or vegetables with your lunch?"

2. Use a Timer
Introduce a visual or audible timer as a countdown to your child as a signal to finish meals or try new foods. This practice can help your child become less resistant and stubborn.

For example, say, "Let's see if we can finish our meals before the timer goes off. This timer is set for 10 minutes!"

3. Positive Reinforcement
Praise and reward your child for trying new foods or following mealtime rules. Positive reinforcement can encourage them to participate more.

Example: Use a chart or a special board with stickers and rewards to track your child's progress when eating different foods.

Step 3: Managing and Controlling Bullying Behavior and Interactions with Siblings

1. Model Empathy and Kindness
Show how to treat others kindly, especially at mealtimes.

For example, say, "How do you think your sister feels when you take food off her plate without permission? How would you feel if your sister did the same thing?"

2. Set Clear Expectations
Talk about appropriate and inappropriate behavior at mealtimes (such as before a restaurant or event) and state your expectations in simple, clear, and reasonable language in advance.

Example: "At the dinner table at a restaurant, we wait for our turn to be served and to receive our food, and remember not to get up from the table before the food is finished!"

3. Role-Playing
Create learning opportunities through role-playing scenarios to teach appropriate behavior in real-life situations.

Example: Pretend you are at a birthday party where you have to ask for something politely or share food with others with kindness and respect.

Step 4: Addressing Behavior in Different Settings

At Home
- Participate in Family Meetings: Hold short family discussions to talk about feelings and expectations of appropriate and inappropriate behavior at the dinner table with your child by example.

- Solve Problems Together: When a conflict arises because of your child's inappropriate behavior, calmly and calmly guide your child to think about correcting their behavior.

Example: If your sibling gets angry at dinner, ask, "What can you do right now to make them happy?"

At Restaurants or Events

Preventive Preparation: Before going out, review expected behaviors and what is appropriate and inappropriate, and practice those behaviors together using simple language.

Bring Comfort Items from Home: For example, a device from home (such as a favorite toy or book) can help a child feel calm and secure outside the home, and this often reduces a child's anxiety in unfamiliar environments.

Positive Reinforcement Outside the Home

Social Contracts: Make a fun "contract" with your child for social events where children agree to follow the rules of behavior. Offer small, immediate rewards for compliance.

Step 5: Respond to Negative Behavior Calmly

1. Stay Calm and Consistent

Modeling appropriate responses to your child's stubbornness is very important. If your child displays negative behavior, calmly, without violence or raising your voice, firmly explain briefly why the behavior is inappropriate.

For example, say, "I can see that you are very upset because you don't want to eat this food right now! Let's take a deep breath together and talk about it calmly."

2. Pause for Reflection

If stubbornness turns into refusal or negative behaviors, taking a break, a short break to calm the child down can often be effective.

For example, say: "If you are feeling too angry right now to eat, you can sit there quietly for a few minutes, take a deep breath, and join us again when you feel calm and ready."

Conclusion

By implementing these strategies and maintaining clear, simple, and unambiguous expectations, parents can effectively manage a child's stubbornness and stubbornness in different situations, minimize bullying tendencies, and create a positive environment for eating together. Creating opportunities to practice and encourage empathy can help children become strong and respectful individuals in life without bullying, violence, and by being assertive and maintaining a calm and composed demeanor. Regular communication and role-playing can facilitate lessons learned. Appropriate and consistent behaviors and create positive habits during meals and afterwards when eating at home, in restaurants or at various events.

7- Training Program for Dealing Appropriately with Inappropriate Behaviors at Bedtime

Establishing a healthy sleep schedule is crucial for children aged 2 to 6, including those with ADHD. Sleep directly impacts their mood, behavior, and overall development.

This is a guide for parents to help them manage their bedtime routines to overcome challenges, tantrums, and behavioral issues related to bedtime, both at home and in different settings, such as vacations or family events.

Below is a practical template to guide parents to help them manage their child's bedtime routines to overcome challenges, tantrums, and behavioral issues related to bedtime, both at home and in different settings, such as vacations or family events. This training program is designed for children 2 to 6 years old with ADHD and includes the following important points:

- Create a regular, relaxing bedtime routine for your child that encourages good sleep habits.

- Address behavioral and stubbornness issues related to bedtime and help children feel safe, prepared, and relaxed for sleep.

Step 1: Establish a Successful Schedule

1. Create a Regular Bedtime Routine
Set a regular bedtime that is consistent with your child getting enough sleep (usually 10 to 12 hours for children aged 2 to 6). Follow a consistent, consistent schedule of activities each night to signal that it's time for bed.

For example, say, "We start our bedtime routine at 6 p.m., which includes bath time, story time, and a quiet cuddle time to help them fall asleep."

2. Create a Calm Environment
Make sure your child's sleeping area is comfortable, dark, and quiet. Use blackout curtains if necessary, or consider soothing sleep music if there is a lot of ambient noise.

Keep electronic devices (such as tablets, phones) away from your child at least an hour before bed to minimize distractions and overstimulation.

1- Suggested Choices
Offer your child simple choices in their bedtime routine. This helps them feel in control and can reduce their resistance.

For example, say, "Do you want to read a storybook or a poetry and songbook tonight?"

2- Use Picture Programs
Create a picture program that outlines the bedtime routine with pictures. This helps your child understand what's coming up and reduces transition anxiety.

Example: Use pictures that show activities like bath time, brushing teeth, and reading a book.

3- Positive Reinforcement
Praise your child for following bedtime routines or trying new things, such as going to bed without resistance. Consider a reward system for consistent behavior.

For example, have a special reward sticker chart or board where your child gets a reward sticker for each night they follow their bedtime routine without fuss.

Step 2: Dealing with Behavior Issues and Stubbornness

1. Calm and Consistent Pattern
Your behavior can set the tone for your child's bedtime routine. Remain calm and consistent in your responses. If your child resists, calmly remind them of the expected behavior.

For example, say, "It's bedtime and we can read a story together. If you're calm, I'll read you a second story."

2. Implement "Light Activity" Time
A calming period before bedtime can help signal rest time. Create short, light, and quiet activities like coloring or playing puzzles to prepare and calm your child before bedtime.

Example: Spend 15 minutes playing a quiet puzzle together and let your child move from the previous active game to the next quiet activity like playing with puzzles.

3. Pause to Reflect on Behavior

If your child becomes too stubborn or starts behaving inappropriately, give him a short break to calm him down before continuing with the bedtime routine. For example, say: "If you are very upset, let's sit quietly together for a moment and breathe. After you feel calm, we can continue with the bedtime routine."

Step 3: Addressing Sleep Behavior Training in Different Situations

At Home

Family Bedtime Discussions: Involve your child in a discussion about the importance of sleep and healthy bedtimes in different situations. Turn the discussion into a fun conversation about what your child finds enjoyable about bedtime.

Problem-Solving Together: Whenever there is a fight or a struggle at bedtime, ask your child what would help them feel more comfortable going to bed.

At a Party or While Traveling

Preventive Preparation: Discuss bedtime expectations before attending gatherings or traveling. Agree on a specific time to start a bedtime routine, even if it is away from home.

Bring your child's familiar and comfortable items with you: Bring a blanket, stuffed animal, or favorite pajamas to help them feel more comfortable and secure and more attuned to different sleep environments.

Step 4: Manage Bedtime Resistance Calmly

1. Be Calm and Confident

Respond to your child's stubbornness and bullying with empathy and understanding. Calmly and calmly address your child's concerns and misbehavior without showing your tiredness or anger.

For example, say, "I know you want to stay up, but getting enough sleep will help you have a fun and less tiring day tomorrow. Let's get ready for bed together!"

2. Use Gentle Reminders

If your child forgets the bedtime rules or starts misbehaving, gently remind them of the bedtime routine and the importance of sleep.

For example, say, "Remember, after brushing your teeth, it's time for a story and then it's time for bed. Let's try to do these things together!"

3. Create a "Magical" Bedtime Routine

Make bedtime a fun, magical adventure for your child so it's not a chore. Provide imaginative elements like "Sleepy Fairy Magic!" by giving them a fabric bag filled with strips of colored yarn to help them mark their bedtime as a game.

Conclusion

By implementing this bedtime training program, parents can create a positive bedtime experience for children aged 2 to 6, including those with ADHD. Establishing a routine, suggesting choices, and implementing calming strategies can significantly reduce stubbornness and behavior problems. Through consistent communication, role-playing, and modeling appropriate behaviors, parents can help their children learn the importance of sleep while also feeling safe, calm, and loved. Over time, continuing these efforts regularly can lead to more restful nights and a stronger, more independent child.

8- A Training Program for Dealing with Stubbornness Appropriately for Children Aged 2 to 6 Years with ADHD and Normal Children

1. Behavior

A normal 2- to 6-year-old child may be stubborn or resist instructions when they want to do something their own way. This stubborn behavior often stems from a desire for independence or resistance to being controlled because they prefer to be in control of their own work.

2. Example

Scenario: A child refuses to wear a sweater on a cold day, insisting that he doesn't need it because "he wants to be comfortable."

Response: Parents can calmly explain why wearing a sweater is important ("It keeps you warm and healthy"), or offer the child a few choices, such as "Which one do you want to wear?" This way, the child feels in control but also receives guidance as they get dressed.

Children 2 to 6 Years Old with ADHD

1. Behavior
A child 2 to 6 years old with ADHD may be stubborn in doing tasks like other normal children, but may get tired and frustrated more quickly or become more emotionally intense. This stubbornness and persistent resistance can be related to the common trait of impatience, impulsivity, or challenges in regulating emotions and feelings.

2. Example
Scenario: A child with ADHD stubbornly refuses to clean up their room and put away their toys, insisting instead on continuing to play. When asked to stop, they may become agitated and angry.

Response: Parents or teachers can acknowledge the child's feelings ("I can see you want to keep playing!") but calmly set clear expectations for the child ("We have to clean your room first before we can play outside"). Also, provide a short break before doing the task ("Let's play together for 5 more minutes, then we'll clean your room together!"). A smoother transition, with a short break, from one activity such as "playing" to the next activity, "cleaning the room," can often reduce children's stubbornness and resistance.

Strategies for Dealing with Stubbornness
1. For Normal Children 2 to 6 Years Old
Reinforce Choices: Offer your child choices whenever possible. For example, instead of just saying, "Let's have dinner here!", ask them, "Do you want to help set the table for dinner? Or help decorate the food?" This gives them a sense of choice and control over what they are doing, and it also gives them a break from the "play" activity to the next "eat dinner" activity.

Be Consistent: If you have set a limit for your child with a previous conversation, remain firm, firm, but kind, and encouraging. If your child resists cleaning, you can say calmly and firmly, without arguing: "It's time to clean up. We can do this together, and then we'll have story time!"

2. For Children 2 to 6 Years Old with ADHD
Use Visual Schedules: Use visual schedules to show a rough outline of the daily routine. This can help your child understand what is coming up next and reduce anxiety and resistance to transitions.

Implement Breaks: For longer or more difficult tasks that may be challenging, offer short breaks or small breaks after completing a small portion of the task. For example, "After you put away three of your toys, you can play for 5 minutes, then continue with your task."

Use Positive Reinforcement: Praise and reinforce immediately when your child tries to follow instructions. For example, if they start cleaning with you, even if it's just a few small items, acknowledge their effort ("Well done! Now let's finish it together!").

Conclusion

While stubbornness can be a normal behavior in children aged 2 to 6, it is important to remember that children aged 2 to 6 with ADHD may need more understanding and support. Strategies may include offering choices, using visual aids, and incorporating time-outs to help manage their unique behavior patterns. By adopting these approaches, both parents and teachers can effectively deal with their stubbornness, foster cooperation, and lead to more positive and appropriate interactions in building and maintaining relationships in their lives.

9- The Training Program for Dealing with Bullying for 2 to 6 Years Old Normal and ADHD Children

Managing bullying behavior among children aged 2 to 6, and especially children with ADHD, is often a significant and difficult challenge for parents and teachers. It is important to approach bullying situations thoughtfully and constructively, without rushing. Rather than using "positive punishment only," which often involves limiting privileges or creating consequences for behavior change, focusing on positive reinforcement along with guidance and empathetic teaching is generally more effective. Here are some strategies for parents and teachers to address this problem, including:

Strategies for Parents
1. Open Communication
Encourage open conversations about feelings and relationships with children. For example, ask your child about their day and who they played with, and make it clear that you want to understand their experiences.

2. Teach Empathy
Help your child understand how their behavior affects others. Use role-play to show and understand how someone might feel when they are being bullied. For

example, give them the role of a child who is bullied so they can understand what it feels like to be bullied.

3. Model Positive Behavior

Model the behaviors you want to see in your child by modeling them in relationships. Show kindness, respect, and acceptance of others in your daily interactions, and allow them to learn by example.

4. Provide Structured Opportunities for Sharing

Set up play dates or small gatherings where children can practice social skills by playing with others. This practice helps them understand and learn from others the consequences of appropriate behavior, such as cooperation, or inappropriate behavior, such as bullying.

Strategies for Teachers
1. Create a Respectful Classroom Environment

Set clear expectations for kindness and respect. Make sure all students understand that bullying is inappropriate, undesirable, and unacceptable behavior, and that respect is appropriate and desirable behavior.

2. Implement Social-Emotional Learning

Incorporate activities that focus on social skills, emotion regulation, and conflict resolution into the curriculum as much as possible.

3. Early Intervention

Address instances of bullying behavior as soon as you notice it. Talk to the child calmly and nonviolently, and in simple, clear language, explain why the bullying behavior is unacceptable and guide him or her toward more positive interactions.

4. Facilitate Peer Support

Encourage teamwork through group activities. This activity helps children learn to cooperate better and strengthens friendships, which can reduce the occurrence of bullying behavior.

Examples
1. Home Event: Birthday Party

Scenario: During your child's birthday party, you notice that they are excluding a friend from playing.

Addressing the Behavior

Before the Party: Talk to your child about the importance of including everyone in activities and games and how it would feel to be left out.

During the Party: If they are bullying during the party, gently remind your child of the previous conversation. Suggest that they invite their friend to join them. If they still refuse, take them to a quiet corner and calmly but firmly ask, "Why are they acting like this? Do they know the consequences of continuing to bully?" This can give the child an opportunity to think about the consequences of inappropriate behavior and to develop empathy and understanding.

2. School Event: Group Project

Scenario: During a class project, you observe a child being left out of a group project.

Addressing Behavior

Before the Project: Discuss with the whole class the importance of teamwork and the value each member brings to the project, and explain in simple, clear language what the consequences will be for any inappropriate behavior or bullying during group work.

During the Project: If you notice bullying behavior occurring, intervene in a kind but firm manner. Show the child who bullied the child the consequences for their behavior in a nonviolent and calm manner, and create a discussion in which the excluded child can express their feelings of discomfort without fear. Guide the group to consider how everyone can participate in the group project, and encourage them to take turns doing their tasks so that all children have an equal opportunity to participate.

Conclusion

Instead of focusing on punishment, both parents and teachers should emphasize teaching empathy, communication, and appropriate relationships with others. By addressing the consequences of bullying behavior with open dialogue with children, positive reinforcement, and structured opportunities for social development, they are more likely to learn and gradually internalize positive and appropriate social behaviors for building lasting relationships, which in the long run will help them reduce bullying behavior and maintain relationships throughout their lives.

Teaching Bullying Appropriate Behaviors to Children 2 to 6 Years Old with ADHD

When teaching children with ADHD aged 2 to 6 how to deal with bullying, there are some differences that often need to be considered between normal children and children with ADHD, including:

1. Impulsivity: Children with ADHD may act without thinking, which can lead to unintentional bullying behavior, such as interrupting or being overly aggressive in play. This impulsive, impulsive behavior can be misinterpreted as bullying.

2. Difficulty with Social Cues: Children with ADHD often struggle to recognize social cues and understand the emotions of others. This can make it difficult for them to assess how their actions are affecting their peers.

3. Emotion Regulation: Children with ADHD may have difficulty managing their emotions, which can lead to outbursts or problems controlling aggressive behavior.

4. Attention and Concentration: ADHD symptoms can affect a child's ability to focus on group dynamics and understand their surroundings, which can lead to social misunderstandings.

Strategies for Supporting Children Aged 2 to 6 Years with ADHD

1. Individual Attention: Provide clear, one-on-one guidance when discussing behavior. Use simple, clear language to explain the effects of their actions and the consequences of the behavior on others. Be clear and assertive about demonstrating the consequences of acceptable and unacceptable behaviors.

2. Visual Aids: Use visual supports such as charts or pictures to illustrate expected behaviors in social situations. These pictures can serve as reminders of appropriate behavior.

3. Role-Playing: Engage in role-playing scenarios that allow the child to actually play out and practice social and problem-solving skills. This activity can help them learn appropriate responses and understand empathy.

4. Positive Reinforcement: Focus on recognizing and rewarding positive, social behaviors rather than punishing negative behavior. This helps reinforce the desired actions and increases their motivation to interact positively with peers.

5. Social Skills Training: Implement structured activities that specifically teach children social skills, such as sharing, turn-taking, and body language recognition. This training can be done in small groups where children aged 2 to 6 can practice individually and receive feedback in a calm, safe environment.

6. Parent-Teacher Collaboration: Parents and teachers should work closely together to monitor behaviors and implement specific, consistent programs that are appropriate for home and school. Sharing observations and teaching strategies between parents and teachers can create a more supportive environment for children to learn.

7. Teach Emotion Self-Regulation Techniques: Provide children with simple self-regulation strategies, such as deep breathing, counting to ten, or using calming toys, to help them manage their impatience or impulsivity by calming themselves down before each activity.

Examples
1. Home Scenario
Play Situation: If a child with ADHD becomes overly aggressive during a game, parents can stop the activity, acknowledge the child's feelings, and suggest alternative ways to express excitement or play.

2. School Scenario
Group Activity: In a classroom group activity, if children with ADHD are constantly interrupting others, the teacher can gently remind them of the group rules (e.g., "Remember, we take turns talking!"). The teacher can then talk privately with the child about how interrupting others can make others feel uncomfortable. The teacher can also introduce and reinforce the practice of waiting to speak with visual aids that indicate turn-taking.

Conclusion

When teaching children with ADHD aged 2 to 6 about bullying and social interaction, it is essential to adopt strategies that are tailored to their unique needs. By fostering understanding, empathy, and social skills through structured guidance and support, both parents and teachers can help these children navigate social situations more effectively, reduce instances of bullying behavior, and promote positive interactions.

REFERENCES

1. Adabla, S.; Nabors, L.; Hamblin, K. A scoping review of virtual reality interventions for youth with attention-deficit/hyperactivity disorder. *Adv. Neurodev. Disord.* **2021**, *5*, 304–315.

2. Amat, A.Z.; Zhao, H.; Swanson, A.; Weitlauf, A.S.; Warren, Z.; Sarkar, N. Design of an interactive virtual reality system, invirs, for joint attention practice in autistic children. *IEEE Trans. Neural Syst. Rehabil. Eng.* **2021**, *29*, 1866–1876.

3. American Psychiatric Association. Diagnostic and Statistical Manual of Mental Disorders. 4. Washington, DC: American Psychiatric Association; **2000**.

4. Anthes, C.; Garcia-Hernandez, R.J.; Wiedemann, M.; Kranzlmuller, D. State of the art of virtual reality technology. In Proceedings of the 2016 IEEE Aerospace Conference, Big Sky, MT, USA **2016**, March **2016**, March, 5–12.

5. Babu, P.R.K.; Sinha, S.; Roshaan, A.S.; Lahiri, U. Multiuser digital platform to promote interaction skill in individuals with autism. *IEEE Trans. Learn. Technol.* **2022**, *15*, 798–811.

6. Bailey, J.O.; Bailenson, J.N.; Obradović, J.; Aguiar, N.R. Virtual reality's effect on children's inhibitory control, social compliance, and sharing. *J. Appl. Dev. Psychol.* **2019**, *64*, 101052.

7. Battistich, V.; Schaps, E.; Watson, M.; Solomon, D. Prevention effects of the child development project. *J. Adolesc. Res.* **1996**, *11*, 12–35.

8. Beidel, D.C.; Tuerk, P.W.; Spitalnick, J.; Bowers, C.A.; Morrison, K. Treating childhood social anxiety disorder with virtual environments and serious games: A randomized trial. *Behav. Ther.* **2021**, *52*, 1351–1363.

9. Bisso, E.; Signorelli, M.S.; Milazzo, M.; Maglia, M.; Polosa, R.; Aguglia, E.; Caponnetto, P. Immersive virtual reality applications in schizophrenia spectrum therapy: A systematic review. *Int. J. Environ. Res. Public Health.* **2020**, *17*, 6111.

10. Blewitt, C.; O'Connor, A.; May, T.; Morris, H.; Mousa, A.; Bergmeier, H.; Jackson, K.; Barrett, H.; Skouteris, H. Strengthening the social and emotional skills of pre-schoolers with mental health and developmental challenges in inclusive early childhood education and care settings: A narrative review of educator-led interventions. *Early Child Dev. Care.* **2021**, *191*, 2311–2332.

11. Bloom, B.; Cohen, R.A.; Freeman, G. Summary health statistics for U.S. children: National Health Interview Survey, 2007. Vital Health Stat. **2009**, 239(10), 1–80.

12. Caponnetto, P.; Triscari, S.; Maglia, M.; Quattropani, M.C. The simulation game-virtual reality therapy for the treatment of social anxiety disorder: A systematic review. *Int. J. Environ. Res. Public Health.* **2021**, *18*, 13209.

13. Carreon, A.; Smith, S.J.; Frey, B.; Rowland, A.; Mosher, M. Comparing immersive VR and non-immersive VR on social skill acquisition for students in middle school with ASD. *J. Res. Technol. Edu.* **2023**, 1–14.

14. Centers for Disease Control and Prevention. National Health Interview Survey. http://www.cdc.gov/nchs/nhis.htm.

15. Cheng, Y.; Huang, C.L.; Yang, C.S. Using a 3D immersive virtual environment system to enhance social understanding and social skills for children with autism spectrum disorders. *Focus Autism Other Dev. Disabl.* **2015**, *30*, 222–236.

16. Coburn, J.Q.; Freeman, I.; Salmon, J.L. A review of the capabilities of current low-cost virtual reality technology and its potential to enhance the design process. *J. Comput. Inf. Sci. Eng.* **2017**, *17*, 031013.

17. Cohen, J. *Statistical Power Analysis for the Behavioral Sciences*, 2nd ed.; Routledge: New York, NY, USA, **2013**.

18. Dahl, R.E. Adolescent brain development: A period of vulnerabilities and opportunities. Keynote address. *Ann. N. Y. Acad. Sci.* **2004**, *1021*, 1–22.

19. Dalgarno, B.; Lee, M.J.W. What are the learning affordances of 3-D virtual environments? *Br. J. Educ. Technol.* **2010**, *41*, 10–32.

20. Dechsling, A.; Orm, S.; Kalandadze, T.; Sütterlin, S.; Øien, R.A.; Shic, F.; Nordahl-Hansen, A. Virtual and augmented reality in social skills interventions for individuals with autism spectrum disorder: A scoping review. *J. Autism Dev. Disord.* **2022**, *52*, 4692–4707.

21. DeRosier, M.E.; Thomas, J.M. *Hall of Heroes*: A digital game for social skills training with young adolescents. *Int. J. Comput. Games Technol.* **2019**, *2019*, 1–12.

22. Dowling, K.; Simpkin, A.J.; Barry, M.M. A cluster randomized-controlled trial of the mindout social and emotional learning program for disadvantaged post-primary school students. *J. Youth Adolesc.* **2019**, *48*, 1245–1263.

23. Durlak, J.A.; Weissberg, R.P.; Dymnicki, A.B.; Taylor, R.D.; Schellinger, K.B. The impact of enhancing students' social and emotional learning: A meta-analysis of school-based universal interventions. *Child Dev.* **2011**, *82*, 405–432.

24. Elsabbagh, M.; Divan, G.; Koh, Y.-J.; Kim, Y.S.; Kauchali, S.; Marcín, C.; Montiel-Nava, C.; Patel, V.; Paula, C.S.; Wang, C.; et al. Global prevalence of autism and other pervasive developmental disorders. *Autism Res.* **2012**, *5*, 160–179.

25. Farashi, S.; Bashirian, S.; Jenabi, E.; Razjouyan, K. Effectiveness of virtual reality and computerized training programs for enhancing emotion recognition in people with autism spectrum disorder: A systematic review and meta-analysis. *Int. J. Dev. Disabil.* **2022**, 1–17.

26. Fernández-Sotos, P.; Fernández-Caballero, A.; Rodriguez-Jimenez, R. Virtual reality for psychosocial remediation in schizophrenia: A systematic review. *Eur. J. Psychiatry.* **2020**, *34*, 1–10.

27. Frolli, A.; Savarese, G.; Di Carmine, F.; Bosco, A.; Saviano, E.; Rega, A.; Carotenuto, M.; Ricci, M.C. Children on the autism spectrum and the use of virtual reality for supporting social skills. *Children.* **2022**, *9*, 181.

28. Fundamentals of SEL. Available online: **https://casel.org/fundamentals-of-sel/** (accessed on 15 November **2023**).

29. Galera, C.; Melchior, M.; Chastang, J.F.; Bouvard, M.P.; Fombonne, E. Childhood and adolescent hyperactivity-inattention symptoms and academic achievement 8 years later: the GAZEL Youth study. Psychol Med. **2009**, 39 ,1895–1906.

30. Guevara, J.; Lozano, P.; Wickizer, T.; Mell, L.; Gephart, H. Utilization and cost of health care services for children with attention-deficit/hyperactivity disorder. Pediatrics. **2001**, 108, 71–78.

31. He, J.; Zhang, H.; Zhao, H. Research on the auxiliary treatment system of childhood autism based on virtual reality. *J. Decis. Syst.* **2021**, 1–18.

32. Hedges, L.V. Distribution theory for glass's estimator of effect size and related estimators. *J. Edu. Stat.* **1981**, *6*, 107–128.

33. Higgins, J.P.T.; Thompson, S.G.; Deeks, J.J.; Altman, D.G. Measuring inconsistency in meta-analyses. *BMJ.* **2003**, *327*, 557–560.

34. Ip, H.H.S.; Wong, S.W.L.; Chan, D.F.Y.; Byrne, J.; Li, C.; Yuan, V.S.N.; Lau, K.S.Y.; Wong, J.Y.W. Enhance emotional and social adaptation skills for children with autism spectrum disorder: A virtual reality enabled approach. *Comput. Educ.* **2018**, *117*, 1–15.

35. Ip, H.H.S.; Wong, S.W.L.; Chan, D.F.Y.; Li, C.; Kon, L.L.; Ma, P.K.; Lau, K.S.Y.; Byrne, J. Enhance affective expression and social reciprocity for children with autism spectrum disorder: Using virtual reality headsets at schools. *Interact. Learn. Environ.* **2022**, 1–24.

36. Irish, J.E.N. Can I sit here? A review of the literature supporting the use of single-user virtual environments to help adolescents with autism learn appropriate social communication skills. *Comput. Human Behav.* **2013**, *29*, A17–A24.

37. Johnson, M.T.; Troy, A.H.; Tate, K.M.; Allen, T.T.; Tate, A.M.; Chapman, S.B. Improving classroom communication: The effects of virtual social training on communication and assertion skills in middle school students. *Front. Educ.* **2021**, *6*, 678640.

38. Jones, D.E.; Greenberg, M.; Crowley, M. Early social-emotional functioning and public health: The relationship between kindergarten social competence and future wellness. *Am. J. Public Health* **2015**, *105*, 2283–2290.

39. Ke, F.; Im, T. Virtual-reality-based social interaction training for children with high-functioning autism. *J. Edu. Res.* **2013**, *106*, 441–461.

40. Kolk, A.; Saard, M.; Roštšinskaja, A.; Sepp, K.; Kööp, C. Power of combined modern technology: Multitouch-multiuser tabletops and virtual reality platforms (*PowerVR*) in social communication skills training for children with neurological disorders: A pilot study. *Appl. Neuropsychol. Child.* **2023**, *12*, 187–196.

41. Kondrla, P.; Lojan, R.; Maturkanič, P.; Biryukova, Y.; Gonzalez Mastrapa, E. The Philosophical Context of Curriculum Innovations with a Focus on Competence Development. *J. Educ. Cult. Soc.* **2023**, *14*, 78–92.

42. Kondrla, P.; Maturkanič, P.; Taraj, M.; Kurilenko, V. Philosophy of Education in Postmetaphysical Thinking. *J. Educ. Cult. Soc.* **2022**, *13*, 19–30.

43. Králik, R. The Influence of Family and School in Shaping the Values of Children and Young People in the Theory of Free Time and Pedagogy. *J. Educ. Cult. Soc.* **2023**, *14*, 249–268.

44. Kuriakose, S.; Lahiri, U. Design of a physiology-sensitive VR-based social communication platform for children with autism. *IEEE Trans. Neural Syst. Rehabil. Eng.* **2017**, *25*, 1180–1191.

45. Lahiri, U.; Bekele, E.; Dohrmann, E.; Warren, Z.; Sarkar, N. Design of a virtual reality based adaptive response technology for children with autism. *IEEE Trans. Neural Syst. Rehabil. Eng.* **2013**, *21*, 55–64.

46. Li, C.; Belter, M.; Liu, J.; Lukosch, H. Immersive virtual reality enabled interventions for autism spectrum disorder: A systematic review and meta-analysis. *Electronics.* **2023**, *12*, 2497.

47. Liber, D.B.; Frea, W.D.; Symon, J.B. Using time-delay to improve social play skills with peers for children with autism. *J. Autism Dev. Disord.* **2008**, *38*, 312–323.

48. Loe, I.M.; Feldman, H.M. Academic and educational outcomes of children with ADHD. *J Pediatr Psychol.* **2007**, *32*, 643–654.

49. Lorenzo, G.; Lledó, A.; Arráez-Vera, G.; Lorenzo-Lledó, A. The application of immersive virtual reality for students with ASD: A review between 1990–2017. *Educ. Inf. Technol.* **2019**, *24*, 127–151.

50. Lorenzo, G.; Lledó, A.; Pomares, J.; Roig, R. Design and application of an immersive virtual reality system to enhance emotional skills for children with autism spectrum disorders. *Comput. Educ.* **2016**, *98*, 192–205.

51. Lorusso, M.L.; Travellini, S.; Giorgetti, M.; Negrini, P.; Reni, G.; Biffi, E. Semi-immersive virtual reality as a tool to improve cognitive and social abilities in preschool children. *Appl. Sci.* **2020**, *10*, 2948.

52. Maenner, M.J.; Shaw, K.A.; Bakian, A.V.; Bilder, D.A.; Durkin, M.S.; Esler, A.; Furnier, S.M.; Hallas, L.; Hall-Lande, J.; Hudson, A.; et al. Prevalence and characteristics of autism spectrum disorder among children aged 8 years—autism and developmental disabilities monitoring network, 11 Sites, United States, 2018. *MMWR Surveill. Summ.* **2021**, *70*, 1–16.

53. Malhotra, N.; Ayele, Z.E.; Zheng, D.; Ben Amor, Y. Improving social and emotional learning for schoolgirls: An impact study of curriculum-based socio-emotional education in rural Uganda. *Int. J. Educ. Res.* **2021**, *108*, 101778.

54. Merchant, Z.; Goetz, E.T.; Cifuentes, L.; Keeney-Kennicutt, W.; Davis, T.J. Effectiveness of virtual reality-based instruction on students' learning outcomes in K-12 and higher education: A meta-analysis. *Comput. Educ.* **2014**, *70*, 29–40.

55. Mesa-Gresa, P.; Gil-Gómez, H.; Lozano-Quilis, J.-A.; Gil-Gómez, J.-A. Effectiveness of virtual reality for children and adolescents with autism spectrum disorder: An evidence-based systematic review. *Sensors.* **2018**, *18*, 2486.

56. Montoya-Rodríguez, M.M.; de Souza Franco, V.; Tomás Llerena, C.; Molina Cobos, F.J.; Pizzarossa, S.; García, A.C.; Martínez-Valderrey, V. Virtual reality and augmented reality as strategies for teaching social skills to individuals with intellectual disability: A systematic review. *J. Intellect. Disabil.* **2022**, *27*, 1062–1084.

57. Mosher, M.A.; Carreon, A.C.; Craig, S.L.; Ruhter, L.C. Immersive technology to teach social skills to students with autism spectrum disorder: A literature review. *Rev. J. Autism Dev. Disord.* **2022**, *9*, 334–350.

58. Newbutt, N.; Sung, C.; Kuo, H.-J.; Leahy, M.J.; Lin, C.-C.; Tong, B. Brief report: A pilot study of the use of a virtual reality headset in autism populations. *J. Autism Dev. Disord.* **2016**, *46*, 3166–3176.

59. Parsons, S. Authenticity in virtual reality for assessment and intervention in autism: A conceptual review. *Educ. Res. Rev.* **2016**, *19*, 138–157.

60. Pastor, P.N.; Reuben, C.A.; Loeb, M. Functional difficulties among school-aged children: United States, 2001–2007. National health statistics reports no. 19. Hyattsville, MD: National Center for Health Statistics. **2009**.

61. Riva, G.; Davide, F.; Ijsselsteijn, W. Being There: The experience of presence in mediated environments. *Being There Concepts Eff. Meas. User Presence Synth. Environ.* **2003**, *5*.

62. Rosenfield, N.S.; Lamkin, K.; Re, J.; Day, K.; Boyd, L.; Linstead, E. A virtual reality system for practicing conversation skills for children with autism. *Multimodal Technol. Interact.* **2019**, *3*, 28.

63. Rosenthal, R. The file drawer problem and tolerance for null results. *Psychol. Bull.* **1979**, *86*, 638–641.

64. Rowland, A.S.; Lesesne, C.A.; Abramowitz, A.J. The epidemiology of attention-deficit/hyperactivity disorder (ADHD): a public health view. Ment Retard Dev Disabil Res Rev. **2002**, 8 ,162–170.

65. Sarver, N.W.; Beidel, D.C.; Spitalnick, J.S. The feasibility and acceptability of virtual environments in the treatment of childhood social anxiety disorder. *J. Clin. Child Adolesc. Psychol.* **2014**, *43*, 63–73.

66. Satu, P.; Minna, L.; Satu, S. Immersive VR assessment and intervention research of individuals with neurodevelopmental disorders is dominated by ASD and ADHD: A scoping review. *Rev. J. Autism Dev. Disord.* **2023**.

67. Shi, J.; Cheung, A.C.K. The impacts of a social emotional learning program on elementary school students in China: A quasi-experimental study. *Asia-Pac. Edu. Res.* **2022**.

68. Skjoldborg, N.M.; Bender, P.K.; Jensen de López, K.M. The efficacy of head-mounted-display virtual reality intervention to improve life skills of individuals with autism spectrum disorders: A systematic review. *Neuropsychiatr. Dis. Treat.* **2022**, *18*, 2295–2310.

69. Soltani Kouhbanani, S.; Khosrorad, R.; Zarenezhad, S.; Arabi, S.M. Comparing the effect of risperidone, virtual reality and risperidone on social skills, and behavioral problems in children with autism: A follow-up randomized clinical trial. *Arch. Iran. Med.* **2021**, *24*, 534–541.

70. Strine, T.W.; Lesesne, C.A.; Okoro, C.A.; McGuire, L.C.; Chapman, D.P.; Balluz, L.S.; Mokdad, A.H. Emotional and behavioral difficulties and impairments in everyday functioning among children with a history of attention-deficit/hyperactivity disorder. Prev Chronic Dis. **2006**, 3, A52.

71. Taylor, R.D.; Oberle, E.; Durlak, J.A.; Weissberg, R.P. Promoting positive youth development through school-based social and emotional learning interventions: A meta-analysis of follow-up effects. *Child Dev.* **2017**, *88*, 1156–1171.

72. Tsai, W.-T.; Lee, I.J.; Chen, C.-H. Inclusion of third-person perspective in CAVE-like immersive 3D virtual reality role-playing games for social reciprocity training of children with an autism spectrum disorder. *Univers. Access Inf. Soc.* **2020**, *20*, 375–389.

73. Wang, Y.; Yang, Z.; Zhang, Y.; Wang, F.; Liu, T.; Xin, T. The effect of social-emotional competency on child development in Western China. *Front. Psychol.* **2019**, *10*, 1282.

74. Weare, K.; Nind, M. Mental health promotion and problem prevention in schools: What does the evidence say? *Health Promot. Int.* **2011**, *26*, i29–i69.

75. Wehmeier, P.M.; Schacht, A.; Barkley, R.A. Social and emotional impairment in children and adolescents with ADHD and the impact on quality of life. J Adolesc Health. **2010**, 46, 209–217.

76. Wu, B.; Yu, X.; Gu, X. Effectiveness of immersive virtual reality using head-mounted displays on learning performance: A meta-analysis. *Br. J. Educ. Technol.* **2020**, *51*, 1991–2005.

77. Xiong, J.; Hsiang, E.-L.; He, Z.; Zhan, T.; Wu, S.-T. Augmented reality and virtual reality displays: Emerging technologies and future perspectives. *Light Sci. Appl.* **2021**, *10*, 216.

78. Zhao, H.; Swanson, A.R.; Weitlauf, A.S.; Warren, Z.E.; Sarkar, N. Hand-in-Hand: A communication-enhancement collaborative virtual reality system for promoting social interaction in children with autism spectrum disorders. *IEEE Trans. Hum. Mach. Syst.* **2018**, *48*, 136–148.

79. Zieher, A.K.; Cipriano, C.; Meyer, J.L.; Strambler, M.J. Educators' implementation and use of social and emotional learning early in the COVID-19 pandemic. *Sch. Psychol.* **2021**, *36*, 388–397.

80. Zins, J.E.; Weissberg, R.P.; Walberg, H.J.; Wang, M.C. *Building School Success through Social and Emotional Learning*; Teachers College Press: New York, NY, USA, **2004**.

Further Reading

ADHD Changes in Children as They Grow and Develop
https://www.nationwidechildrens.org/family-resources-education/700children/2018/05/adhd-as-a-child-develops

Your ADHD Child's Real Age: Emotional Maturity, Executive Function
https://www.additudemag.com/real-age-adhd-emotional-maturity-executive-functioning/

ADHD: Current Concepts and Treatments in Children and Adolescents
https://www.ncbi.nlm.nih.gov/pmc/articles/PMC7508636/

Social Emotional Learning: Activities and Strategies for ADHD Kids
https://www.additudemag.com/social-emotional-learning-activities-kids-adhd/

Why Children with ADHD Can Be So Emotional | Psychology Today
https://www.psychologytoday.com/us/blog/mythbusting-adhd/202210/why-children-adhd-can-be-so-emotional

Attention-Deficit/Hyperactivity Disorder (ADHD) in Children
https://www.stanfordchildrens.org/en/topic/default?id=attention-deficithy-peractivity-disorder-adhd-in-children-90-P02552

ADHD and Social Skills: What to Know | Psych Central
https://psychcentral.com/adhd/adhd-social-skills

The impact of ADHD on the health and well-being of ADHD children and ...
https://www.ncbi.nlm.nih.gov/pmc/articles/PMC5083759/

Social and emotional difficulties in children with ADHD and the impact ...
https://www.ncbi.nlm.nih.gov/pmc/articles/PMC3489829/

How ADHD May Be Impacting Your Child's Social Skills and What You Can ...
https://www.foothillsacademy.org/community/articles/adhd-social-skills

ABOUT THE AUTHOR

Dr. Mina Khatibi is a senior Educational Psychologist with many years of experience in the field of Educational and Child Psychology. She is also an expert in the following fields:

1- Child and Adolescent Art Therapy

2- Yoga Therapy

3- Impact of Mindfulness in Children and Adolescents

4- Sound Healing Therapy

Email: drminakhatibi@gmail.com

Website: drminakhatibi.com

www.ingramcontent.com/pod-product-compliance
Lightning Source LLC
Chambersburg PA
CBHW081426270326
41932CB00019B/3116